Rambling Experiences in Scotland

A Collection of Historical Walking Accounts from the Highlands, Hebrides and Other Areas of Scotland

By

Various Authors

British Library Cataloguing-in-Publication Data
A catalogue record for this book is available from
the British Library

Contents

CHAPTER IX

BRAERIACH IN MIDSUMMER

AFTER the prolonged heat and drought of a recent May, the month of June brought to the central Highlands unusually cold and boisterous weather, with much heavy rain in the glens and snow on the tops.

On the morning of June 26 I made the ascent of Braeriach from Loch Einich, a remote loch lying nearly 1,700 feet above sea level, and found conditions more resembling mid-winter than the longest days of the year. The Bennaidh, issuing from Loch Einich, was rushing in semi-spate under the now long-discarded sluices which were used in former times to dam back the loch in order that the timber from Rothiemurchus and the surrounding forests might be carried down to the sea in an artificial spate. At the end of the loch many burns were rushing down dark Coire Odhar, the largest of them having its birthplace in Loch nan Cnapan, on the Moine Mhor. Sgoran Dubh, near its summit, was powdered with snow, which covered the young green of the blaeberry shoots and the black rocks in a uniform garb of greyish white.

Within two hundred yards of the upper bothy of Glen Einich a deep bed of winter's snow still lingered, but as a whole the hills were exceptionally free of old snow for so early in the summer. A bitter wind blew up the glen from the north, as, following the stalking path which winds up the shoulder of the hill past Coire Dhondail until it emerges on that wild plateau known as the Moine Mhor, or Great Moss, I came upon the fresh snow at an elevation of 3,000 feet. At first it lay in small patches, but gradually became continuous. The severity of the previous night's frost

1

could be judged by the fact that large icicles hung from the rocks on which a cluster of globe flowers were bravely holding their blooms to the icy wind—an extraordinary contrast for late June. From some boulders a hen ptarmigan emerged, reluctantly leaving her brood, which she had taken from the grass to the rocks for more shelter and warmth.

Just before emerging on the plateau one crosses a small burn having its source on the summit plateau of Braeriach. To-day this burn, swollen as the result of the recent rains, presented a wonderful spectacle. The strong wind had blown the water over the surrounding stones, and the frost had frozen this spray, so that each boulder was encrusted in a sheet of transparent ice. Each blade of grass fringing the burn also bore this icy covering, so that it was many times magnified in size and sparkled in the light. A few days before the storm the plateau had been gay with many plants of the cushion pink, in all the glory of their flowering. To-day the blooms presented a sorry sight, for they had been destroyed almost beyond recognition by the polar wind. Even the grass had lost some of its greenness—and the grass on the high grounds was unusually good that season.

At a height of perhaps 3,500 feet I came across a hen ptarmigan covering two chicks on a small snow-free patch, and moved on as quickly as possible in order that the mother might return before the cold had numbed the young. A little farther on a ptarmigan's nest, from which the young had been hatched, just showed through the snowy surroundings.

As I reached the summit plateau of Braeriach, a few hundred yards from the Wells of Dee, the scene was a truly polar one. Mist clouds hurried southwards, just touching the plateau, and everywhere was snow and ice. The Wells of Dee were half-covered with snow and in places drifts lay two feet in depth. On the extreme summit of the hill—about a mile to the east—mist still lingered, and across the dark rocks of the Garbh Choire, Ben MacDhui could be seen, its summit also powdered with white. Owing to the fact that the storm had come from the north, Cairn Toul had escaped lightly, and no snow lay even on its highest slopes.

Shortly after midday the most sudden change that I have ever seen on the hills transformed the whole face of the country from Ben MacDhui to the far distant Atlantic. As though by magic the mist everywhere lifted, and from a sky of deep blue the sun shone brilliantly. Near the head of Horseman's Corrie I lay awhile, sheltered from the wind. Westwards countless hills formed the horizon. Ben Lawers, above Loch Tay, was plain, and the cone of Ben More above Crianlarich. Even the snow-beds on Ben Nevis were clear, and I imagined I could see the sharp peak of Ben Cruachan sloping away to Loch Awe. Then to the west of far-distant Ben Nevis I could make out what I think were the high hills about Kingairloch, or even the Island of Mull itself. It has been asserted that from Braeriach the Cuchulain Hills in Skye can be made out. I do not think this is the case, but the sharp hills which lie about Knoydart may have been mistaken for them.

In Horseman's Corrie the drifts of fresh snow were extensive and blotted out the large field of winter's snow which I had seen there earlier in the week. The air, out of the wind, was now quite warm, and the blaeberry plants were giving off their fine scent about me. Several ptarmigan rose from their broods, and an indication of the severe weather was given by the fact that in two instances but a single chick survived, while in another—and I think this bird was the same as the one I had flushed five days previously with a brood of six—only two now remained. By evening, except for a few wreaths, the snow had entirely gone, and every hill burn was running fast and full. Thus came and vanished a storm of midsummer snow, and one hoped that a spell of fine and windless weather might now come to the high grounds for the sake of the deer and the mountain birds, whose existence, even under favourable circumstances, is a hard and almost incessant struggle against the elements.

CHAPTER XIII

THE early months of that season, while bringing to the low country a mild and early spring, had clothed the Cairngorm hills with snow to an even greater extent than usual. Even with May there came no break in the wintry conditions, and up to the 23rd of that month the high plateaux were spotlessly white. Indeed, a stalker with more than twenty years' experience of these hills told me that he had never seen the Cairngorms carry such a depth of snow so late in the season. May 23 was sunny and mild, with a strong breeze of south-west wind. That evening the breeze fell away, and scarce a breath of air stirred the next morning as I left Glenmore Lodge, near the shores of Loch Mhorlich, for the summit of Cairngorm. The western Cairngorms that spring carried much more snow than those hills of the same range lying farther to the east. Indeed, round the summit of Cairngorm itself little snow remained, though fringing Coire Chais was the usual extensive semicircular drift. But to the westward the Snowy Corrie, or Coire an t-sneachda, as it is known in Gaelic, was still filled almost entirely with snow, and Coire an Lochan near it wore a mid-winter aspect.

From Glenmore Lodge the track, after crossing some boggy pasture land, where curlew trilled this morning of late May and oyster-catchers piped, enters the pine forest and emerges on the shoulder of Cairngorm. The first ptarmigan were seen before the 2,500-foot contour line was reached. By their anxious behaviour the cocks we passed showed they had sitting mates near, for they refused to fly far, and stood perched on prominent boulders looking anxiously around.

But it was only the lowest nesting ptarmigan that had begun to brood as yet. Even at 3,000 feet the birds—and ptarmigan were very plentiful on Cairngorm this still and sunny morning —were still going in pairs, and throughout the whole of the day, during a walk over many miles of ptarmigan country, I came across no nesting birds until on the slopes of Creag na Leacainn, under 3,000 feet, late in the afternoon. Just below the summit of Cairngorm were several pairs of ptarmigan together, sheltering from the strong south-east wind which swept the summit, and enjoying the warm sunshine. The summit cairn was reached shortly after midday, and from it a wild scene of Arctic character extended. From Cairngorm to the rounded summit of Ben MacDhui there stretches a great plateau, which to-day was almost entirely covered with enormous fields of snow. Beyond the plateau the upper slopes of Cairn Toul and Braeriach rose up, spotlessly white, and with great cornices, in which rents and cracks were appearing as a result of the rapid melting of the snows fringing the summits.

Though the sun shone warm, a thick haze blotted out any distant view, but soon the wind shifted from south-east to a point or two west of south, the haze cleared away to a considerable extent, and the sun shone forth with great heat from a cloudless sky. Each burn on the plateau was flowing for almost the entire length of its course beneath the snow, and one could thus cross the streamlets anywhere on these snow bridges. Not a vestige of growth as yet was stirring amongst the hill plants. The creeping azalea, which should, before the first days of June, be showing its beautiful crimson flowers in profusion, was as browned and withered as in December, and the clumps of cushion pink were dried and apparently lifeless. It was curious, on such a day of summer warmth, to find the plateau still as in midwinter, and difficult to realize that only a day or two previously the first breath of spring had not penetrated thus far.

On the snowfields were the roosting-hollows of ptarmigan

—some of them quite freshly excavated—and on one of these snowfields I found an oak leaf lying. It had evidently been carried up thither from Speyside, or maybe from the valley of the Dee, but anyhow, a distance of many miles, by a furious winter's gale when the surface of the snow was hard and dry.

Despite the Arctic conditions of the plateau, insect life was fast awakening under the sunshine. Humble bees flew strongly hither and thither, searching perhaps for honey from non-existent flowers, and spiders crawled near the snow.

Just beyond the deep hollow where lay Loch Avon, Beinn Mheadhon, with its stone-studded top, carried little snow, but to the westward of that hill, Loch Etchachan, in Mar, was still frozen half across, with a strong breeze ruffling the liberated waters. An eagle crossed the plateau near me, making as though for the great precipices in the neighbourhood of the Shelter Stone, where was, and probably still is, an eyrie of these fine birds. Flying against the breeze, and speeding past me like an arrow, a dotterel winged its way south, having apparently just come up from the low country.

It was curious, as one crossed a snowfield, to feel the instant lowering of the temperature. The glare from the snow was dazzling, so that, arriving at the bare dark ground beyond, one seemed to enter a region of twilight, so great was the sudden transition. Each burn, where it could be seen, was running full and clear—for snow water is never coloured. The streamlet known as the Feith Bhuidhe, swollen by the melting snows, could be heard from afar. The lochan —Lochan Buidhe, or the Yellow Lochan—where the stream has its birth was still covered with snow and ice, and for the first part of its course the burn ran completely under the snow. Then it emerged for a few yards, was again imprisoned, and finally ran free, with great ice floes lining its banks. A wonderful scene for the last days of May, and one which must be rare in Scotland at any time.

Ptarmigan croaked on the plateau. Their season of nesting had been retarded by the late snows, and it would be a fortnight yet before the hens were brooding. As I sat in a sheltered part of the hillside I noticed a couple behaving in a curious manner. Through the glass they were seen to be two cocks, and the birds were evidently rivals for the affections of a hen somewhere near. In great excitement they pursued each other backwards and forwards across the hill face, now flying low over some great snowfield, now racing at express speed above some rocky scree. Anon they would alight together in the snow, pause a moment, perhaps for breath, then run rapidly across the snow parallel to each other, with wings outspread. Then one of them would once again take hurried flight and the other would pursue him. Once the birds passed not more than six feet from where I sat, and so intent were they on their own affairs that they paid not the slightest attention to me. From time to time one of them disappeared, and I imagined that the dispute had been settled, but a few minutes later the pursuit was as furious as ever.

Near Lochan Buidhe a couple of hinds were spied crossing a field of snow. From the direction of their tracks they seemed to have come from the Glenmore side, attracted to the tops, probably, by the sudden heat, for here there was as yet no grazing of any kind. At Lochan Buidhe the watershed is very narrow. Within a hundred yards of the birthplace of the Feith Bhuidhe burn, the March burn (which appears in the Lairig Pass as the Pools of Dee) rushes down the rocky face of Ben MacDhui, so that waters which flow respectively into Spey and Dee almost mingle at this point. Looking down into the Lairig beneath me, I could see that even here winter still lingered. Two of the Pools of Dee were still buried beneath snow and ice, and big snowfields covered the steep face of Sron na Lairige.

But the most remarkable scene for the season of the year lay towards Cairn Toul and the Garbh Choire. The latter was quite filled with snow, and round the top of the rocks everywhere great cornices hung. In Cairn Toul there lies, sheltered from sun and wind, a gloomy hill loch, Lochan Uaine. To-day this loch was entirely covered with a sheet of unbroken ice over which there spread great cracks. The last occasion on which I had seen this loch was on the preceding November 7, when it was frozen hard, so that it had been in the grip of the ice for close on seven months. Crossing by the ridge of Creag na Leacainn, I descended to the Lairig, just before the commencement of the wood that extends up the pass a little way from Rothiemurchus. On my descent I passed many ptarmigan, and was interested to find at elevations ranging from 2,800 to 2,700 feet quite a number of small and stunted specimens of the Scots pine—*Pinus sylvestris*. I had once found an isolated specimen at this height in the Garbh Choire, but had never seen a number of trees growing at such an altitude. The seed had probably been blown up from the pines which grow in the Lairig, not far from the hillside.

In the glen the heat was intense, and Allt na Beinne-Moire was in full flood with the melting of the snows. All around was the aroma from many pines and birches, so that it was a pleasure to pass through the woodlands filled with the young growth of springtide. Two capercaillie rose at my feet, and redstarts flitted from tree to tree as I passed. At Aviemore that night the temperature at 9 p.m. exceeded 70 degs. Fahr., and not a breath of air stirred. Spring had been backward, but she came at length to the hills in the form of full summer, and it was not long ere the snows had gone, and in their stead the high tops were clothed with green hill grasses and tinged with the flowers of many plants of the creeping azalea and the cushion pink.

*   *   *   *   *

Less than a fortnight later a great change had taken place on the hills. From May 27 until the morning of June 5 the high tops were almost continuously hidden by mist and rain; but on June 5, after a cold and misty morning, the sun broke through the clouds shortly after ten o'clock, and the remainder of the day was beautifully clear and sunny. Though mist had hidden the hills during the fortnight since my previous visit to the high tops, the air had been mild, and there had been no frost.

From the great plateau stretching from Ben MacDhui to Cairngorm the snowy covering by now had disappeared, with the exception of a few large snowfields in sheltered hollows. The Feith Bhuidhe burn was now snow-free almost throughout its course, and Lochan Buidhe was unfrozen except for a little ice and snow at its western end. All the burns of the high plateau had shrunk remarkably in size. For example, the March burn, where it passes on its way down the hill face of Ben MacDhui within a hundred yards of Lochan Buidhe, was on May 25 a big rush of water. By June 5 it had dwindled to a mere trickle. This had resulted mainly through the melting of the snows, but partly from the considerable drop in temperature during the first days of June, when the melting of the remaining snowfields was considerably slowed down.

Although the high ground was now comparatively snow free, there was as yet no growth amongst the upland vegetation. The previous year, in early June, even the highest grounds were green, and *Silene acaulis and Azalea procumbens* were in flower. I should say that in the season of which I write—1920—the plants of the high hills were almost three weeks later than in previous years.

Most of the ptarmigan had now commenced to sit. One nest I saw from which, judging by the feathers lying around, the sitting bird had been captured by a fox; the eggs lay in the nest, but all had been sucked.

Cairn Toul, a fortnight earlier, had been almost entirely snowclad, as seen from Ben MacDhui. Now, however, much of the snow had gone from it, and from Lochan Uaine the ice had melted, with the exception of a few half-submerged icebergs. The Garbh Choire was still almost filled with snow, and on Braeriach great fields and cornices remained. The distant hills were distinct, and the large snowfields on Ben Nevis were prominent. Big snow wreaths could be seen covering the high ground above the Dubh Loch on Lochnagar, but Beinn a' Ghlò was almost free of snow, and Beinn a'Bhuird and Beinn Avon were also in like case as seen from the west.

As usual, the eagle was at his hunting above the plateau, and sailed across the grass-grown corrie known as Coire mhor na Lairige. Scarce a breath of wind stirred, and the sky was of a very deep blue and almost cloudless, except where, far to the south, a layer of white cumulus clouds gathered.

In Coire an Lochan of Cairngorm, a fresh avalanche of great frozen blocks of snow lay piled up near the lochan.

Late that evening the hills were extraordinarily clear, but before dark a strong and cold northerly wind brought mist once more to their tops, and this continued to hide them for some days.

CHAPTER XV

LYING a little to the north-west of Cairn Toul, and reaching an elevation of just under 4,000 feet, is the wild and storm-scarred point known in the Gaelic as Sgor an Lochan Uaine, or the Cliff of the Small Green Tarn.

Eastwards, the ground dips sheer to the Garbh Choire beneath; westwards the land flows away gradually, and two hill burns have their birth in the hollows known as Clais an t' Sabhaill and Clais Luineag respectively. A wild and barren peak is this, which gives a home to no bird or beast; to few plants even can the exposed rocks offer a foothold. At times an eagle, sailing across from Mar perhaps, or from Rothiemurchus, may alight for awhile on its stony summit, or a ptarmigan may shelter behind the rocks on its leeward face should the wind blow strong and cold from the Garbh Choire beneath, but still it is a place altogether desolate, and given over to the storms and to the hurrying mists.

But when fine June weather comes to the hills, and when the sun shines full on ridge and corrie, the grim sternness of this weather-beaten point is softened somewhat, and amongst its granite rocks plants of *Silene acaulis* burst into life and carpet the ground with a profusion of beautiful flowers of crimson or pink, while in the crannies parsley ferns gradually uncurl their fronds of softest green.

It was early one afternoon of June that a companion and I left the shores of Loch Einich—that fine hill loch lying beneath the dark rocks and green corries of Sgoran Dubh—and made our way over Coire Dhondail to the wild expanse of high and comparatively level ground stretching away to the west of Braeriach, and known as Moine Mhor or the Great Moss. In the corrie much snow still remained where it had been drifted in before a winter's gale from the southeast, and near the ridge a large snowfield hid the track near its steepest and most rocky point. A cock ptarmigan rose ahead of us at an elevation of not more than 2,000 feet—an unusually low level at which to find these birds on the Cairngorms—and no doubt he had a sitting mate near.

Great fields of snow still lingered in Coire Odhar and fringed the corries of Sgoran Dubh—Coire Mheadhon, Coire na Cailliche and Coire nan Each—the brilliant whiteness of the snowbeds contrasting strikingly with the fresh green grass and blaeberry plants growing just beneath them. Sailing along the ridges of Braeriach in the teeth of a northerly breeze, a golden eagle passed us by, and on the hillside were the feathers of some luckless ptarmigan he had captured. The track reaches the plateau of the Moine Mhor at about the 3,000-foot level, and from here a magnificent view lay westward—Ben Lawers, Schiehallion, Ben Alder, Ben Eibhinn, all stood out, their east-facing corries very heavily marked with the winter snows. Away behind them rose Ben Nevis, and, bearing northwards, and still more distant, the sharp peaks of Knoydart. At our feet lay Loch nan Cnapan, with ice and snow still covering its western shore, and perhaps a couple of miles east of it, Loch an Stuirteag, on the march between Mar and Glenfeshie. All the high ground carried considerably more snow than usual for the time of year, and vegetation was unusually backward. In Horseman's Corrie —named, so it is said, after a former tenant of Glenfeshie forest—the usual extensive snowfield remained, and from it flowed a large and swift-flowing burn of beautifully clear water.

Clais Luineag, on its western side, was almost entirely beneath snow, and here, beside the source of the burn—which for the first mile of its course was flowing beneath a continuous snow bridge—we pitched our tent at a height of about 3,600

Sunrise from Sgor an Lochan Uaine

feet above sea level. Towards sunset the wind died away, and the stillness was intense. No croak of ptarmigan was to be heard in the corrie—the snows had driven them lower for their nesting—and no song of the snow bunting was carried down to us from the scree above. At 1.30 a.m. we left the tent, making for Sgor an Lochan Uaine, just above us. Though by Greenwich time the hour was but half an hour after midnight, the sky in the north-east was already bright, while low down on the western horizon the bright warm light of Jupiter contended with the dawn. Gradually the light strengthened, but it was not until seventeen minutes past three (Greenwich mean time) that the sun, rising from behind the high ground midway between Cairngorm and Ben MacDhui, transformed the great snow cornice fringing Sgor an Lochan Uaine, so that it was bathed in a pale rosy light.

From the time the sun first appeared until his red ball was fully above the horizon exactly five minutes elapsed, and during this time his rays had reached Monadh Mor, with its great snowfields, and Beinn Bhrotain, with deep corrie facing away towards the valley of the Dee. For perhaps half an hour before the sun actually appeared, the horizon northeast burned brightly, and one single ray shot high into the sky. The waning moon had by now risen above the scree on the western slopes of Cairn Toul, and momentarily paler did she seem in the fast increasing light. About this time the western sky was strikingly and unusually beautiful. Along the horizon lay a bank of dark grey haze. Above that was a wide band of a greenish tinge, merging into a dull pink, which reached almost to the zenith. Singularly fine did the eternal snows of the Garbh Choire seem when flooded by the rays of the rising sun. Right beneath us lay dark Lochan Uaine, but newly freed from its icy covering. So still were its waters that it was hard to distinguish them from the surrounding corrie, and in them lay reflected the images of many snowfields. Then across the wide and rock-strewn Garbh Choire one saw the infant

F

Dee showing for a few hundred yards down the precipitous face of Braeriach before abruptly plunging beneath the snows, which held it imprisoned throughout almost the whole of its early course.

It was shortly after sunrise that there commenced to form away down in Glen Geusachan, far beneath us, a tiny wisp of thin grey mist. Increasing steadily in size, the small cloud, as it rose, caught the rays of the sun with fine effect. Gradually filling Glen Geusachan, the cloud overflowed west through the dip in the hills where lies Loch an Stuirteag, wafted by the lightest of easterly breezes which had now sprung up. At the same time a like cloud was forming in the Garbh Choire, and away towards the south and south-west similar clouds were lying in the valleys, especially towards the Forest of Gaick. Although the air was apparently mild, a keen frost was now binding the ground, so that the sphagnum mosses were crisp under foot, and a layer of black ice was formed on the water issuing from each snowfield, the snow itself being as hard as iron to the foot.

For some time past a cock ptarmigan had been croaking from the boulders of Clais an t' Sabhaill. Evidently his mate was brooding somewhere near, and the presence of intruders was affording him no little anxiety.

The sun was well above the horizon as we reached the plateau of Braeriach, and the hill looked very fine in the clear morning air, the young grasses contrasting strongly with the granite-strewn plateau on which snowfields still lingered. On the plateau an old hind was grazing on the tender grasses. She was remarkably tame, allowing us to approach to within a few yards, and then walking on ahead of us with evident annoyance at being so unwarrantably disturbed at her feeding; but after about fifteen minutes she suddenly got a whiff of our wind, and with this confirmation of the presence of her hated enemy she galloped instantly across the shoulder of the hill and beyond our sight.

By nine o'clock, from the precipices of Braeriach, the

Sunrise from Sgor an Lochan Uaine

Garbh Choire presented a wonderful sight. The whole of the corrie and the Lairig were filled with a soft billowy mist, on which the sun shone with almost dazzling brilliance. From this sea the upper reaches of Ben MacDhui emerged and the top of Cairn Toul. Gradually, imperceptibly, despite the power of the sun, the mists rose higher, and as we watched, all ground below the 4,000-foot level was enveloped, though above us the sky was still of an unclouded blue. South-west we saw, one by one, the tops of the high hills disappear; Ben Lawers and Schiehallion for a time kept their summits mist-free, but gradually were forced to yield to the advancing vapours. Due west, however, the cloud layer did not appear to reach beyond Ben 'Alder, and across the intervening mists Ben Nevis towered, its height seeming enormous from the clouds that lay low on hill and glen between us and it.

At length, shortly after ten, the mists, in their unrelenting upward course, appeared on the plateau of Braeriach itself. At first only in halting wisps did they venture thus far, and the sun dispelled them easily. But ever denser did they press forward, and more quickly too, so that the sun battled in vain against the invading force, and soon the plateau was shrouded in gloom and clammy vapours, through which came from time to time the croaking of an unseen ptarmigan, and the murmur of the rushing Dee in the Garbh Choire far beneath.

CHAPTER XVII

CLISHAM: A CLIMB IN HARRIS

ON the Island of Harris are many hills, and the highest of them all is Clisham, which reaches an altitude of 2,622 feet. No great height is this, as compared with the big hills of the Cairngorm range—Ben MacDhui, Braeriach, and Cairn Toul—yet it is nevertheless the highest hill in all the Outer Hebrides, and from its summit in clear weather a view unsurpassed may be had across hill and sea. Much weather of a very wet and misty character was experienced in the Hebrides throughout the second week of a recent July, and I do not think that during this period the summit of Clisham was once free of cloud. The morning on which I made the ascent opened promisingly enough, and when, accompanied by a companion, I left Tarbert, Harris, the sun was shining. But before we had made much progress along the northern shore of West Loch Tarbert, a freshening southerly breeze brought with it heavy clouds, and rain commenced to fall.

Our way for the first four miles led along the margin of the sea loch, but near the whaling station of Bunavon Eader—where, owing to the heavy sea running outside, the past few days had been unproductive—the road winds up a steep hill face to where, at a height of 600 feet above sea level, a chain of three lochs lie, surrounded by big hills. It was here that we left the Stornoway road, and struck up the face of Clisham, the upper reaches of the hill being shrouded by hurrying mists, but the sky southward giving promise of better things to come. As compared with the Cairngorms, these high hills of the Outer Hebrides are singularly devoid of bird and animal life. A few yards from the road we flushed a somewhat sickly-looking cock grouse; but during the whole climb we saw, with the exception of the seagulls, no birds but a pair of meadow pipits. No curlew or golden plover cheered us with their musical cries; even the buzzard, which in the Island of Mull is numerous, seems quite absent here. About the summit of Clisham one or two pairs of ptarmigan are still said to be found, but during our climb we came across no trace of them. The eagle was formerly to be found here, but has not, so I am informed, been seen for several years. There is scarcely any heather on the hill; grass extends from base to summit, and even at a height of 2,600 feet wild thyme was in flower.

During our climb the weather gradually improved, until the summit cairn was mist free ere we reached it. The cairn of the hill was moss-grown, and amongst the rocks saxifrages bloomed, with an occasional violet near them. Not many yards from the cairn are the remains of a rough shelter which the surveyors inhabited for three months some fifty years ago when making a survey of the district. For fuel they burned peats, and a certain sturdy Highlander carried a sackful of peats every day from the low ground to the summit of the hill, receiving for this very hard work the modest sum of £1 per week.

During the time we spent on the hill-top the mist was never far above us, but was never really down on the hill. Curiously enough, Clisham, although the highest hill in Harris, was at this time the only one free from mist, due probably to the fact that it lies further removed from the influence of the Atlantic than the surrounding tops. This mist curtain extended all round except northward, and while giving some very fine effects, greatly restricted the view. At our feet lay West Loch Tarbert, the sun shining on its waters, ruffled by a southerly breeze, which seemed fresher at sea level than where we stood. Across the loch the large island of Taransay was prominent, with many rocky islets, known

Clisham: A Climb in Harris

as the Taransay Glorigs, extending northward from it. Southward of Taransay, the Atlantic swell broke slowly on the wild headland known as Toe Head, and on the broad stretch of sands—Traigh Scarasta and Traigh an Taobh Tuatha— the sun shone brightly. Beyond that again were the islands of the Sound of Harris, Pabbay, by reason of its hill, Beinn a' Charnain, being most noticeable. In the distance could be seen, stretching out into the Atlantic, the north-west point of North Uist. Westward the view did not extend far beyond West Loch Tarbert, though on a clear day St. Kilda can be seen from Clisham, the distance being roughly sixty miles. Almost at our feet there nestled the two small islands of Soay Mor and Soay Beag, close in towards the northern shore of the loch. A little north of west many hills stood between us and the Atlantic. Close to us, across Coire Dhubh, rose Mullach fo Dheas, less than 200 feet lower than Clisham (or *The* Clisham, as it is known to the natives) itself. Farther west Ullaval and Turga Mor (2,227 feet) were hidden in dark clouds. North lay Loch Roag, with its many islets, and had the weather been clear we should have seen, far out to sea, the group of the Flannan Islands or the Seven Hunters. Immediately below us the great Loch Langabhat lay blue in the sunshine, a strong breeze ruffling its waters.

The peninsula of Eye, with Tiumpan Head at its eastern extremity, could be seen indistinctly; but the view in this direction did not extend so far as the Butt of Lewis, or Rudha Eorrapidh, as it is known in the Gaelic language.

South-east lay Loch Seaforth, that long arm of the sea that penetrates inland, following a devious course, a distance of close on twenty miles. Sailing on its blue surface were two small boats, their crotal-dyed sails showing up as dark specks against the waters. Out into the Minch lay the group of the Sennt or Shiant Islands, soft sunshine lighting up their grassy slopes, where sheep graze. Near them a deep-sea trawler was steering north, making perhaps for the Iceland fishing grounds, her mizen set, and smoke trailing lazily from her funnel, with a fair breeze on her quarter.

South-east, and set far into the Minch—it is nearer to Skye than to the Harris coast—was the lonely Isle of Fladda Chuain, where is said to be the site of a chapel of St. Columba. Beyond it rose the high ground of the north of Skye, and more to the south we could make out the flat-topped hills known as MacLeod's Tables. The Cuchulain Hills were indistinct, and their topmost slopes hidden in mist.

Alpine plant life was scarce on Clisham. One missed the delicate flowers of *Silene acaulis* and *Azalea procumbens*—the latter an essentially granite-loving plant, and so unlikely to be found here. A few plants of the Alpine willow were growing round the summit of the hill, and from a ledge of rock a plant of rose-root bloomed.

As we left the hill and reached the small tarns beneath, the wind had dropped to the faintest of breezes, and northward the sky was dark and thundery. At the loch side a sandpiper with young broke the stillness with shrill cries of alarm, and far above us a raven circled and croaked, while on tireless wings the tribe of the gulls sailed high above the hill-tops, or, soaring downwards, alighted on the waters of the quiet hill loch, their plumage seeming the whiter against its peat-stained waters and the grim black rocks that towered behind it.

Highlands, Highways
and Heroes

I

FROM MY WINDOW

Call of the blood in the open road,
    Whispering winds from the sea.
Call of the glens and the lonely bens—
    You call to the heart of me !

THE open road calls to most hearts when the spring
sun mounts high. Whether we are gangrels at the
core for all our black coats and business affairs, I
cannot say, but there is a something deep-rooted
within us which sends the blood coursing again when
we hear a mavis in the garden or read a tale of the
hills.

This morning I suddenly realised that winter was
now over, and if the snow still caps the bens, or lies
here and there like a white patch on a dark hill-side,
the roads are open and the burns are singing a free
song again.

The frost is sweirt to go and still powders the
morning grass, but the sun is growing stronger and
braver, and a strange unrest is apparent amongst
the birds. Very soon, at this rate, the foolish
March hare will commence his amorous gambols
on the brae-side and the lark will trill again against
a blue sky.

HIGHLANDS, HIGHWAYS & HEROES

My old tortoise is out and about, and I saw him amongst the dead leaves at the garden-foot this morning, as if even his sluggish blood feels the urge to be up and out of doors.

The thrushes have taken the grassy patch into their control, and brave fellows they look in their brown-and-white waistcoats; while in the old elms that back the garden—grey old veterans which have seen many seasons come and go — the rooks are making quite a fuss over some domestic affairs, and there seems no end to their squabbles.

To me it is the sweet o' the year, and I share the universal unrest—the urge to go afield amongst the glens or hedgerows.

The dark days are past ; a cosy fire and the drawn curtain have lost charm when everywhere brown is giving place to green and sap is bringing new life to the moribund woods. The snell east wind has enjoyed its season, and now—

> It's a warm wind, the west wind,
> Full of birds' cries.

From my window as I sit I can see the hills. Not the stern, rugged bens, purple clad, but hills green even in the distance, where white moving specks which I know are sheep crop all the day long in the home of the whaup and the peesweep.

To-day they are quiet and lonely enough ; peaceful too in the spring sunlight, and behind them reaches a blue haze of distance.

On one hill-side is a white farm-house, and in the autumn it grows in size as a landmark as the stack-yard gradually fills ; but now the fodder is con-

COVENANTER COMMUNION CUP

LUSS VILLAGE AND BEN LOMOND

23

sumed and it seems shrunken and derelict. Too far off to observe smoke from its chimneys, as the gloaming creeps over the country-side and a light suddenly springs up in a window, I know the long day is over, the kye are bedded down for the night, and the rest hour has come.

Perhaps it acts as a beacon to some late traveller on the moorland road, and it looks bright and homely, poor lamp as it must be, but long before my bedtime arrives it suddenly disappears, the last sign of life away there on the hill, and another clean, healthy day has come and gone.

I know, although it is far off from where I sit, how utterly silent it is away there on the brae-side. Still to eeriness, but for the occasional querulous cry of the peesweep, suspicious alike of friend and foe and restless as the sea.

Some say the peesweep has a guilty conscience and cannot rest like other flesh and blood. There is one eerie story about it having mocked the Saviour on the Cross, but that apart, its misdeeds of later years are enough to haunt it for generations yet to come, and some country folks look upon it as accursed.

The lore and legend of the past is gradually dying out, but the score against this beautiful bird—and it is one of the most beautiful, I think—is too full to be easily forgotten or forgiven.

The hills I see through the glasses from my window were Covenanting country in the bad old days. Many a poor, starving, outlawed creature sought refuge amongst their hollows, hunted through moor and moss-hag, clinging to life when all but life was taken from them, and then the pees-weep would whirl and wheel and cry about their hidieholes, so that the dragoons might hunt them down.

No wonder the simple country people of those days looked upon the bird as an enemy spy, an emissary of the evil one, and still believe that its ill conscience deprives it of peace and rest.

Over there, hidden from my view to-day, was the home of Pollok, author of " The Course of Time," a man whose work is being forgotten but can never die.

> He entered into Nature's holy place,
> Her inner Chamber, and beheld her face.

Amongst the moorlands lies Lochgoin, the home of John Howie, with its relics and mementoes of the " Killing times."   Not far away is the little village of Fenwick, where it is said the dragoons played at football in the street with a martyr's head.   It may be so, I cannot tell, so many are the tales, so lichen-grown by time that one must accept these traditions on faith, or agree to forget or ignore.

An old kirk-yard epitaph records the incident :

> Here lieth one whom bloody Inglis shot,
> By birth a monster rather than a Scot,
> Who that his monstrous extract might be seen,
> Cut off his head, then kicked it o'er the green ;
> This was the head that was to wear a crown,
> A foot-ball made by a profane dragoon.

They had a dreadful time these same Covenanters, and some of the privations they voluntarily endured form a remarkable epoch in Scottish Church history.

Strange turn of the wheel that John Knox and
Bloody Claverhouse should both take their brides
from under the same Ayrshire roof !

One of my cherished possessions is a Communion
Cup used at open-air Conventicles. Formed not
unlike a modern egg-cup, the stem unscrews and
it all fits into one piece again so as to be easily concealed or carried on the person.

The intimidating " Highland Host " which swept
Ayrshire and Galloway districts would doubtless
return to their native glens by the Fenwick moor
roads. Loaded with booty and the pillaged treasures of many a farm and cottage, they thought it
no crime to oppress the Whigs.

" Bloody Clavers," who was looked upon in
the western Lowlands as a demon incarnate, a man
whose very soul was stained with innocent blood,
whose fiendish cruelty nothing could appease, was
viewed from a totally different angle by the Highlanders. To them he was " Ian mor nan Cath," or
" Great John of the Battles," a mighty leader and
a loyal champion of the King.

Indomitable, fighting men all ; who would change
a page of the sometimes harrowing history of the
West, for it formed character, bred a hardy independence which has stood their descendants in good
stead on many occasions and throughout the world?

The feuds in Ayrshire and Renfrewshire were as
bitter and ruthless as any amongst the hot-blooded
Highland clans, and the King's writ was of no more
account in Carrick and Cunningham than in the
outermost isles.

To us to-day, living in an environment where the

B

law is all-powerful and no man can carry on a blood feud with his neighbour, these bad old days seem almost incredible—or at least to belong to romance. But not so—and this tale of bloodshed engendered by a sheep's head is a rather grim jest !

The scene was on Lugarside, that Ayrshire stream made classic through the fastidious taste of a Burns' contemporary, because in the beautiful song associated with this river the original water was the Stinchar, but as it did not sound euphonious enough for the poet's critical friends, he altered it to Lugar, but there was nothing of poetic fire or fancy associated with " the moors and mosses many O " when the neighbouring feudalists fell out !

The two families in question were the Auchinlecks (or Afflecks) and the Colvills, and they were at one time on the most friendly terms, as behoved such close neighbours.

The home of the Auchinlecks and the castle of the Colvill family stood on opposite sides of the river, and so intimate were they that a rope provided a means of communication between the two, messages and letters being thus exchanged.

And then one day the neighbours quarrelled over some trivial matter, and intercommunication ceased.

Auchinleck, with savage humour, or failing to realise the consequences of his ill-timed joke, one day gave the signal that a communication was being dispatched to the enemy stronghold.

It took the form of a small parcel, and was duly sent along the rope and taken to Colvill to whom it was addressed.

The haughty old gentleman received it with

surprise, but his curiosity soon changed to rage when he discovered the contents—the remains of a sheep's head off which his correspondent had that day dined !

Calling his retainers he gained access to the enemy stronghold, and slew his one-time friend and neighbour.

The matter did not end there, however. Auchinleck was sib to the house of Douglas, and that redoubtable warrior could not brook such an insult to his blood.

Soon the Douglas faction were knocking at the Colvill door, and ere long the castle was a smoking ruin and the owner a prisoner. Why the Douglas burdened himself with the captive I do not know, but apparently he changed his mind on their ride home, and Colvill was summarily slain.

The Tethering of the Sow was an affair of an altogether different complexion—battle for the sheer joy of conflict.

For generations a blood feud, bitter in its intensity, had existed between the great Ayrshire families of Craufurd and Kennedy. Many attacks and counter-attacks, forays and personal exploits had passed between the rival houses.

One day, in the far-off fifteenth century, a herald or scion of the Bargany Kennedys made his way to Kerse, the home of the Craufurd chief, then an old man whose fighting days were past.

His message to Kerse was that on a certain day the Kennedys would tether a sow on the Craufurd lands, and not all the armed might of that proud family could remove it !

Such were the times that it is needless to state the challenge was accepted with alacrity, and so Kyle and Carrick were again to measure strength.

Each side called up its hardy warriors and every preparation was made, the Kennedys to defend the sow they carried to the tryst, the Craufurds to drive it out of their domain and avenge the insult offered to their name.

The fateful morning arrived and the struggle began. All day the battle raged, and before nightfall the Craufurds drove the aggressors and their sow from their lands, each side suffering heavy losses.

Honour was satisfied—and the sow was "flitted"!

Think of the bloodshed and bitter hate engendered over a sheep's head displayed in ridicule—or the tethering of a sow on a certain piece of land on the longest summer day, with the taunt that the other faction could not "flit it." Puerile they seem to us now, but men played that game in the days when war was a ploy.

The story of the Westlands is one long tale of such deeds and encounters, foolish in modern eyes, but the real adventure of life in the times when spear and prowess alone protected house and name.

But where is there no trace of war or feud in this old land of ours? No man need go far afield in quest of old romance—he can find it in full measure at his very door an he will.

Scarce a furlong from my own window lies a battle-field—a turning-point in Scotland's stormy history, for there a queen lost her throne, and with it her head.

All around, the street- and place-names are commemorative of the event and of those who took a part on that fatal day.

Here it was that the Regent Moray forever blighted the hopes of his half-sister, the ill-fated Mary Queen of Scots, who flits across the pages of our history with a wan and ghostly attraction. Had Mary but fled to France while the way was open instead of delivering herself up to the English warden, many a fell chapter would never have been written.

One of the streets hereabouts, with a peculiar irony, is named Lochleven Road, and mayhap few of the citizens dwelling there give a passing thought to the nomenclature of their neighbourhood and the how and why of it all.

What a wealth of romance and incident clings to the older Glasgow streets; what stirring tales could be told of the surroundings, now busy and populous suburbs.

And here is one of note!

Near-by, on the south-east, still stand the ruins of Cathcart Castle, hidden now by tall tenement buildings, past which clang electric cars; a district busy with the rush of everyday affairs, but perpetuating at its street corners the names and deeds of other days when the sword was mightier than the pen, and personal daring brought greater reward than do stocks and shares!

History tells us that from this old castle Mary gazed anxiously from a window, following the fortunes of her gallant little army until she saw her hopes forever blasted and her prospects melt like mist on the distant Ben Lomond.

The story that Mary viewed the battle from a window in Cathcart Castle is not merely possible, but indeed probable. Sir Walter Scott, however, definitely tells us that she " beheld this final and fatal defeat from a castle called Crookstane," but had that been possible all the incidents would require to be recast, as the reputed battle-field could not have been witnessed from Crookston.

Perhaps Scott confused Cathcart and Crookston, because at this latter Mary and Darnley are supposed to have spent their honeymoon. What a tragic bit of history it all forms ! Crookston, now also lending its name to a growing suburb, had many adventures in its time, and was besieged in the old feudal days, Mons Meg being dragged thither to add force to the argument.

Face west and pass Camphill — only a year or two since and it was a mask of wild hyacinths, known as " the Bluebell Wood," but now a crowded suburb—and you will come by Seton Avenue, in turn leading to Maitland and Lethington Avenues, each name significant, but now, like an old moss-grown milestone, meaning little to the fast-moving world.

Men gave àll—and willingly—when they fought for lost causes in those days. Lord Seton for the part he took was forced to flee to the Continent, and was reduced to such straits that he acted as a common waggoner before his ultimate rehabilitation and return to Scotland.

Go a step farther and you are in Crossmyloof, a strange name for a city suburb, but one with a romantic traditionary origin. The story is probably quite without foundation, but it is not devoid of interest.

When Mary's leaders found themselves out-generalled and out-numbered by Moray, they advised caution, and indeed delayed in forcing the issue.

With that impatience which was such a marked characteristic of her race, the Queen insisted in putting the issue to the trial. When her councillors remained obdurate, Mary took from her bosom a crucifix, and placing it upon her open palm said: " As sure as this crucifix crosses my loof I shall this day brave the Regent."

The Queen's Park marches with Crossmyloof, and opposite was the Moray Park, a vacant space now also covered with suburban dwellings.

Strathbungo, slightly north, finds its origin, or rather its appellation, from a much older circumstance. It is, or at least so I have been told, a corruption of Strathmungo, because Glasgow's Patron Saint approached what is now the city from that direction, crossing over towards the eastern district where the Cathedral now stands, and his old-time pathway is now that busy district Crosshill.

And so within a square mile or two out of the many, we have tracks and traces of Saints and Kings, Queens, Regents and Warriors.

The tall old elms which blank my library window have witnessed many changes, but even they had not broken the ground until centuries after St Mungo had passed, so far back in the annals of time lies the origin of the city !

But the low-lying stretch of green hills which

form the distant background to the view must have witnessed it all, and more if they could only tell.

The call of the hills is strong in the blood of most true Scots. I know a man who comes from Argyll, a keen business man, immersed in affairs of importance six days of the week, but when he goes out of an evening to take the air, his footsteps lead to a high-lying part of his suburb from whence he can look out over the Clyde valley to the distant hills of home. The hills call to him, stir something in his blood, the feeling Stevenson expresses so finely in the lines :

> Be it granted me to behold you again in dying,
> Hills of Home.

Glasgow is ringed by hills, Highland and Lowland. Her story and traditions are linked and intermingled, and the whig and wearer of the tartan have equal share in her fame and achievements.

If the south road leads to the land of Wallace and the Bruce, on the west the Highland line entices and the heather hills beckon from many quarters.

In the West lie the silent lochs and the great bens, where red tartan warred with green, and the lonely glens are haunted by the deeds of past years. There Rob Roy held his own by the power of his blade, and from the same hill-sides was taken the gentle Cameron, last man to suffer for his part in the 'Forty-Five. Before his day the Clan Gregor, the Campbells, Macfarlanes and Colquhouns slaked their vengeance and righted their wrongs all independent of the King's writ ; Montrose harried

FROM MY WINDOW

Argyll, and a man's tartan was his passport ór his snare.

And so to-day when the sun is mounting and the birds are mating, when the dead bracken is still clinging to the slopes, either you cannot understand or your blood will tell you why Masefield sang :

It's the white road westwards is the road I must tread,
To the green grass, the cool grass, and rest for heart and
   head,
To the violets and the warm hearts and the thrushes' song,
In the fine land, the west land, the land where I belong.

II

ON THE ROAD TO INVERSNAID

Follow the road to the great wide spaces,
　Where high in the corries the free winds play ;
There you will find in the distant places,
　Peace at the close of day.

EVERY morning a little robin comes and sings his matins at my bedroom window. Shrill, yet sweet, but not by any means a song of peace or goodwill. Indeed, a more pugnacious little rebel amongst his feathered peers I have yet to meet.

When his notes are expended he cocks his head to one side, looks into the room with the cheekiest expression imaginable, and seems to say : " Was not that effort worth a crumb or two of comfort ? "

On this morning I did not see him, although I left his reward as usual on the window-sill. It was too glorious an awakening to be abed, and so I was up and on the road to Inversnaid before Master Robin Redbreast had left the snug seclusion of the ivy, or wherever his dormitory retreat is to be found.

Soon I was past the last suburban outpost and under the open sky, but early as I was, the plough-boy had forestalled me, and the glistening black furrows bore plenteous testimony of his slow-footed industry.

Gradually I was reaching higher country, and behind me the smoke-pall of the great city was growing more evident as it hung, sullen-like, in the distance.

The air was sweet with the scent of burning wood as I passed through Drymen village. The cottage chimneys were smoking, and a farm-cart rattling along the Balmaha road showed that the world was about its business again.

Back there, under that distant Glasgow reek, I am a member of a club, where on the smoke-room fireplace there is carved the motto, " Gang Warily," and idly I wondered to myself if the busy clubmen who took their midday *aperitifs* there knew the origin of the phrase.

The motto " Gang Warily " links this quiet little village and the busy man's club through a long line of good swordsmen in the Drummond family.

The story is that " Maurice, son of George, son of Andrew, King of Hungary, being in command of the vessel in which Saint Margaret, afterwards Queen of Malcolm Canmore, embarked for Hungary, happened to be driven by storm into the Firth of Forth. Here, on landing, fortune befriended him, for he was made Steward of Lennox, and received from the hand of Malcolm the lands of Drymen, or Drummen, from which was derived the name of Drummond."

Five generations later we find one Sir John Drummond of Drummond, Thane of Lennox ; and his son, Sir Malcolm, obtained from King Robert a grant of land in Perthshire for his great services in the Battle of Bannockburn, where, by his advice, caltrops were first used as a defence against the

English horsemen. In memory of this wise counsel, as Burke informs us, " his descendants bore caltrops upon a compartment of their arms, along with the motto, ' Gang Warily.' "

Loch Lomond and her myriad charms are now in the rear, and away on the right are the hills which seem to circle Stirling like a rampart.

The bog myrtle—the badge of the Campbells—flourishes in profusion, and on rubbing a few leaves upon the palms of the hands, the scent is delicious and refreshing.

Suddenly there is a fleeting glint of silver from the Lake of Menteith, the only lake in this land of lochs and dark waters. Well it is that the very name should be singular and a thing apart, an association black in the record of our land ; for Menteith it was who betrayed Wallace to his enemies and later just missed ensnaring the Bruce in Dumbarton Castle.

It is told that a Menteith once sent his butler for a fresh supply of wine, so that his guests might not be in want. As this worthy was passing the lake he espied two well-known witches, each mounted on a bulrush by the water's edge. They hailed the butler, and he, honest man, mounted a bulrush alongside them, and was immediately transported to France !

He had sufficient presence of mind to hold on to the empty wine-cask through it all, and on suddenly finding himself inside a royal palace, he nimbly filled the cask with the most exquisite wine from the King's sideboard. It is pleasing to note that he also brought home a silver cup engraved with the Bourbon fleur-de-lys, and still more gratifying to learn that Menteith's guests pronounced the wine excellent.

There was a Graham—Sir John—known by the soubriquet " Sir John with the bright sword," said to be an ancestor of the Grahams of Gartmore, bordering on Aberfoyle. He built the Castle of Kilbride, which remained in the possession of his representatives, the Earls of Menteith, for almost two centuries. The Menteith Grahams were for long known by the " by-name " of " The Grahams of the Hens."

Tradition tells us that when the Stewarts of Appin, led by Donald Nan Ord, or Donald of the Hammer, were retreating from Pinkie they passed the Lake of Menteith and stopped at the house of the Earl. A marriage feast was in preparation, the principal dish being poultry, and the hungry Stewarts calmly appropriated the food. They were pursued and overtaken, when a fierce conflict ensued, in which the Earl of Menteith and most of his followers were slain, while it is said that Donald Nan Ord escaped with only one follower. From that date the Menteiths were known as the Grahams of the Hens.

Donald the Hammerer finished his days, full of remorse and regret, as a monk in Iona.

For all his wild life of pillage and bloodshed, the deed which led to his withdrawal from the scenes of his prowess was one committed in error.

When an infant, Donald owed his life to an old foster-mother who tended and looked after him when his parents were slain and his patrimony forcibly taken possession of by one Green Colin of Dunstaffnage.

Donald, for all his warrior ways, never forgot his humble benefactor, and in her old age presented her with a farm where she might end her days in peace and comfort.

One day the Hammerer observed his son doing some work or other on the farm, and incensed that one of his blood should so demean himself as to engage in manual labour, he drew his sword and in great fury advanced towards the young man with the intention of slaying him.

The son fled before his incensed sire, but Donald followed him into the farm-house. Seeing someone lying on the bed, and assuming in his rage that it was his son, he plunged his blade into the body, only to find that he had slain the old foster-mother to whom he virtually owed his all. And so in remorse Donald of the Hammer withdrew from the scenes of his tumultuous life and died in holy office.

Pleasing thoughts these to help one along this uninteresting highway, and then suddenly, as it were, the long straight road comes to an end. Over the little bridge at Gartmore Station, where, this morning, the Forth is ringed by feeding trout—great fellows if the monster glimpsed as I passed is a criterion—round the corner, and Aberfoyle lies below in a curious haze, part smoke, part mist.

A town of great traditions this, open enough to all to-day, but a spot which filled Bailie Nicol Jarvie's heart with nervous dread one morning in the long ago.

Then, as now, Aberfoyle stood as an outpost

betwixt the rich Lowlands on one side—on the other the hills and lochs where the word of a Highland chieftain carried greater weight than did ever edict from the Crown Officers in Edinburgh.

But to those who know its secret, Aberfoyle is an ancient stronghold of more than red tartan and caterans. It is a haunt of the fairies.

But Scott was not quite accurate when he wrote:

'Tis merry, 'tis merry, in Fairyland
When fairy birds are singing;
When the court doth ride by their monarch's side,
With bit and bridle ringing.

For it is not always merry in Fairyland. Many years ago Loch Lomondside was a famous rendezvous of the Sleagh Maith, or the Good People as they were called by those careful not to give offence. But a lazy, wicked curmudgeon of an old man drove them from the bonnie banks by his greed.

This is the true story of his ill-timed act. For although the fairies are never seen nowadays on Loch Lomondside, at one time they dwelt there, and good kind fairies they were too, until frightened or subdued by the bad-tempered old farmer who had a croft not far from Inverbeg.

Here was a burn, and on the bank the fairies used to hold their revels. But it was not all fun and light-hearted dancing either, because at certain seasons the hill-folk brought their wool of an evening and, wishing a wish as to the colour they would like it tinted by the fairies, went off to bed. Sure enough next morning the wool was always nicely sorted and dyed as desired, and the honest farm-folk and the good fairies lived in undisturbed amity.

One day the old man referred to gathered all his soiled, dirty, matted wool, and without washing it or doing anything to help lighten the fairies' task, he dumped it all down at the burn-side, and in a loud grumbling voice ordered the fairies to bleach the wool pure white or he would make it hot for them !

Next morning his wool was beautifully white and clean, but so heavy had been the task and so frightened were the fairies that never again were they seen on Loch Lomondside, and so the Colquhouns must dye their own wool like other folk to this day !

Perhaps these disappointed little folks when they fled in their distress sailed across the loch to Aberfoyle, quite a long journey for such elfin-folk, carrying their queen in a fairy litter. But be that as it may, Aberfoyle has more than one fairy knowe and ring where high revels are held in the light of the harvest moon, the while seven little pipers make merry and the dancing thrives apace.

> And now they throng the moonlight glade,
> Above, below, on every side,
> Their little minim forms arrayed,
> In all the tricksy pomp of fairy pride.

Mortal eye has not seen them in our time, so far as I know, but they were familiar to the Rev. Mr Kirk, who flourished in the latter part of the seventeenth century. He wrote an intimate book on their customs and affairs, and was, in just retribution for disclosing their secrets, carried off by them to Fairyland in the end !

In this queer old volume he described even their food, and, of course, like all mortals who interfere and disclose such secret manners and rituals, they got him at last !

A queer tale it is—and a true one if the one-time gossip of the old clachan, now a ruin, is to be believed.

This reverend gentleman must have lived a full and busy life, and apart from his researches into the lives and habits of fairies, he was a proficient Gaelic scholar, insomuch that he went to London to superintend the printing of the Bible in that tongue. It was translated under the direction of Bishop Bedel, and was published about 1685.

His book on fairies, elves and other supernatural creatures was issued in 1691, under the title, " An Essay on the Nature and Actions of the Sub-terranean (and for the most part) Invisible People, heretofore going under the name of Elves, Faunes and Fairies, etc."

Fairies, according to this gifted authority, possessed " light and changeable bodies of the nature of a condensed cloud."

In the course of his investigations he discovered their homes " in little hillocks, and here they are sometimes heard to bake bread, strike hammers and do such-like service."

The fairy-folk do not appear to reside permanently in one hillock; indeed, for some reason which must be more deeply seated than mere restlessness, they move their habitat every three months or so, and during these migrations they may be seen by those gifted with second sight.

c

Mr Kirk relates a remarkable instance of two women who, unknown to each other, dreamed of some treasure buried in a certain fairy hillock. Not merely did they dream, but to strengthen their belief, voices directed them where to search. Proceeding to the appointed spot, they met and jointly discovered a vessel full of money, and dividing the spoil between them, as it was a time of famine, they were so enabled to buy grain. This was certainly good work on the part of the little people.

But Mr Kirk delved too deeply into those secret ploys, and the fairies bided their time and turned the tables on him. They came upon him, I take it, when he was ill-prepared to defend himself against their magic.

Scott was more accurate this time when he wrote the verse :

> It was between the night and day,
>   When the Fairy King has power,
> That I sank down in a sinful fray,
> And, 'twixt life and death, was snatched away,
>   To the joyless Elfin bower.

The truth is, it was evening, and the clergyman was walking upon one of these fairy mounds, situated not far from his manse, I trust, because he was dressed only in his nightshirt, when he suddenly sank in a swoon. The unenlightened took this for death, but the knowing ones averred that it was produced by the supernatural influence of the much-violated fairy people.

They buried him in Aberfoyle kirkyard, but

later he appeared " as a form " to a friend and told him of his awkward position, furthermore stating that only Graham of Duchray could restore him again to his friends in the mortal sphere, and he explained that at the baptismal ceremony of his posthumous child he would appear in the room, when Graham of Duchray was instantly to throw his dirk over his apparition, and he would at once be restored to his mortal form. True to promise, the spectral apparition materialised at the ceremony, but so astonished was Duchray that he altogether omitted to throw the dirk, with the result that Mr Kirk is still held in thrall by the fairies, whose tricks he did so much to expose !

But the minister of Aberfoyle occasionally took part in more stirring affairs than even the tracking and outwitting of elves and fairies.

One local affray at least was conducted in the presence not merely of the parish minister, but also of the elders.

The Earl of Airth, being anxious to serve certain papers upon Graham of Duchray, and finding, like many another man in these days, that it was one thing to obtain authority from the Court, but another matter to enforce it, learned that Duchray's son had arranged to have a child baptized on a certain date.

Assuming, and rightly, that Graham in person would be present at the ceremony, the Earl gathered his friends and retainers and escorted one, Mushat, the attendant messenger-of-arms, to the spot.

The Duchray party were crossing the old bridge

as the Earl's party arrived on the scene, and not wishing to precipitate matters, the messenger, with his own attendants, advanced towards Duchray and informed that gentleman that he must consider himself under arrest.

Without further ado the baby was set upon the ground, and the Duchray faction drawing swords and pistols, informed Mushat that those of the Earl's party who were not killed would be drowned in the river, and so pressed to the attack.

No great damage was done, although one or two of the Airth men were wounded, one man losing two fingers, while in sequel Graham of Duchray was bound over to keep the peace with the Earl and his tenants.

However, to revert to the fairies ere we leave their familiar haunts, another approved authority, one Martin by name, gives intimate details of the "men of peace" or fairy denizens of this district.

His pronouncements, if he may be accepted as an authority, and he writes with weight, are sadly against all my preconceived notions of fairyland.

Ponder well on these words if you are ever tempted to change your state for the more ethereal realm of elfland : " The *Daoine Shi*, or men of peace of the Highlands, though not absolutely malevolent, are believed to be a peevish, depressing race of beings, who, possessing themselves but a scanty portion of happiness, are supposed to envy mankind their more complete and substantial enjoyment. They are supposed to enjoy, in their subterraneous recesses, a sort of shadowy happiness—a tinsel grandeur ;

LOCH LOMOND FROM ABOVE ARDLUI

INVERSNAID PIER—GLEN ON OPPOSITE SHORE LEADS TO LOCH SLOY

which, however, they would willingly exchange for the more solid joys of mortality."

He too, like our ministerial friend, the Rev. Mr Kirk, gives full particulars of their abodes, and tells how many people were afraid to pass their homes beside Lochcon—on our road to-day—after sunset.

He tells how, if anyone is daring enough to go alone on Hallow-eve and walk round one of the fairy hills nine times towards the left hand, a door shall open and he may enter the subterraneous abode. Many have done so and been sumptuously entertained and regaled with choice and delicate viands and rare wines. Furthermore, the lady fairies " surpass the daughters of men in beauty."

Ever, then, take my advice and have nothing to do with it—there is always a snag somewhere, cropping up when the prospect seems fairest, and true it is : " But unhappy is the mortal who joins in their joys, or ventures to partake of their dainties. By this indulgence he forfeits for ever the society of men, and is bound down irrevocably to the conditions of a *Shi'ich*, or man of peace."

But even then, worse is to follow. Our author tells of a woman who carried out the prescribed formula and was admitted to the " secret recesses." There she met many mortals now held in thrall and powerless to escape. One of these transformed semi-humans, if I may so name them, warned this adventurous person of her fate, and advised her to abstain from eating and drinking for a certain period; when her fairy hosts would lose their power over her and she would be released and sent back to join her fellow-mortals.

This advice she followed, and so in due time she found herself back on earth. Apparently she had retained what the Scots call her " grippin' senses," because on being restored she had brought with her the food she wisely abstained from consuming. Let me add, " When she examined the viands which had been presented to her, and which had appeared so tempting to the eye, they were found, now that the enchantment was removed, to consist only of the refuse of the earth."

All of which only goes to prove that fairyland is no better than it should be, and I for one intend to leave its fascinating people alone and unvisited.

Sir Walter Scott stayed at Aberfoyle for a time, gathering data for his " Rob Roy." Indeed, they say " The Lady of the Lake " was originally to find its setting here, but the minister, his host, was busy on a history of the district, and with his native courtesy Scott moved his plot to Loch Katrine.

It may not be true, but the lady who gave me the story was quite indignant against the minister for taking this extra glamour and romance from her beloved country-side !

No district which acted as the stage for the exploits of such a picturesque figure as Rob Roy MacGregor need feel the pangs of jealousy. His fame is as firmly fixed as is old Creagh Mhor himself, with one eye on the clachan and the other on Jean M'Alpine's, keeping guard betwixt and between with his head in the clouds and his feet in the Forth.

Even Wordsworth wrote a stave to his memory,

and compared him with his southern counterpart, Robin Hood:

> A famous man is Robin Hood,
> The English ballad-singer's joy !
> And Scotland has a thief as good,
> An outlaw of as daring mood ;
> She has her brave Rob Roy !
> Then clear the weeds from off his Grave,
> And let us chant a passing stave
> In honour of that hero brave !

The old clachan, or what is left of it, lies behind the main road, and the modern houses and shops quite conceal the traces of that former generation from the passer-by.

Once past Loch Ard, and on leaving behind the clustering villas which form the west-end of Aberfoyle, there is suddenly revealed the real West Highland beauty. On either side are hills and woods, the narrow road winding beautifully amid scenery painted at this season with lavish colours.

The russet-brown of the bracken, with here and there purple patches of the hard-dying heather, the whole view a patchwork of red, gold and brown, crimson and green. Dame Nature paints with a wonderful palette in Scotland, and nowhere more picturesquely than amongst the hills and glens.

A little farther on is an old mill. Tired and faded it looks this bright morning, like an ancient who has spent his days in hard work and craves to sit with weary, half-closed eyes and watch the younger world bustle past.

To the right, a few paces up the hill-side, is all that now remains of the inn where Bailie Nicol

Jarvie put up such a valorous show with a red-hot poker.

Many a plot would be hatched in Jean M'Farlane's Inn over a glass of usquebaugh, innocent of duty. A muttered warning in Gaelic, and the red tartan was off again to replenish that ever-aching maw of Rob and his freebooters.

Not so very long ago, if my memory serves me aright, a very old man lived in this ancient rickle of stones. There was no chimney, and the peat-reek escaped by the door—no very comfortable dwelling-place. He had some small fame as a breeder of dogs, and looked for all the world like a man who might have the second sight. But to-day the place knows him no more.

On passing Loch Chon, shining like a silver mirror in the morning sun, and studded with lovely green islets, on the right, some hundred yards or so from the highway, an old bridge, surrounded by tall bracken, spans the mountain burn.

It is well worth the time spent in diverging from the path for a moment or two, for this is a General Wade bridge, the work of that industrious law-keeper who made so many roads and opened up so much of the then untrodden lands. The centre or keystones have been removed, I suppose to prevent its further use now that the king's high-way runs clear alongside, but even now the hill-track, for it is nothing more, winds away across the mountain-sides, a lasting tribute to the toil and sweat which created it.

I remember once an old shepherd pointing out the ruin of an ancient bridge on what was for generations the main road from Girvan to Ballan-trae. Here again, to deter anyone from still using it, the keystones had been removed, and so well was it built that it took the roadmen two days to dislodge the first stone !

A great man General Wade, pioneer of hill-roads and Patron Saint of those who explore the land of mighty bens and dark lochs.

The other day I was reading about Wade, and my author claimed that the kilt, as we know it to-day, was invented or originated by an army tailor who accompanied the General's forces in Scotland in 1719 !

Back to the main Inversnaid road again, and soon is reached a cluster of dwellings, surely ill-assorted neighbours, yet blending wonderfully with their setting. The tin house amongst the trees is the manse, and on the right is a whitewashed farm-house, quiet and peaceful in the morning sun, on the spot where once frowned the Garrison of Inversnaid, erected to keep the lawless MacGregors in their place ! Here, perched on a little knoll, in the heart of a beautiful Highland glen, stands all that now remains of the old fort. Wolfe, after-wards famous for his victory at Quebec, was in command.

The ruin, whose walls are some three feet in thickness, is now used as a sheep-pen, one half filled with cut bracken from the near-by hills.

Alongside is the old burial-place of the soldiers. Deep sunk under the grassy moss, only the tops of the stones are visible. Gone are the records of the men who held the fort against the kilted outlaws, and the only stone decipherable—and soon it, too, will fade under stress of weather—is that erected by the Duke of Montrose, that implacable enemy of the Rob Roy faction.

The inscription reads :

ERECTED

BY

THE DUKE OF MONTROSE

TO THE MEMORY OF THE

NON-COMMISSIONED OFFICERS AND MEN

OF THE

2nd, 3rd, 4th, 12th, 13th, 14th, 15th, 16th, and 17th, 19th, 20th, 21st, 23rd, and 31st and 43rd Regiments, who died while on duty at Inversnaid Garrison 1721–1796.

And though no stone may tell
Their name, their work, their glory,
They rest in hearts that loved them well,
They grace their country's glory.

Above the disappearing gravestones in this old God's acre, where literally " heaves the turf in many a mould'ring heap," are to be found, amongst other modern appurtenances, a hen-coop and a child's swing !

On my return through the glen I carefully picked a beautiful little fern from the garrison wall, for soon the few remaining traces will be gone, and its memory will live only in tradition.

Wolfe, who commanded here for a spell, was an honoured enemy. No man in the Hanoverian army was held in higher esteem. At Culloden, Wolfe refused to shoot the wounded clansmen ; in fact, tendered his commission rather than do so.

So perhaps the Heights of Abraham were won on Drumossie Moor in the generous hearts of his Highland heroes!

Just before coming to the deep descent which leads straight down to the loch-side, and the hotel which now adorns the spot where Rob Roy had his home, stands the beautiful little kirk with its wonderful stained-glass windows.

There is a strange little outside tower here with the kirk bell suspended, and every Hogmanay, just on the stroke of twelve, the elder (who is also church officer and sexton in one) rings a merry peal to tell the few scattered inhabitants and the startled deer that another Good New Year is being born to a glad world at peace.

And then when night fell, as I stood at the hotel door, the moon forming a silver pathway across the loch, the everlasting hills ringing me round and the breeze carrying the softly-whispered secrets from tree to tree, the world's turmoil seemed very far away.

Suddenly among the bracken there was a scream so human that for a moment it startled me. What it was I know not. Perhaps a rabbit with a weasel on its trail, perhaps the shouts of the Macfarlane ghosts from that ancient fort on Inveruglas Isle, still turning its empty sockets on Rob Roy's Cave. And then again silence.

As I stood there I thought for a moment of the many feuds this place had seen—of the Bruce—of Rob Roy and the wild clansmen who peopled it in bygone days. And then came to my memory a quotation from Jerome's " Three Men on the

Bummel." Here are the exact words, judge if they fit :

" In this land of many ruins, that long ago were voice-filled homes, linger many legends, and here again, giving you the essentials, I leave you to cook the dish for yourself. Take a human heart or two, assorted ; a bundle of human passions—there are not many of them, half a dozen at most ; season with a mixture of good and evil ; flavour the whole with the sauce of death, and serve up when and where you will. ' The Saint's Cell ' ; ' The Haunted Keep ' ; ' The Dungeon Grave ' ; ' The Lovers' Leap.' Call it what you will, the stew's the same."

When the drovers are returning from Glasgow, having delivered their charges to the buyers there, they come home to the distant west via Inversnaid, cross the loch by ferry, or landwise by Ardlui, and carry on straight as the crow flies across the hills. A hard, weary way it must be, but shortening the journey by half.

Mentally I journeyed with them by Ben Vorlich and Loch Sloy, and then, promising myself to follow in their path to-morrow, I turned my back on the still beauty of the night and went to bed.

GLENFALLOCH—THE ROWAN ROAD

FALLS OF FALLOCH

LOCH SLOY

We are bound to drive the bullocks,
All by hollows, hirsts and hillocks,
Through the sleet and through the rain,
When the moon is beaming low,
On frozen lake and hills of snow,
Bold and heartily we go.

Lifting the Cattle

MOST folks who know anything about Scotland, or at least about the beautiful, romantic Westland, have heard of Loch Sloy, but not many take the trouble to search it out, hidden away as it is in the bosom of the hills, with Ben Vorlich, Ben Ime and Ben Vane as rugged guardians.

When found, it is not an impressive sight, but perhaps that is because one must pass Loch Lomond or Loch Long to reach it, and it suffers by comparison. But if it is not enshrined in song like Loch Lomond, or open to adventurers by deep waters like her sister, Loch Long, Loch Sloy is embalmed in the history of a clan known in the annals of midnight raids and cattle-lifting exploits, who went into battle with its name upon their lips.

" Loch Sloy " was the rallying or battle-cry of the Macfarlanes in the old days when " lifting " cattle was a sport and a business combined, and this particular part of Scotland was never very safe for any man who wore an alien tartan.

Macfarlanes, MacGregors, M'Lachlans, Colquhouns, Campbells, not to mention one or two
neighbouring septs or clans, formed a fitting population for the rough hill-side and loch-studded
country now bereft of its feudal excitements, but
still wild and untamed as Nature formed it.

The Macfarlanes have a "gathering" tune,
"Thogoil nam bó" or "Lifting the Cattle," while
their near neighbours, the MacGregors, rejoice in
one "Ruaig Ghlinne Freoine" or "The Chase of
Glen Fruin." Each has a tale which we shall see
about later.

This morning, when I set out in quest of Loch Sloy,
I went by Loch Lomondside, through the Colquhoun
country, some twenty miles of winding beauty, all
haunting vistas, too wonderful almost to be real.

There is another road past Dumbarton Castle,
the scene of so many stern encounters in bygone
days, up Loch Longside, past Arrochar, and thence
to Loch Lomond. It goes through a pass to-day
thronged with motor traffic, where of yore the
boats of Haco and his wild Norsemen were dragged
overland to spoil the Lomond homesteads, until then
considered safe from the raiding sea-warriors.

But reach it as you will, the first part of your
journey must take you for a mile or two alongside
the busy Clyde and past the Kilpatrick hills, where
even since the days of Bannockburn the citizens
paid a yearly tax to be protected from the wolves
which infested the district.

If there were wolves and thirsty claymores on the
land, the waterways were by no means safe. Indeed,
about the time of Cromwell's death, piracy was

rife hereabouts. There was one Glasgow pirate whose ship carried seven guns, and who lay at the mouth of the Clyde and robbed foreigners going to or coming from Ireland.

He took seven vessels in one week, and General Monk wrote the English Admiralty to " capture and clap him in some secure place." Whether they ultimately captured him I cannot say, but such a fearless rogue deserved at least to fall in fair fight on his own quarter-deck.

Morally, he does not seem to me to be more outrageous than the worthy Glasgow merchants who fitted out a privateer and sent her to harry the Dutch. The *Lion* by name, she was a great vessel of 60 tons burthen, manned by a crew of sixty, with five guns, also muskets, half-pikes and pole-axes. She captured several prizes and brought them in triumph to Port Glasgow.

Indeed, it was with relief that I left behind me the old bustling roadway of kings and merchants, and made for the still calm of the sanctuary of Luss.

Robert the Bruce it was, I think, who ordained this lovely spot a sanctuary—where no man carried warlike implements—later to be ignored in some blood feud when passions raged high.

When I reached the Fruin Water, a burn which to-day runs peacefully into the loch, I paused for a moment and let my mind travel back adown the years. Is there any other language which in a word paints a picture like the Gaelic ?

Unfortunately my knowledge is too sparse to enable me to enter that wonderland of the Gael and enjoy the mysteries which have been handed down for generations, but I believe the Fruin Water means the " water of sorrow."

Many generations ago two MacGregors were returning to their native glen and their way took them by Loch Lomondside. Darkness was approaching, they were tired and hungry, and so they killed a sheep and feasted ere moving on again with the rising of the sun.

The sheep was a black wedder with a white tail. When in the early morning a Colquhoun came upon the remains of their ill-gotten meal and raised the alarm, the MacGregors were pursued, captured, and ruthlessly hanged.

Sheep were plentiful enough, and the crime was not an unusual one had not ill-feeling between the tartans magnified the offence. It was an ill-deed for the Colquhouns, and brought a pitiless return on their clan.

When the MacGregors heard of this summary justice, as was to be expected, revenge was their urge, and for some forty or fifty years reprisals, raids and forays were the rule.

Following the hanging of their two clansmen, the MacGregors did not long ponder on their course of action, and shortly one, Patrick MacGregor of Leggarnie, carried off a herd of cattle from Luss.

The Macfarlanes appear to have joined blades with the MacGregors in their forays, and so from time to time the Colquhouns were made to realise that a blood feud was active.

But worse was to come. One February morning in the year 1603 the Colquhouns had advice from their spies or watchmen that a MacGregor force, some three hundred strong, was advancing towards Glenfruin. This time it was evident that the MacGregors meant no mere cattle-raiding escapade, but were intent on war to the knife, because they were led by their regular captain, Alastair MacGregor of Glenstrae. With them were some Macfarlanes and a few Camerons—fighting men all.

The Colquhouns at once took the field, probably nothing loth, led by Sir Alexander, their chief, but they were a poor match in strategy or warlike fervour compared with their opponents.

The defenders greatly outnumbered the Mac-Gregors, their forces being some three hundred horse and four hundred foot, or fully two to one, but mere numbers were not to save the day.

The MacGregor divided his forces—one party allowing the Colquhouns to pass and attack what they understood to be the full enemy force, when they, in turn, fell on the enemy's rear. Soon the issue was joined, but the practised blades of the MacGregors quickly settled the affray in their favour. Great slaughter was done, and Loch Lomondside was ravaged and spoiled by the victorious avengers.

One man, Allan Oig MacAntuach, it is said, became so frenzied with blood-lust that when the Colquhouns had fled, he rushed upon a party of students and non-combatants who had assembled to witness the battle, and slaughtered some forty of them in cold blood.

There is more than one version of this incident, and there is perhaps doubt about it, but probably some untoward incident did take place. One of

D

the unarmed citizens said to have been murdered was a Tobias Smollett, a bailie of Dumbarton, and doubtless an ancestor of the novelist.

The victorious MacGregors drove off the cattle, sheep and goats, and harried the district thoroughly when they were at it, "with the haill plenishing, gudes and geir of the four-score-pound land of Luss, burning and destroying."

The Government of the day was harsh and cruel in their repression as a result of this affair. The very name MacGregor was proscribed. No minister could marry or baptize one of the name, and they were hunted and harried from place to place.

If any man outlawed for crime killed a MacGregor of equal rank, he obtained not merely a free pardon, but in addition a reward of a thousand pounds Scots. In this way was the majesty of the law upheld, and it was many years ere a MacGregor could openly pass under his own name and yet freely mix with his fellows. Many of them assumed other names— Stewart, Grant, Cunningham, Drummond, and so on—but through it all,

> MacGregor despite them shall flourish for ever !

Scott, in whose words so much Scottish national history is enshrined, by whose pen so many otherwise forgotten incidents are recorded, puts the following stirring lines into the mouth of one of the clansmen :

> Proudly our pibroch has thrilled in Glenfruin,
> And Bannachra's groans to our slogan replied ;
> Glen Luss and Rossdhu, they are smoking in ruin,
> And the best of Loch Lomond lie dead on her side.

LOCH SLOY

Widow and Saxon maid long shall lament our raid.
   Think of Clan Alpine with fear and with woe ;
Lennox and Leven-Glen quake when they hear again
   Rodreigh Vich Alpine dhu ho ieroe.

Matchless on the field of battle, the MacGregors were powerless against a schemer like Argyle, who now took a hand in the game. The MacGregor surrendered, and under promise of a safe-conduct across the border delivered himself to the honour of the Campbell chief. Argyle played him false, and once his treacherous word had been fulfilled and MacGregor was safely over the border, he was then arrested and brought back to execution in Edinburgh.

By virtue of his position as Chief, MacGregor was hanged his own height above his clansmen, eleven in number, but all twelve paid the last penalty on one gallows.

A curious incident is related in connection with this wholesale execution. A young Edinburgh citizen, by name James Hope, who was amongst the crowd witnessing the affair, suddenly fell down, having lost the power of his body. The real truth probably is that he took a shock, but he maintained that one of the Highlanders had shot him with an arrow.

It took a long spoon to sup with Argyle, and what his neighbours gained by prowess in the field they invariably lost in the council chamber.

To-day, under the genial sunshine in this smiling country-side, it is hard to think that such deeds of blood and evil were enacted not so very long ago as history reckons time, but such are the facts.

The calm ripple of the loch, the haunting aroma of peat-reek were far removed from war and slaughter.

Many a time I have puzzled at the miniature stacks of peculiarly-shaped wooden blocks which used to stand, built by a craftsman's hand, opposite a little cottage near-by this spot. More than once I have paused to look at them and wonder at their meticulous curves, in the belief that somehow they were used for salmon nets or something of the sort.

To-day the little stacks were gone, and on inquiry I was told that they were the handiwork of an old man, a survivor of the ancient craft of clogmakers, and that the wooden blocks were destined to make soles for Lancashire lasses !

Keen anglers tell me there is a peculiar species of fish which is only known to this loch. It is for all the world like a herring, and will not take the fly no matter how deft the fisherman may ply his rod.

The theory is that Loch Lomond was aforetime a salt-water loch, but some great cataclysm separated it from the sea, and so by degrees as the water became fresh the denizens gradually acclimatised themselves to the changed conditions. This I leave for geologists to decide, but I think it is correct to state that the bones of whales have been discovered near-by, and this adds colour to the theory !

Of course every Scottish loch has traditions of some sort, and one of those associated with the " bonnie banks " of Loch Lomond is that of a floating island ! Maybe it was on this island that a young M'Lachlan met with a mysterious end.

LOCH SLOY

It appears he was on his way to Dunblane, and having dined at Inverbeg and being impatient for the ferry to take him across the loch, he built a huge fire on the foreshore. In response to the signal a beautiful maiden approached, but the M'Lachlan's companion, detecting something uncanny, refused to enter her boat.

Against his reason, but unwilling to be parted from his charge, he at last reluctantly took his seat. On approaching an island they heard beautiful music, and the M'Lachlan stepped ashore with his enchanter. A huge wave overturned the boat, and while his companion managed to cling to it and save his life, the daring young chieftain and his fairy bride disappeared, never to be seen again.

Superstition does not get much credence in these matter-of-fact days, but it has left us some wonderful tales and traditions.

Loch Lomond's near-by rival, Loch Katrine, has also some wonderful romance woven round the name. Indeed, the one-time valley which is now the loch was for long the home of a race " virtuous and wise." Ben Venue at this time possessed a well of pure spring water, much prized by the inhabitants, and the glen folks placed the well in charge of a young maiden named Katrine.

One evening, while employed in her task of guarding the well, a handsome young Highlander approached Katrine and gave her some cordial to drink to his health. The girl fell instantly into a deep slumber, and the winning young Highlander at once changed into his natural shape, that of a demon who haunted the mountain. He cut the sluices and the water rushed down the hill-side, drowning all the people in the valley.

On recovering from her trance, and observing the calamity her carelessness had produced, the maiden threw herself into the water, which from that day has been named Loch Katrine.

On dark winter nights the demon can still be heard shrieking and howling among the hills—but whether in sorrow at the results of his action or in fierce exultation at his misdeeds will never be known.

Almost every loch has some queer story or dark legend, more fitting as fireside tales than for this springlike morning when the snowdrops are nodding as I pass, and soon the banks will be a fairy-haunted mass of wild hyacinths. Primroses will ere long peep from under the bank, to give place in turn to tall, graceful fox-gloves, festooned in many varieties of moss and fern. How beautifully nature paints her canvas here at every season of the year !

As I paused for a moment to admire old Ben Lomond, still wearing a rakish white mutch although spring was in the air, I spied what at first glance appeared to be a mouse. Suddenly the stillness was broken by a shrill, stabbing trill, and then I knew my sudden visitant was a wren. A careless movement of my foot and the little brown songster disappeared as mysteriously as he came.

Earl Grey of Fallodon, that delightful authority on bird life, once said that he endeavoured never to let a month pass without hearing the wren sing. So clear, so defiant, so sweet a note has he, this tiny knight-errant of the hedgeside.

The wren has many associations, varying throughout Britain, but in some Highland districts there is a tale that he is greater than the eagle. One day the two birds had an argument as to which could soar highest, and the cunning wren perched unnoticed on the eagle's back.

Up went the king of birds, higher and higher, until the earth was far below. "Where are you now, Mr Wren?" he cried, exulting in his height and power. "Here," answered the wren, springing off his back and hovering above him.

Dryden puts the story in verse:

> Fool that I was! upon my eagle's wings
> I bore this wren, till I was tired with soaring.
> And now he mounts above me.

The golden eagle is not by any means extinct, and one forenoon, not so very long ago, a mother bird and two young sailed majestically over the town of Greenock. The mother had a large gull in her talons, and its moaning cry attracted attention. Probably this prey was being taken alive to some hill-bound eyrie to serve as a cruel but necessary object-lesson in wild-craft to the youngsters before they, too, embarked upon their own adventurous careers.

Lunch-time thoughts grew urgent just as I arrived at Tarbet, and here the talk was of sport. A native had the previous evening shot a fox! Shades of Clan Macfarlane I was prepared to face (this was an apparent danger when molesting their old-time rallying place and hunting ground), but the ghost of John Peel was more than I could risk, so after a hasty snack I was on the winding road again, and now almost at the parting of the ways, the point where the king's highway must be left for the heather-clad sheep track.

A wild road this ; indeed, after the first mile or so the pathway, which merely led to a lonely farmhouse, entirely disappeared.

Here on the bleak, bare track reads a notice against fishing in Loch Sloy, signed by a Colquhoun factor. "The world has many turns." How obvious it is that the Macfarlanes are a broken clan when trespass notices are erected on their old clanground by the ancient enemy.

The notice served one good purpose at any rate. It gave me assurance of being on the right way to find the loch, as a more deserted, bleak landscape it would be difficult to imagine. The hills were snowcovered and the ground underfoot was mere bog.

On glancing back ere finally saying farewell to all apparent animate life, I had a most enchanting view of Inversnaid across the loch. Somewhere below where I stood the Bruce must have landed with his followers, some five hundred stout warriors.

After the Battle of Methven the Bruce and his small army were making for Cantyre when they were hard pressed by the MacDougalls, and in error found themselves on the east side of Loch Lomond. They had gone astray somewhere in Glen Falloch, and now must cross the loch or be attacked by their enemies.

Douglas, the King's lieutenant, had the good fortune to discover an old leaky boat, but willing hands soon patched it up and Bruce was first to cross over. The boat held only three men, and so it took all night to transport them, but every one was safely landed.

To keep up their spirits, Bruce regaled his men with tales of chivalry, until the Earl of Lennox, coming unexpectedly upon the Scottish King and his followers, relieved their fast and pointed the way to safety.

Meanwhile I was squelching through peat and moss. The pathway had suddenly deserted me, unless that were it changed to a mountain burn, and there was not so much as a bird on the sky-line.

No sound but the ripple of water, and there was plenty of it and to spare. Here and there a wild-eyed sheep would suddenly emerge from among the huge rocks and boulders, look as if it were going to make vocal protest at my intrusion, and then as suddenly disappear into its native fastness.

The weather had altogether changed. The spring sunshine of an hour ago was gone, and the wind was bitter cold, and slowly it occurred to me that perhaps no such place as Loch Sloy actually existed.

A bad place to go astray on a dark night with more snow to come. Be it said, the Boots at lunch-time had given me careful instructions, but here was no living soul to guide or direct. Right in my path lay a sheep, dead, but what had gone wrong with the poor beast I could not tell. It had not been long dead, and while neither living bird or beast was in sight, the eyes had already been picked out, and the empty sockets gave it a ghastly, forlorn look! To pass I had to desert the path for a moment, to sink ankle-deep in peat moss.

Later I began to think that even if there were
such a loch, what good did it do me to get soaked
and tripped and chilled to see a sheet of water ?
Still, on I went, and in due time came reward.
There lay Loch Sloy, screened by rocks and suddenly
breaking into vision. It was starting to snow again,
and a mist was coming down off the hills, and while
the distance from the main road is really nothing,
the going underfoot made it essential to get back
safely ere daylight departed.

> The evening mists, with ceaseless change,
> Now clothed the mountains' lofty range,
> Now left their foreheads bare.
> And now the skirts their mantle furl'd,
> Or on the sable waters curl'd,
> Or on the eddying breezes whirl'd,
> Dispersed in middle air.

In the strath somewhere near the loch a party
of Athole men were burned to death by a band
of Macfarlanes, under one Black Duncan. Hereabouts, too, the MacGregors were hunted with
hounds, and these dogs sometimes wore a light coat
of mail as a protection against arrows.

The Macfarlanes also carried on a feud with the
neighbouring Buchanans, and on one occasion one
of the latter was tortured for a long day before
being put to death. So that, taken all over, it
must have been an exciting environment for a
generation or two.

They were great cattle-lifters in their time, the
Macfarlanes. The full moon is even yet known
in the West as " Macfarlane's lantern," because by

its light the rievers got busy and drove bestial, which was wealth gained not by work or toil, but in a gentlemanly way pillaging one's neighbours, or the tempting near-by Lowlands.

To-day there is nothing to indicate life, past or present. No mournful cry of peesweep, not even the bleat of a sheep or the whirr of a grouse to break the bleak, awesome silence, and it was a relief to come abreast of the lonely little sheep farm again, and to find a dry path back to the roadway.

IV

TO CRIANLARICH—
THE ROWAN ROAD

So wondrous wild, the whole might seem
The scenery of a fairy dream.

Lady of the Lake

FROM the spot where the Uglas burn sings its merry farewell to the hill-side and loses its identity in Loch Lomond, the road is a sheer delight to every open-air sense.

I could quite as easily have tramped alongside Loch Sloy and come out somewhere near-by Ardlui, but it meant sacrificing the wonderful winding roadway with its beauties and its charm, and that could not be thought of.

Here, just where I deserted the hill-side for this panoramic roadway—for only so could I name it—is to be seen a most interesting example of the power of growth, the hidden, irresistible force of Nature. A huge rock weighing many tons has been split in two by a sturdy holly tree, which grows between the halves severed by the surprising and almost unbelievable strength of its roots.

Soon, too soon, so wondrous is its thrall, Loch Lomond will be passed, and over there a last glance reveals the rocky bank where Rob Roy's cave is hidden.

TO CRIANLARICH

To-day the rocks haunted by spirits of the old-time clansmen are given over to the wild goats, and they, in truth, can be no more sure-footed than were the old-time Gregarach; no more wary of a strange footstep in their fastness.

An old friend who resides hereabouts offered me a kid as a pet, but it looked too much a creature of the wild to be taken from its natural environment; as well cage a golden eagle as hem such a creature from its free, untrammelled life, and I regretfully declined.

He informed me the goats were there, so many per farm, to protect the sheep from injury. Agile and sure-footed as wild cats, they delight to browse among the almost inaccessible rocks and crop the available verdure, and so remove the temptation for the sheep to adventure and perhaps come to grief! Whether this is usual or not I cannot say, but certainly it holds good in this quarter, and, moreover, adds still another picturesque touch to the story.

The black cattle, which formed the wealth of the rievers, the itch for which gave rise to so many daring forays, have to-day given place to the hardy sheep.

When the sheep began to invade the hill country, so little was their culture understood that a law had to be passed prohibiting the wool being *plucked* instead of shorn, indeed the ignorant, rather than definitely cruel, practice was quite a usual custom in some parts.

Just after passing the " dripping rocks," easily found by virtue of the water which eternally drips

down their face on to the roadside, we pass the
" Pulpit Rock." A glance at this curious stone is
not wholly without interest, but the gradual growth
of trees is shielding it from the public eye, and
in these days of speed many old-time landmarks
go unnoticed.

There are so many misty tales and traditions
about this rock that it is difficult to know just
what to believe. Some say it was in use during
the Covenanting period and that the minister of
Arrochar preached to his faithful flock, using the
peculiar pulpit-like cave, some four feet above the
ground-level, for this purpose. This might well
be, as the Macfarlane clan fought on the Moray
side against Mary Queen of Scots at the ill-fated
Battle of Langside, and later in the " Killing times "
there were many strange pulpits in use.

Of all the tales of the rock, the one I prefer
savours more of war, or rather of individual combat, and is older than any of them.

You can doubt it if you will, but some hundreds
of years ago a fierce black bull of Scotland met a
great red bull of England on the side of Ben Vorlich.
How that came about I cannot say, but you must
accept the fact on faith.

They engaged in mortal combat, and in the
course of this conflict of giants, the huge Pulpit
Rock was dislodged and sent tumbling down the
mountain-side. The Scottish bull overcame and
dispatched his English rival, but still sometimes
the knowing ones call the rock the Stone of the
Bulls.

Every autumn I pass along the loch-side road on

my way to Crianlarich to gather rowans, and all this district is verdant with the graceful trees, so beautiful at every season. The oak, the fir, the silver birch are plentiful and wonderful in their own way, but for me the rowan has always held a fascination, a charm not merely for its graceful beauty, but for its place in song and tradition.

Lady Nairne has immortalised it, and if no other verse had ever been written, her words alone have appointed its place in the heart of all lovers of this fairest of our trees.

> Thy leaves were aye the first o' Spring,
> Thy flow'rs the simmer's pride ;
> There wasna sic a bonnie tree
> In a' the country-side.

That old song is known wherever a Scotsman goes. What village lad did not find it part of his Friday afternoon curriculum in the schooldays of auld lang syne ? What if the beautiful simple melody was slightly mutilated, enthusiasm for the cause raised it above such petty considerations, and its soul-haunting melody must often awaken slumbering chords in the heart of many a wanderer. And here is a profusion of the graceful tree— miles of beautiful scenery made lovelier by its presence.

Some say the Cross was fashioned of rowan, but this I know, this tree brings good luck and wards off evil spirits, and for this purpose it was planted at cottage doors ; and so it is fitting that it should flourish in dark glens and on sombre hill-sides.

If the rowan has a serious rival hereabouts it is

in the glistening evergreen holly which also abounds, but notwithstanding their prevalence in this district, neither has been adopted as the badge of a local clan.

That of the Macfarlanes is the cranberry; the MacGregors sport the pine; the symbol of the Colquhouns is the dogberry, and the Campbells have the sweet-scented bog myrtle.

How beautiful everything seems on a morning like this! The catkins give an added charm, and there is a very profusion of *yellow* bloom. Strange that Nature tends so much towards yellow at this season. The graceful daffodil, the shy primrose, sturdy whins, and every roadside starred with colt's-foot.

Some of the colt's-foot duly found its way into the vasculum, to be dried and held in readiness against the colds and chills of next autumn. A sovereign specific this for these common ailments, and one not appreciated as it deserves!

But now we are mounting, a happy lilting burn on the right, and Glen Falloch opens before us serene and perfect in its loneliness.

It was down Glen Falloch brave Bruce and his gallant little army came that day they missed the path and found themselves on the wrong side of the loch. And oftentimes since their day has this old glen given back the answering defiance as MacGregors followed their war-pipes, or Macfarlanes drove their lifted cattle at the run in the white moonlight.

Here, too, might be met from time to time Athole men in peace and war; Camerons, clansmen of more than one contending faction when the Fiery Cross called them forth with claymore and targe to redeem their wrongs or maintain their rights. How many tired warriors have slaked their thirst or bathed their wounds at that tumbling, foaming hill-burn; to-day, as then, leaping in silver cascades on the mountain-side?

MacNabs, Campbells, Stewarts—what tartan has not at one time or another used this silent sombre pass to the Lowlands and the open world beyond?

> As wild and as untamable
> As the rude mountains where they dwell.

Down the same glen one morning adventured three Athole men on a private mission of vengeance.

They came to find one Duncan Dhu, and punish him for the part he had taken when some of their clan were burned in a hut by that warrior and his friends.

Coming upon a man splitting the trunk of a tree, they questioned him about the whereabouts of this Black Duncan, unaware that they were addressing him in person.

Under promise of secrecy and reward, Duncan agreed to point out their man if they would first help him to complete his task.

The Athole men readily agreed, and the wily Duncan requested them to hold the split portion of the tree while he drove the wedge deeper. They grasped the huge trunk, but instead of driving in the wedge, Duncan, with an upward blow, released it, and the trunk closed on the hands of the three clansmen, holding them fast in a vice-like grip. With a cry of exultation Black Duncan speedily dispatched his enemies.

E

But if the day of feud and harry among men is over, Nature still carries on her ruthless ways. For a moment I stopped to watch a hawk, suspended like a huge spider, and then so sudden was its swoop that it was gone ere it seemed to move! On the right a trout leaped—a perfect beauty he was—and there was a fly the less in the world. Shortly a weasel, intent on some evil design be sure, ran with peculiar motion across the roadway and was lost in the stone dyke. If man has been tamed, fur and feather carry on the old savage pitiless quest, and war is still rife in this apparently quiet and peaceful glen.

Rowan trees guard the wayfarer all the while to Crianlarich, that village junction of the roads to the open spaces of the West. And here too, of an autumn afternoon, every approach, almost every cottage garden, is bright with the beautiful berries, and old Ben More must find his trusteeship an easy task with such wards of good fellowship flourishing at his feet.

From Crianlarich on, my trail is a secret one—for here, with three gallant companions, I go to camp—away from the dust and rush and strife of the outer world. So secluded is this haven among the hills, that for some seven or eight years the same derelict sheet of corrugated iron has acted as wind-screen for our fire.

On the right is a long, not too steep, hill-side; in the autumn afire with rowan berries, the scarlet hips of the dog rose, and purple heather. To-day the whins will be bursting into yellow patches and the background of last year's bracken will look like burnished bronze.

TO CRIANLARICH

On the left is a rock-strewn hill, also with its gallant trappings of rowan, but here many years ago a huge wound was cut to supply whinstones for the road surface.

In front, the roadway takes a sudden turn, the trees step briskly into line, and the impression from even a few yards off is that a fir wood bars further progress.

It is here that we bivouac—in a small grassy depression at the side of the miniature loch, hidden from the few passers-by, and sheltered from the breeze by the tall Scotch firs.

The last mile always provides a tense moment or two. What if someone has chanced upon our spot to picnic, or even halt for an hour? But no one ever has, and the fears surely are groundless.

Round the corner we go—and the first glance shows a flurry of blue-grey smoke, the pungent, sweet scent of a wood fire. The worst has happened, our fears are realised, someone has to-day forestalled us!

A man is using our corrugated sheet to stifle his fire before moving on. A yard or two down the road a woman with a child's perambulator, loaded only with personal effects, is waiting her lord's pleasure.

" Leave it, please," I shouted, running towards him; " it will save us making a fire, and we'll camp here for an hour." In an instant the iron sheet was kicked aside, a handful of twigs from the plenty around, and the merry crackle was joy to our hearts.

Soon the kettle sings a merry tune and the lunch is spread and waiting. Delicious scones, gleaned from a farm kitchen on the journey, figure largely in the menu, and never did West End chef have more appreciative patrons. And then to lie back on the cut bracken and smoke with a contented mind—can life hold more, I wonder ?

A damp, mossy bank on the loch-side is rich in peculiar fungus-like growths, brilliant crimson in colour, with black or white spots, and as large as tea-plates.

Someone told me this fungus grows and lives on dead matter, and that but for its development the fallen leaves would mount and increase until growth would be stifled. It may be so, and more every day is it brought home to me that Nature does nothing without a purpose ; that everything is part of the mosaic we call life, ever changing but always working to a preconceived plan and pattern : however, to me their strange, vagrant beauty is excuse enough.

So clear is the water that by standing quite still for a moment we can see the lazy-looking trout moving about in aimless fashion, to whisk out of sight when a movement disturbs them.

But no one is here to molest their solitary domains, and as I moved away from the quiet little loch, with its dark mantle of firs, it was to leave it all to an undisturbed, almost primeval silence.

The winding path leads on to a land of mighty bens and deeper lochs : a land where great deeds found their stage in the years that are now but a memory ; where the ready claymore was the arbiter between clan or sept, and prowess was the final judgment, and so, carefully extinguishing the embers of our fire, we took the North road.

LOCH LUBHAIR. GLENDOCHART

BY GLENDOCHART TO KILLIN

Here the war-pipes' music shrill,
Strengthened thew and heart.
Echoed back the hills the wild refrain.
Dark and lonely now the glen,
Gone the gallant fighting men,
Still in loyal hearts their deeds remain.

As I left Crianlarich the air was redolent of scents sweet and haunting as a summer afternoon, and through it came a whiff of peat-reek, true indication of Highland lodgings.

Ben More stood gaunt and silent on the right, green with the coming of spring, and once again the roadway was a winding vista of charm and beauty, a lilting happy stream on the left, hills sloping away on the right, not dark and forbidding, but in the bright sunshine flashing signals of peace and goodwill when the rays scintillated on the snow patches which mosaiced the landscape on every side. In fact, genial as the morning was, bright and powerful the sun, snow seemed loth to lose its hold on the hill-sides, and clung precarious in the hollows and rocky clefts.

Loch Dochart springs suddenly into view as you come round the bend; to-day its only tenants one or two squalling gulls. There is good fishing here, as evidenced by the row of boats, a dozen or so, each chained to its post and awaiting " the gentle-man from London," or other sporting tenant.

But I had no eyes for fish this morning, although here and there one jumped cleat in his exuberance. In the centre of the loch is a rocky, tree-grown island with the ruins of an old-time fortress standing staunch and upright, foursquare against all comers.

It was a Campbell retreat at one time ; indeed, if the tale is true, one of seven strong places in the possession of the Campbells of Loch Awe, built by Sir Duncan of that ilk.

This particular fortress, guarding its island site so arrogantly this peaceful morning, was supposed to be impregnable, and might well have been in some districts, but here MacGregors or MacNabs were not clans to sleep soundly when vengeance was still unslaked or wrongs called for redress, and so one night the MacGregors sacked it when the Campbells were in residence : a dear lesson on the advantages of keeping watch and ward when such dangerous clansmen were on foray.

It was winter, the loch was frozen, the oppor-tunity too golden to pass. The MacGregors crept silently across the ice-bound loch, no more than shadows from the sinking moon, surprised the fortress, and put all the inmates to the sword !

Great clansmen the Gregarach ; and even this morning, as I photographed the solid-looking old relic, the boat I stood in was named the *Rob Roy*. If there are any Campbell ghosts about, preserve me from fishing from a boat of that name some moon-light night ! Every owl in the woods above would make my heart leap, every rustle amongst the

island trees bring sudden visions of Campbell
vengeance on those who dared to embark on their
territorial waters in a barque bearing a MacGregor
name !

In the days of the great Montrose and his arch-
enemy Argyle, this district was naturally in an
uproar. The MacGregors and the MacNabs were
for Montrose, and some Campbells, joined by
Stewarts, Menzies and others invaded Glendochart
to the number of fifteen hundred men. They
ravaged the island keep and proceeded towards
Strathample, where they laid siege to the castle,
but retreated towards Menteith on the approach of
the Athole men led by Graham and Drummond.
The forces met near Callander, and some eighty of
the invaders were slain ere they made good their
escape towards Stirling.

Montrose himself passed through the glen on his
way to carry terror and devastation to the Campbell
lands of Argyle.

But wild nights and keen blades seemed far away
this glorious morning. Beside me a bank of nestling
velvety wild violets, and a very myriad of wood
anemones growing in a rich soft carpet of moss and
dainty little ferns, while the repeated, seemingly
endless, call of the cuckoo—the first I have heard
this year—echoed across the loch as clear as a bell.
A droning old bumble-bee grumbled around for
a moment or two, and an early squirrel kept a
questioning eye on my movements for quite a
time considering how busy he appeared to be !
I dallied here too long, but the silent beauty and
charm of the place made it difficult to leave.

Again the winding, roundabout road, only an odd hundred yards visible at a time, but of itself so full of charm that one can spare the longer view.

Over behind those western hills, a road we do not traverse to-day, lies Dalree, intimately associated with an incident which might well have altered the whole history of our land.

The Bruce, you remember, slew the Red Comyn at Dumfries, and as that gentleman was related by marriage to the Lord of Lorn, Chief of the MacDougalls, that clan was inspired with an implacable hatred towards the King.

After hiding in the wild Athole and Breadalbane country with his almost dispirited army, now little more than three hundred men, the royal force was endeavouring to reach Argyle. Approaching Dalree they were attacked by Lorn, who had under him some thousand fighting clansmen. The odds against Bruce were too heavy, and he was forced to retreat, contesting every foot. Bruce was in the rear, and at length, coming to a narrow pass, the King, single-handed, guarded his men, who were now more certain of escape.

Three of the MacDougall faction, a father and two sons, determined either to slay or take their chief enemy prisoner. Bruce was mounted, and one of the sons grasped the rein, but the King killed him. The second of his attackers endeavoured, by grasping his leg, to unseat him, but his horse, being spurred, gave a forward bound and knocked his assailant to the ground; as he rose Bruce struck him with such force as to cleave his head in two. The father, now desperate with fury at the death of his sons, grappled with Bruce and held him so closely that he could not wield his sword. Drawing a hammer which hung at his saddle, the Bruce struck and vanquished his third foe by dashing out his brains. Even then, the dying Highlander maintained his fierce grip, and the King had to unfasten his cloak to free himself, and thus the famed Brooch of Lorn fell into the hands of the MacDougall family.

Here again, the MacGregors, when fighting was afoot, had to play their part, and a band of that restless clan took part with the MacDougalls against the King.

Later, when power came his way, the Scottish King did not omit to collect his debt from the MacDougall faction, and to establish his sovereignty over his fierce vassals. He drove John of Lorn out of his country, and presented a considerable part of it to one Sir Colin Campbell, first of the feudal family of Argyle, a name destined to become known in many ways as the centuries passed.

The MacNabs, on whose clan ground we now are, also took part with the MacDougalls, and the Bruce paid them back in kind at a later date when his star was in the ascendant.

It is said these two clans took sides with the invaders against the Scots at Bannockburn, their hatred of the Bruce being stronger than their patriotism.

When leaving Crianlarich, if the south and west shoulders of Ben More were green and verdant, a backward glance revealed that his broad back was still white, and with the dying of the sun a snell wind would spring up.

HIGHLANDS, HIGHWAYS & HEROES

Somewhere hereabouts a MacNab who had been out in the '45 was believed to be hiding, and the redcoats were sent to burn down his house. It was duly fired, but on moving off someone noticed that the flames were apparently extinguished. A man was sent back to re-kindle it, and MacNab, who had been on the watch and had quenched the flames, shot him dead. The soldiers rushed to take the outlaw prisoner, but three were shot before he was dislodged. Taking to the rocks, he managed to account for a further three, when the soldiers retired, and for the time being, at least, left him in possession.

The same wise old hills look down on us to-day, storied in tales we may never know, rich with the romance of forgotten deeds no man can now trace, gone for ever like the smoke of last night's fire.

A lonely little lochan breaks into the roadway, its sole possessor, so far as I have ascertained, one trout, seemingly as proud of his domain as any Highland chieftain, and in his sudden leaps showing like a bar of rainbow.

Just here the railway—was ever railway so beautifully and unobtrusively situated—suddenly changes its position. One moment it forms a silent guard on the right, and as we dip under the bridge, almost as if by magic, it marches on our left.

In front the vista is now magnificent in its stretch and charm. Bare rock-strewn hills on the right, beautifully wooded slopes on the left, with the Dochart hurrying through the glen, the sun and some wonderful cloud effects above—and amidst it all a great silence.

BY GLENDOCHART TO KILLIN

Just above stands what you might well mistake for the falling ruins of a commonplace cottage, but it is one with a history attached, because at one time it was the home of Rob Roy.

Scramble up the bank and examine it and you will agree the site was well-chosen, indeed one more admirable for a man who might have to flee from his enemies at any moment would be hard to find. From here the glen is open for miles, and the giant bulk of Ben More affords shelter from the winds, protection against a sudden attack in that quarter, and a ready retreat in case of emergency. Behind, the hills are rock-strewn, and it would be difficult to track a nimble hardy man who knew every secret path and hidie-hole. At the very door lies a deep, bracken-clad gash in the hill-side, just the place for slinking off to cover unnoticed.

Here in the olden days a man might live his life free and unfettered, his every need supplied from the land at his door.

> Low down by yon burn that's half-hidden in heather,
>   He lurked like a lion in the lair he knew well;
> 'Twas there sobbed the red-deer to feel his keen dagger,
>   There pierced by his arrow the cailzie-cock fell.

Another enchanted mile or two and there, a few hundred yards from the roadway, stands what appears to be a solitary sheep-pen, guarded by an ancient tree. Something about it attracted, and on approaching I found it to be a burial-place of the MacNabs.

Here on this little knoll, quaint and silent amongst the hills, lie the kilted warriors of a bygone day—

the stones, those not under the moss of a century are too lichen-covered to be clearly decipherable. On a number of these old tombstones are carved queer, bearded faces, and I thought of the far-off times when the coronach would wail for the chiefs who are gone—unknown to-day to all but their direct descendants.

Opposite is Suie Lodge, and on making inquiries at the smiling, soft-tongued Highland woman in charge, she could give me no information, but suggested I might inquire at the hotel a little farther up the glen.

There, in Luib Hotel, with its golden eagle guarding the rods, baskets and waders, they told me something of its story and the prestige of the Clan MacNab.

Many are the tales told of the clan, and in truth this district more than holds its own in cruel deeds and relentless feuds.

Here is one incident of the less grim order told of the MacNab, who was prone occasionally to get into financial difficulties. One evening a sheriff-officer called to present a summons, but before he could perform his duties the laird invited him to enter his abode and partake of refreshment. Whisky was, of course, produced, and the officer was well plied with it, while, acting on instructions, some of the men hastily constructed an effigy and hung it upon a tree at a little distance from the fortress.

In the morning the man of law bethought him of his legal duties, but on glancing out of the window he was horrified to observe the dummy body swinging from a branch.

ROB ROY'S COTTAGE, GLENDOCHART

LOCH TAY FROM KILLIN

" What is that ? " he asked, falling into the trap so artfully prepared for his special benefit.

" It's nothing," replied his hearer ; " just a messenger of some kind who tried to force a summons on the laird."

The messenger-at-arms left for Edinburgh without undue delay, and took his summons back with him, having no wish to grace in turn the dule tree of a Highland gentleman !

While smiling and peaceful to-day, the glen can assume at certain seasons a wild and almost savage desolation. More than once have I seen the winding burn break its bounds and spread to the dimensions of a small loch, here or there a semi-submerged tree pointing the depth and overflow of the turbulent waters.

One old authority who explored the district in the last years of the eighteenth century tells of the rapid climatic changes to which Glendochart was subject. Sometimes the snow lay deep ; at other times the glen was swept by torrential rains. Severe frost held it in a vice-like grip—then suddenly and without warning came the thaw. Oftentimes huge avalanches of snow and rocks would come tumbling down the hill-sides, carrying everything in their path to ruin and destruction.

He relates how one evening night had hardly fallen, when one of these mighty snowfalls came tumbling down the hill-side. In its path lay a cottage, and the family were gathered round the peat-fire awaiting their evening meal. In a moment they were overwhelmed and buried beneath a mass of snow and rocks, everyone that is, except the mother, who was probably in another part of the cottage busy with her task.

But to-day there is no hint of storm or terror—every prospect is bright and fair.

St Fillan had associations with this district, and just hereabouts, where the roads diverge, was enacted a scene strange even in the annals of the Westland.

More than usual mystery surrounds the burial-place of St Fillan, even allowing for the lack of actual knowledge of what happened in the far-off seventh century, midway through which the Saint took farewell of the world.

When St Fillan died at Dundurn, the natives naturally desired his bones to rest in their midst, but there were other claimants. He was carried through Glenogle until the bodyguard arrived at this road-junction near Killin, and there a fierce altercation arose as to the direction in which the cortege should now proceed. Claymores were drawn and blows exchanged, so determined were the two factions to secure the honour of providing sepulture.

And then a miracle was performed. Where before one coffin had lain there were now two, and each party, reverently raising one, carried it off in opposite directions !

As the road gets narrower and more winding the great bulk of Ben Lawers, snow-capped and stark, becomes more dominant, dwarfing his neighbours.

Surely no town ever had more picturesque approach than this old-time Highland village of Killin. Guarded by a narrow bridge, on the left the falls of Dochart, a wonderful series of broken steps and, even this morning when anglers are complaining of low waters, a sight to remember.

The Dochart here divides into two channels and so creates a small, coffin-shaped island, hallowed ground inasmuch as it forms the burying-place of the MacNabs.

The approach is guarded by a locked gate, but the keeper of the keys was not to be found, so vaulting the dyke I easily gained admission by going underneath the bridge and crossing the stream by some large stones.

Here is peace. The ground deep in beech mast, the sanctuary screened by trees—surely an ideal place to rest until the great day when clan feuds shall be forgotten and all tartans will rank alike.

There is one outstanding tree amongst the many guarding those who sleep — a tall birch. Its branches droop as if in mourning for its charges, and sadness is depicted in every twig. It may seem fanciful, but if ever tree spoke by outward sign and symbol, this old birch mourns the clansmen it has seen laid at its feet for generations past.

The name Killin means, according to some authorities, the burial-place of Fingal, and as he was a great Celtic warrior in his day, I went to view his grave.

It stands on a brae-side midway through the village, and to reach it one must pass a tradesman's yard. Here I found a man busy painting a sign, and to " pass the time of day " I asked him whose grave that was in front.

" Rob Roy's, I think," said he !

The headstone has every appearance of great age, and undoubtedly the formation of the ground is reminiscent of a grave, but I believe the place was probed or examined many years ago and no urn or remains were discovered.

Still, let us preserve our traditions and beliefs, and for sentiment's sake I hope the great Prince of Morven, so immortalised by his son Ossian, is really resting there !

There is another monument here, also erected to a saint, but of much later date, one James Stewart, who flourished here as minister in the middle part of the eighteenth century. His life is notable for the fact that he translated the New Testament into Gaelic, and partly completed a like work on the Old, finished by his son, Dr Stewart, who was minister of Luss, on Loch Lomondside.

Alexander Campbell, whose " Journey from Edinburgh through Parts of North Britain " was published in 1802, has much sage advice and information to impart, and, like all who want to see the beauties of the land, he visited Killin. He has devoted considerable space to this place, even to quoting prices charged for provisions at the time of his visit, and tells us that beef, mutton, veal and pork averaged 3d. per lb. of $17\frac{1}{2}$ oz. ; butter 9d. per lb. of 22 oz. ; and cheese from 5s. to 7s. per stone of 22 lbs.

But it is when he waxes eloquent about the people, their customs and feuds, that I like him best.

Here is a literal quotation, which is not uninteresting, and it will be observed I have not departed from his spelling. The italics, too, are as the author placed them :

" The *Macdonells* of Keappoch, a brave and resolute race of warriors, and the *Campbells* of Braidalbane, a numerous and no less warlike people, were continually making inroads on one another's lands. A desperate conflict took place on the hill rising immediately above the church of *Killin*, called *Stronachlachan*, undertaken by the brother of Keappoch, and a number of his followers, against the inhabitants of *Bunrannoch* and *Strathtay*.

" The *Macdonells*, who had travelled from their fastnesses in *Brae-lochaber*, over the mountains, through *Rannoch*, and Glenlion, had carried off all the cattle on their way southward ; and returning with their booty, by the heights of *Deiffer*, which run along the South side of *Loch-tay*, they had ascended *Stronachlachan* ; when tidings of their progress reached a party of *Campbells* who were assembled in the Hall of *Finlarig* at a christening.

" Fired with indignation at so daring an insult, they instantly rushed forth, ascended the hill, and attacked the foe, but were repulsed with loss.

" The *Macdonells*, triumphant, pursued their route ; but the Campbells receiving a reinforcement, as well they might on their own lands, followed the enemy, and came up with him on the braes of *Glenurcha*, where they overpowered him by numbers, recovered the booty, and returned in triumph, having accomplished their revenge."

This wild affray really arose, I believe, from the fact that the reivers (they were actually the Macdonalds of Glencoe) were attempting to drive

F

their booty across the Breadalbane lands without paying the customary " road collop."

This " road collop " was a certain percentage of the spoil due to another clan through whose territory a drove of " lifted " or stolen cattle was driven. In its time the custom gave rise to many wild occasions, indeed one notable example of its far-reaching possibilities was a battle-royal between the M'Intoshes and the Munros.

A party of the Munros were returning from Edinburgh to their homes in the far North.

They were mounted, for the journey was a long and tiresome one, and on their halting for the night somewhere in the Athole country, the owner of the land, when darkness fell, had the tails cut off their horses !

This was of course an unforgivable insult, but the Munros were not in sufficient strength to take immediate action, and so proceeded on their homeward journey.

Arriving at their chief stronghold, the Fiery Cross went round, and soon an eager band of armed men came south to pay their clansmen's debts ! And in full measure did they carry out their self-appointed task. Houses were given to the flames, no living soul who crossed their path was spared, and a great drove of cattle was carried off as spoil.

On passing through the M'Intosh lands the usual " road collop " was demanded.

Then followed some argument, summarily ended by Munro stating that he would give no more, and if the quota was not considered generous enough he would withdraw it altogether.

The M'Intoshes were not at strength and withdrew, threatening to return and take all.

Munro knew they would honour their threats, and so ordering the least able of his following to drive the cattle straight across the hills for home, he and his fighting clansmen kept to the road, which passed not far from Inverness.

Soon the M'Intoshes were hot-foot on the wake of their enemies, and a desperate conflict ensued. M'Intosh and more than half of his clansmen were slain, but not without considerable loss to the Munro faction.

Never have I seen such a profusion of daffodils —only rivalled by the primroses which flourished everywhere—while the blackthorn formed a snowy mass of scented blossom.

No one can sojourn in Killin without visiting the ruins of Finlarig Castle, at one time a principal seat of the Breadalbane Campbells.

An avenue of ancient beech trees leads towards this old fortress, and time-worn as they are, they are guarded by the stumps of a former generation, planted, it is said, by one Donnacha Dubh a Churichie, or Black Duncan of the Cowl, a heartless warrior who for long occupied the place.

To gain admittance one rings a bell, suspended from the main gate, and supposed to be the nose of a shell used in the Egyptian war !

A quaint old stone sundial stands here, although now long past its duty days, a mere curio from the past. At one time I understand it not merely told the hour, but also gave the moon and tides.

It is said to be the only survivor of its kind in Scotland.

Scarcely less interesting is the fleur-de-lis carved on the guardian wall.

Indeed it is a warlike environment.

In front of the castle entrance is a pit, some six or seven feet deep, paved throughout and still furnished with two massive iron chains. On the edge is a stone with a hole in the centre, and captives whose birth or estate forbade hanging were allowed the honour of placing their heads on the stone, when the executioner soon relieved them of further worry in this world.

Inside the castle proper are a number of ancient stones and carvings, one particularly pointed out being that of a knight spanking his wife, so that the domestic hours in those old times were no less exciting than those spent on the field or in the chase !

The old gallows tree still flourishes notwithstanding its awful past, but the branch from which Black Duncan's victims made their exit from the world, and on which the mark of the rope was said to have been quite distinct, was blown down on the night of the Tay Bridge disaster. The trunk is now a mere shell, and some stormy night the ghosts of Black Duncan's victims will gather round it, and when the day breaks the locals will talk of how the wind seemed to shriek round the castle that night and the old gallows tree was blown down. Its stormy end, as I forecast it, will never occur to them, and they will never know how retribution came to Finlarig !

OLD STONE FIGURES IN FINLARIG CASTLE

102

EXECUTION PIT, FINLARIG

BY GLENDOCHART TO KILLIN

If the invasion comes from the proper airt the great tree will lie prone at the foot of the justice knowe, surmounted as it is by the old holly tree under which Black Duncan sat and delivered his ruthless judgments of pit and gallows, and where justice was rarely tempered with mercy. It will be a mete end to its iniquitous old career.

The newer leaves of the venerable holly are prickly and fresh, but those on the aged branches are smooth and dull, bald with their burden of years.

Here every ben has given back again the echoes of the fierce clan slogans and the clash of steel, but as I turned my back on the ancient citadel and came down the steep narrow path, not even a bird broke the silent stillness, and only the century-old trees seemed to whisper in the shadows of the coming night.

> The shades of eve come slowly down,
> The woods are wrapped in deeper brown.

The beech leaves of last summer rustled on the path, the old giving place to the new; an owl screeched from somewhere in the gathering darkness—and then a light glinted through the trees, and I knew the hotel was just across the wooden bridge.

VI

PONTIUS PILATE'S BIRTHPLACE

There's naething but the sheep tae see—or deer upon the hill,
The cloud-scarves waivin' roun' the ben—the liltin' o' a rill ;
Just miles o' purple heather—an' the bracken on the brae,
But it's a' that I wad ask for in the langest day.

IT is, I think, admitted that Pontius Pilate probably first saw the stars in Britain, and as tradition has settled on Fortingall as his birthplace, for the glamour of the thing I am taking it for granted. After all is said and done, it is quite likely, and many claims are nowadays projected which rest on more gossamer foundations.

Be that as it may, to-day my road led by the winding side of Loch Tay, but at the moment the Lochay was my companion, and its garrulous chatter was counter-balanced by the silent heather-clad braes on the left.

Black Duncan of the Cowl was patron of this district, and ruled and rustled it with the best. Patron he may have been—but saint he certainly was not.

One thing I will say for him—land-grabbing Campbell as he was—his heritage of trees (for he was a master arboriculturist) was his good deed in his day.

That he was a true friend I doubt, but there were no two minds about his hatreds. A lovelace, he was survived by some thirty children, and combined with his feuds and forays the skill of a scheming statesman and the light gift of the poetaster.

As has already been told, he used to sit in judgment under his ancient holly, sending his captives to the right or left as seemed best in his sage opinion. His edicts would probably be carried out on the instant, so that, on one hand, his victims would adorn the old oak tree while, on the other, the blade would drink deep in the pit. Doubtless he would gloat over the untimely end of many a brave fellow whose tartan was for the time in ill-favour with the lord of Finlarig and his nefarious plots and schemes.

To-day such scenes are far down the avenue of history, and the charming tree-lined roadway is peaceful enough in the moist August sunshine.

For the moment mighty Ben Lawers with his attendant Beinn Ghlas, which for the past hour have dominated the view, are hidden by the verdure.

The rowans are plentiful : yellow where they fight for precedence with their strong growing competitors ; scarlet where the sun has touched them, but always charming to the eye.

Loch Tay, which for the past mile or two had hidden amongst her sentinel trees, now came dramatically into the open.

Larch, chestnut, oak, ash, silver fir and the fruitful rowan make the way gay and beautiful, till once again the loch sinks behind the host of trees and hides for a little as if conscious of the wealth of charm she has to contend against, only once more to appear in a long silver streak, more reminiscent of a wide embracing river than a Highland loch.

Trees are always graceful things, but I cannot remember any season when they looked so radiantly beautiful, due perhaps to the heavy rains. Indeed, this summer has produced a garniture of flower and berry, rich in fragrant colouring, which has made the field and hedgeway, moor and woodland, a special joy and pleasure.

Loch Tay must be traversed twice, once either way, ere it can be appreciated, even by the casual passer-by; but so much is secret, hidden by the woods and hills, that only a lifetime's acquaintance will enable you to understand.

But all is dwarfed by Lawers, a great rambling hulk of a mountain, which looks even mightier and more majestic at a distance.

On the farther shore the towering hills are tree-clad at the base, giving way to a purple stretch and shading off to a brilliant green again at the higher altitudes.

So land-locked does the loch appear here that for a little I lost it completely; nothing on either side but sloping braes, thick in sturdy bracken, with the bold and irrepressible peak of Tullich crowning all.

Round the bend, and once more the full stretch of the loch, now carrying a slight mist which adds to, rather than detracts from, its charm.

Ben Lawers now towers above us, an easy hill to climb and a paradise for the botanist.

There is a tale that at one time the men of this

district were veritable Samsons for strength. When engaged on military duty, strict orders were given that no man was to pass a certain milestone, under severe penalty. Now it so happened—and perhaps that may have been the reason for this restriction—that the inn was situated some little distance on the wrong side of the boundary. Anxious to enjoy its forbidden delights, and yet afraid openly to break bounds, one of the men, big John, carried the milestone with him—and so kept within his orders !

Shortly after we pass the Ben there opens up the most beautiful vista of all. The road starts to wind slowly downhill, the loch opens out—the right arm stretching as far as one can see until it merges in the vision with the dark woods which appear to stand knee-deep in the water; the immediate foreground a range of huge bens, green, purple and black as the sun kindles them, sombre and awe-inspiring.

Mark the spot, because here you will find something of interest. The roadway is bordered by a moss-clad stone dyke, and in the field above stands a noble tree, easily distinguished by its bifurcated trunk. Almost under its spreading branches you will find a stone, older probably than its guardian. It is an interesting relic, and the inscription runs :

TRADITION SAYS THIS STONE
IS THE FAIR OR MARKET
CROSS OF FERNAN.
AND THE LEGEND IS
" CURSED BE HE WHO REMOVES IT "
BREADALBANE.

The panorama is now a changing prospect of loch, wood and hill, almost every step producing a new and varying picture.

Here I parted company with the loch and took the narrow road for Fortingall, and almost at once a token of bygone days meets the eye. Under a plane tree, open and unprotected save by the goodwill of the passer-by, stands an old stone baptismal font, brimming to-day with soft rain-water from the Glenlyon hills.

It is all that now remains to mark the spot where in other generations stood a church dedicated to Saint Ciaran.

The river which runs alongside is the Lyon, dashing its crystal amber waters into foam in its anxiety to join the loch, while around, the hills seem to crowd suddenly together, adding a black sombreness to the scene.

On the left is the forbidding entrance to Glenlyon, once a Clan Gregor stronghold, but lost by that tragic clan in the old turbulent days of the past.

Glenorchy's proud mountains, Kilchurn and her towers,
Glenstrae and Glenlyon no longer are ours,
   We're landless, landless, landless.

Sometimes of a winter's evening, when thinking of the lonely hills and glens, my mind dwells for a space on dark Glenlyon, and I wonder if any poor mortal is groping his way along its stygian paths. In summer, one of the most winsome roads I know, but with a sudden trick of changing to an awesome dreary way when the mists gather and the sun hides. Below the roadway the dark turgid stream ;

on either hand trees in abundance, while towering above are the purple hills.

To walk alone through Glenlyon in the gloaming, rain and mist competing, never a living soul to hail, is only in small measure to realise the trials and miseries of a broken man in the days when the strong arm alone ruled. It is impossible to appreciate fully what life meant in those times, but whatever wrongs were committed when greed and secret council went hand in hand, to me Glenlyon seems a stage to suit the tragic stories of the past more fittingly than most.

Never can I forget one September evening traversing the glen which beckons to one at Bridge of Balgie, some miles up Glenlyon, and joins the main road again where the little church looks down on Loch Tay.

What a wondrous glen-road it is ! Its startling beauty is almost unreal, so haunting is its charm.

Picture a huge cleft amongst the hills, shaped like the letter V. From top to base on either side a thick quilt of purple heather, the narrow track, clinging and winding for miles in front, the only break in the hill-side. Below, a brawling stream, every foot white and foam-tormented, for all the world like a long tortuous waterfall. No other feature intervenes until a lonely mountain loch appears. Rarely is the silence violated by so much as a bird. Beautiful—grand—no words of mine can paint or do it justice. Sit for an hour and smoke—for you are away from the world, immured completely, alone with the hills.

If fate places you amongst her favoured ones and

you visit this glen of peace and silence, go afoot, for the road is like some you may know amongst the Galloway hills, too narrow for vehicles to pass in safety—a land made only for those who wish sanctuary and peace.

But that by-way has led away from Glenlyon and the task in hand; still, who would grudge or mar the pleasure of mentally re-treading the old roads of yesterday—roads that come back unbidden to the mind at times with a keener zest and a greater joy than was to be obtained even in the actual tramping of them!

It is on the borders of two hundred years since Pennant adventured through Scotland and wrote his interesting account of the country and its characteristics.

He visited Glenlyon, on horseback I feel sure, and refers to a great clan battle which took place here between the MacKays and the MacGregors, and so fierce and bloody was the conflict that the waters were darkened with blood when the victors washed their weapons.

Another authority tells of a " great battle " which also found its stage in this glen, the contestants on this occasion being the notorious Wolf of Badenoch and the Clan MacIvor, and yet again the river was stained with the blood of the slain.

Campbells, Stewarts, Camerons, Athole men, to name only a few of the fierce brotherhoods, have in turn tried issue here.

And before their day, the great Fingall, renowned as a warrior, had twelve castles in the glen, or at

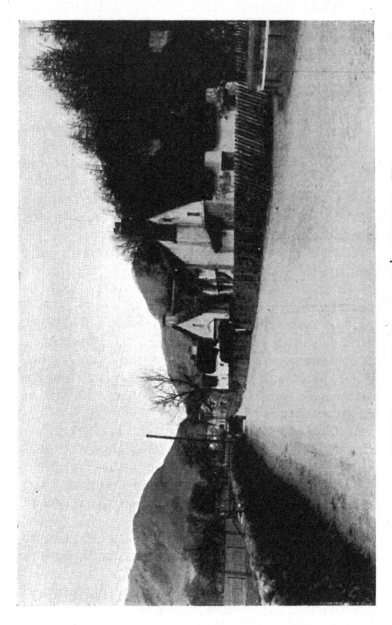

FORTINGAL—PONTIUS PILATE'S BIRTHPLACE

IN GLENOGLE

least so the tale goes, and perhaps that may have
been the reason for its original name of Cromghleann-
nan-clach or the Crooked Glen of the Stones, but
that I cannot say.

But now the thatched roofs of Fortingall peep
amongst the trees and the little old-world clachan
draws near.

Right away sinister memories are awakened by
the sight of Glenlyon House, which guards the
approach to the village. For this was the home of
Campbell, the man who carried through the blackest
deed in Scottish history; from here he went to eat
bread which could be ill-spared, to feign friendship
with his hosts—and cut their throats by way of
thanks. Aye, Glencoe was a bad blot on the page
of Scottish history, and the terror of that night in
the Glen o' Weeping is never likely to be effaced so
long as heather grows or tales are told. A black
business indeed.

> Leave the blood upon his bosom,
>   Wash not off that sacred stain;
> Let it stiffen on the tartan,
>   Let his wounds unclosed remain,
> Till the day when he shall show them,
>   At the throne of God on high,
> When the murderers and the murdered,
>   Meet before the Judge's eye!

Charles II is supposed to have said " there never
was a rebellion in Scotland without either a Campbell or a Dalrymple at the bottom of it," but this
was far worse than an open rebellion. Only, perhaps,
after the '45 was such calculating, heartless cruelty
again conceived, and even Cumberland, bad as he

was, might have stopped short at such nameless treachery. As Campbell himself admitted on one awful occasion, the curse of Glencoe followed him through the years. Some considerable time after the Glencoe horror, he was present at a military execution. A reprieve had arrived for the poor fellow under sentence, and when Campbell was drawing it from his pocket, his handkerchief dropped to the ground. This was the prearranged signal for the firing-party, and so the man was shot ere Campbell was aware of his mischance!

Fortingall, as we know it to-day, owes much to the late Sir Donald Currie. If neat, trim houses be the standard, then that model landowner did much to be thanked for. Personally, I like to see the typical crofter's home, with its low doorway and thatched roof, but I suppose comfort and a higher standard of living must come before picturesque effect, even in a Highland clachan!

For a place so steeped in tale and tradition, Fortingall has an unassuming exterior.

But if you saw in it just an attractive little village, a place in which to loiter for an hour and then pass on, you would be wrong.

There are several points of interest here, not least to me the old yew tree, probably the arborial veteran of Europe.

Go in by the gate which guards the little kirkyard, pass the model church, and there you will find this ancient yew, caged behind stone and railing to protect it from the thoughtless.

At one time it was wholly surrounded by masonry, but careful observers noted signs that such confinement was having an evil effect on the veteran, and so part of the wall was taken away and iron railings, admitting light and air, substituted.

Such a souvenir of other days wants careful nursing, and when its time comes to wither and die, the very hills will feel that they have lost a companion of their youth. I peered through the railing and examined it from every angle, because here was age in stark reality, a living thing which had braved life for two thousand five hundred years, indeed that may underestimate its age.

It would be a full-grown, matured citizen of the forest world some six or seven hundred years before Pontius Pilate was born, and yet here it is, green and fresh, a link with days so distant that we have lost their record !

No wonder its heart looks bad, its trunk here and there a mere shell, and that its back is slightly bent in part ; the burden of two thousand five hundred years is a heavy load to carry.

Pennant, already referred to, mentions the old yew tree, and gives its measurements as " fifty-six feet and a half in circumference."

But he gives other interesting figures which throw an illuminating light on the intervening years. On one side of Loch Tay, " within a radius of fifteen square miles, there lived seventeen hundred and eighty-six souls ; on the other side, almost twelve hundred."

The road which winds round the opposite side of the loch is one of the most beautiful by-passes in Scotland. It is, or should be, a preserve for the man with the haversack however ; at least it is not a good road for cars, and fortunately no provision is allowed for buses, and so it remains secluded and picturesque, a haven for the lover of beautiful paths and lovely trees, where walking is still a real pleasure, undisturbed and free.

Studded with ruined cottages—perhaps the one-time homes of the families Pennant speaks of—laced with rushing cascades, hazel patches and wild flowers in profusion, at every season a rambler's joy, no wonder it is a favourite land for brush and palette. More than once I have been astonished at the abnormal size of the hips—or fruit of the wild rose —hereabouts, and indeed in the autumn season they form a distinctive colour feature with their bright crimson and scarlet splashes against the fern banks.

Last time I passed that way, and a heartening walk it is, I was entertained by the sight of a model rock-garden adorning one of those ideal little residences which so often surprise one in out-of-the-way spots, and to observe two fat porkers rooting about amongst the plants !

No human soul was in evidence, and the magic of hill and loch threw a spell over the scene. To my mind the real charm of Loch Tay is only fully appreciated from this winding narrow pathway.

They were an industrious people on Lochtayside in Pennant's day, and when tending their cattle on the hill-sides they took their spinning-wheels with them and annually sold some fifteen hundred pounds worth of yarn at Taymouth fair.

But Taymouth, too, has lost its old-time glory. The home of the Breadalbanes is now a modern hotel, and golfers in plus-fours smoke cigarettes and discuss the merits of steel shafts underneath the crests and arms of men who played with sterner weapons.

The Breadalbane family name is Campbell, and the founder of the line arrived here somewhere about the end of the sixteenth century—Sir Colin of that ilk.

This gentleman, when it was pointed out to him that his house, instead of being in the centre of his land, had been erected at the eastern extremity, explained that he hoped to make the site the centre in due course, but his pious intentions were frustrated.

Chambers tells a good story of a Breadalbane who flourished many years ago.

When in London this young Earl fell in love with a daughter of the Earl of Holland. The young lady possessed in her own right a fortune of ten thousand pounds, and was the richest prize in the matrimonial market of her day.

His suit prospered, and soon the happy couple were wed.

After the ceremony, Breadalbane brought his young bride home to the ancestral hall—and the manner of their journey was strange, even for that day.

The Earl mounted his Highland sheltie, while his bride climbed up behind; on the other of his two ponies he had the ten-thousand-pound dowry in gold, guarded by their retainers, and so they made their strange, intriguing journey to the North !

But all that is beside the point and takes me away

G

118

for the moment from the old yew tree and the task in hand.

Another ancient tree grows close by, a chestnut, laden with "burs" enough to delight half the school lads in the parish. But old and mellow, as we reckon time, it is a stripling as the old yew counts the years, and its gently swaying branches are the mere exuberance of youth as compared with the stiff rustling of the ancient one.

At the church door stands what to me has the appearance of an old baptismal font; doubtless it too has witnessed many a strange affair in its day, weather worn with its weight of years.

In a field immediately opposite the hotel is to be seen a green mound, surmounted by a stone.

It is a grave, a community burial-place, with its rather gruesome story of a strong-minded heroine.

In the dark days of the plague Fortingall was no more fortunate than many other places. Death was abroad, and found many victims in this out-of-the-way Highland clachan. So rife was it that soon the dead outnumbered the living, and one old woman, carrying on with indomitable spirit, brought the victims to this green spot and day by day added to the hecatomb. It is said she placed them on horseback—a patient old white horse—or dragged them on a rough sledge, and so was enabled to perform her self-appointed duty to her fellow-villagers.

It took one of strong character to act her part, and terrible as was the load fate placed on her shoulders, faith must have filled her heart and attuned her mind and will to her ghastly heritage.

That is the story as tradition hands it down, but later I was told a strange tale by one who is dowered with second sight.

My informant was passing Fortingall one bright sunny day and saw walking in the field beside the stone twelve nuns. They were dressed in garments composed of some rough cloth, but otherwise their habits were much the same as at the present time.

They appeared so natural that this gentleman supposed they were nuns staying in the village for a holiday or rest.

On his glancing at the other side of the road for an instant and looking towards the field again, the nuns had disappeared. By looking away he had lost the correct focus.

He got the impression that the stone marked their burial-place, and that they had lost their lives while nursing the villagers during the Black Plague. That impression was given to him by some outside influence which he could not describe or account for.

That indeed was not his only occult experience in this district. Last summer, accompanied by his wife, he was walking from Killin to Bridge of Lochy. They were walking by the road which leads up the left side of the Lochy. It was a bright summer day, without a shadow or cloud in the sky.

On his passing a mound of stones in the field just before reaching the farm, something there attracted his attention.

My friend's wife suddenly said: "Don't you see figures of men sitting on these stones?"

"Yes," answered my friend; "there are quite a

number of them : they all wear the kilt, and their leader has on a steel helmet."

His wife also noted these facts, and apparently conscious that they were observed, the leader came to his feet and gave the salute.

My friend informed me that many years ago a fierce clan battle was fought on the spot and that the stones cover the burial-place of the dead, who, according to him, are for some reason earth-bound.

To me the second sight is an uncanny thing, but be that as it may, later, as I stood at the hotel window and again saw the green mound in its lonely field, but now in the gathering darkness and under a drenching rain, I could scarce forbear a shudder as I turned towards the glowing peat-fire.

VII

THROUGH GLENOGLE
TO BALQUHIDDER

Long before the towns were built,
   Far behind the years,
Came the Roman cohorts in their pride.
   Here the kilted clansmen,
   And the hardy lowland spears,
Fought their way to freedom e'er they died.

SOME weeks, months almost, were to pass ere I was on the open road again.

Spring, with her promise, was over. Summer, heavy with fulfilment, was gradually losing her ornate tints, and the wind this morning had a bite, early in August as it was.

The dog roses, which had rioted in such profusion of pink and white, no longer made the hedgerows gay with colour, while their compensating heritage of hips still lacked the crimson polish. Like the fruit of the hawthorn—haws beloved in boyhood days—they hung in dull brown clusters—a mere promise of beauty to come when the last lingering hedgerow blossom had disappeared.

Gone, too, were the primroses and daffodils where before their yellow carpet, flanked by flaming whin and more delicate broom, had been a delight to the eye.

   Lowliest of lovely things are they,
   On earth that soonest pass away.

But Nature had merely changed her colour scheme, and to-day the foxglove flaunted her banners beneath the scented honeysuckle while the air was heavy with the perfume of queen-of-the-meadow.

In my own garden, ere I left, the Michaelmas daisies were on the point of bloom, a sure harbinger, in this district at least, that autumn tints of crimson, russet and gold would early displace the more delicate bounty of the wayside flowers.

The changing season brought one new glory—the heather was rioting over every hill-side, forming a purple garment which boded ill for the old cock grouse that nodded so complacently to me as I passed.

Poor old cock grouse—little did he wot that the sheep I met on the roadside a mile or two back were being moved to make his slaughter more certain.

It is necessary to retrace one's footsteps for a mile or two before leaving Killin and to pass once again Inchbhuidh, where the MacNabs sleep so soundly.

As the wild MacGregors were to the Colquhouns, so stood the MacNabs of other days to the Clan Neish.

The Clan MacNab, probably no worse than their neighbours in the old times, had certainly no monopoly of the virtues. One incident in their records can take its place with most.

For many years the MacNabs and the Neishes were at active and bitter feud. Long were they opposed, and open or covert acts of aggression and hatred seemed to keep the ill-blood at fever-heat.

On this memorable occasion they met openly in battle array and fought with such bitter ferocity that when the day was done only a remnant of the Neishes was left alive.

These men, about a dozen in number, sought refuge on an island in Loch Earn, acting under command of an old Highlander, a blood relative of their slain chieftain.

They lived by ravage and plunder, and as they possessed the only boat on the loch, their position was thought to be safe from all comers.

The MacNab chief of those days was a vindictive, unscrupulous old savage who could not stand to be crossed or contradicted, and whose rule was brutal and absolute.

One day a servitor, having been dispatched by MacNab to Crieff to purchase provisions for the Christmas festivities, was met and robbed by the Neishes; was indeed fortunate that his life was spared.

When the ghillie returned from his fruitless errand to the rocky stronghold of the MacNabs, the old man went almost demented with rage and venom, and brooded on his wrongs until, the day of the feast arriving, viewing his own scanty board, and thinking of his blood enemies carousing at his expense, he could contain himself no longer.

Turning to his twelve stalwart sons, he said, " the night is the night if the lads are the lads," a hint which required no stronger expression !

The twelve instantly got ready for their task,

and fully armed with pistol, dirk and claymore, they sallied forth to do their father's bidding and revenge their wrongs.

Knowing that without a boat their mission would prove a fruitless one, led by Smooth John, so called in irony because of his rough manner, they mounted their own boat on their shoulders and so carried it from Loch Tay to Loch Earn over mountain and burn, a seemingly impossible task. As a matter of fact, were it not vouched for, the undertaking seems beyond human endurance, but hatred of their enemies and an unholy enthusiasm gave them super-human endurance.

Never do I visit this region but that night's work comes uppermost in my thoughts. What men these brothers must have been. Strong, brawny, determined ; feral and remorseless as the weasel which crossed their path—also engaged on its blood-thirsty expedition, but if anything on a higher moral plane, because it followed blind instinct in its blood-lust, not revenge and rapine.

Arriving at Loch Earn, they launched their boat and craftily approached the island, where the Neishes resided in a low-roofed hut.

But silence was unnecessary. With the exception of the ancient leader their enemies were in an intoxicated stupor, contributed alike by the MacNab plunder and their sense of security.

Bursting open the door, Smooth John and his brothers soon made short work of their hereditary foes.

Seizing the old leader by his white hair, John twisted his head and severed it with his claymore, while his brothers slaughtered the sleeping clansmen. Only a little boy escaped, by hiding near-by.

On their return, the MacNabs resolved to carry back their boat, but becoming fatigued—and little wonder—they dropped it on the hill-side, where it lay for many years, until in time it rotted and disappeared.

They took the severed head of old Neish with them and presented it to their stern old sire, who called for whisky, and, it is stated, in common with his warrior sons, got drunk with joy !

From what I have gleaned, the MacNabs of bygone days were a fiery, quick-tempered race who brooked no interference with their rights and privileges—real or fancied.

A story goes that on one occasion a laird of MacNab, with a company of what were then known as the Breadalbane Fencibles, was proceeding from the West to Dunfermline, and in addition to their lawful baggage there was concealed a considerable quantity of whisky ! Some spy or traitor had given away the secret, and when the Fencibles were somewhere in the vicinity of Alloa, a party of excisemen that had been lying in wait came forward to appropriate the smuggled whisky. Mac-Nab, as a chief who placed a high value on his personal position, was marching in a stately manner some little distance in advance of his party, when one of the men hurriedly approached and informed him what was toward.

" Did the lousy villains *dare* to obstruct the march of the Breadalbane Highlanders ? " he shouted, and immediately hurried to the scene of operations.

Asking the officials, in none too polite terms, who they were and what they wanted, he was told by their spokesman, " gentlemen of the excise."

" Robbers and thieves, you mean," shouted the enraged MacNab, and insisted on the production of their commissions.

Not expecting any such contretemps, they had not considered it necessary to bring documentary evidence of their status.

" Just what I thought," roared the laird; " a parcel of highway robbers and thieves." And turning to the baggage party he shouted, " Prime ! load ! " but the excisemen did not await the third order, and made for Alloa at top speed.

" Now, my lads," said the laird, " proceed—your whisky's safe."

But to the road. To pass under the railway bridge is like opening the door of another room. The setting at once changes, and the green hills guarding Glenogle stand arrayed on every side. The roadside was garlanded with bloom. King's-bedstraw, harebells, foxgloves, meadow-sweet, and a profusion of our own hardy, dauntless Scotch thistle.

What a defiant-looking plant this same old thistle is, almost conscious of its dignity as the national emblem. But the burden seems to weigh lightly on its rugged head, and its " touch-me-gin-ye-daur " attitude is alike uncompromising for Scot or foreigner, friend or foe.

I stopped to admire one particularly splendid

specimen carrying aloft its many purple crowns, and thought of the noble work its progenitors did so many centuries ago, so that to-day it is looked up to by every true native as his guerdon and exemplar. It has a lesson for most of us, this rugged old flower.

Its sturdy independence, thrawn purple-faced old Scot as it is, makes it worthy of Maclagan's verse :

> Hurrah for the thistle, the bonnie Scotch thistle !
> The evergreen thistle of Scotland for me.
> Awa' wi the flowers in your lady-built bowers,
> The strong-bearded, weel-guarded thistle for me !

In any case there are no lady-built bowers here-abouts ; indeed Glenogle is one of the wildest spots I know. At one part in particular, so studded it is with huge rough boulders that I sometimes wonder how the avalanche which seems so imminent does not sweep down the mountain-side and carry the railway line to chaos in the burn below.

The Scottish Kyber Pass, Queen Victoria is reputed to have aptly named it.

The road got wilder as it ascended, with a fine white-flecked, peaty-looking burn brawling along on the right.

The day had promised rain since early morning, and just as I passed Lairig Cheile, nestling alone here by the roadside, down it came.

No gentle smirr, but a very deluge. Mist suddenly enveloped the hills, and on the other side of the glen, in the distance, it seemed to drift along like huge clouds of steam.

But where I was it was no picturesque drift; rain evidently meant to do its worst, and in a few minutes white foaming torrents were rushing down the hill-sides, turning almost cream-colour in their rage. Rarely have I seen such heavy rain, and the mist on the hill-tops made the scene dark and wild. There was no thunder, unfortunately, to add solemnity to the setting, which became more desolate the higher I mounted.

In half an hour, after everything, myself included, was saturated and in a thoroughly miserable condition, the mists rolled away, the sun smiled, and disclosed the rows of hills and bens towards which lay my goal.

The sun was shining again, but Loch Earn was carrying white horses as I passed. Unfortunately my road to-day led away from the loch-side, and a beautiful vista of tree-spanned, troubled water was my only reward.

The bare hill-sides now gave place to roadside trees and wooded slopes, where on the left lies Ardvorlich, now home of the Stewarts.

There was little traffic; indeed the place seemed deserted until one hurrying motorist arrived and caused commotion enough during his momentary passing; indeed never until to-day did I know that a hen had so many feathers.

Quietly walking along the highway, which at this point is straight and level, I saw a sedate-looking white hen on the roadside. A car, coming at speed, appeared at the bend, and just then the hen, in that wayward manner germane to the species, took thought to cross the road. Part running, part flying in a heavy manner, it was too slow for fate, and the oncoming car caught it on the radiator. The impact was quite audible, and of a sudden the camber was white with feathers, for all the world as if someone had emptied a bolster.

Of the hen I had seen my last, and it was being borne towards the city on the bonnet or wings of the car.

After one passes Balquhidder station the view is as perfect as I can imagine. Green hills, richly wooded at the base, tall bracken, and guarded in the distance by blue-black mountains, rugged and stern. Every change of light or shade varies the scene, but morning, high noon, or evening, it is to me a wonderful picture.

A mile or two of this rapture-compelling scenery, and then Kingshouse. Here I left the main highway and took the by-pass towards Balquhidder. In front lie the Braes o' Balquhidder, sung so sweetly by Tannahill:

> Now the summer's in prime,
>   Wi' the flowers richly blooming,
> And the wild mountain thyme,
>   A' the moorlands perfuming.

The whole place seemed deserted, void of human activity, when quite unexpectedly I came upon a beautiful little church. Surrounded by a high wall, with trees growing it seemed to the very door, so small that it appeared almost as if some architect had made a model for a beautiful cathedral—for a cathedral in miniature it verily looked—and left it

here to be called for. The wall was too high to
scale, the huge iron gates were securely locked, and
so I had to content myself with gazing longingly
through the bars. What a difficult thing it is to
gain access to a Scottish church unless a service is
in progress! No church door stands invitingly
open to anyone who wants to worship quietly alone.
Always you must be one of a crowd, with an
organist perfunctorily stumbling through the ill-
chosen music. Tired nerves—heavy hearts—find
little peace in such surroundings, and the sanctuary
of a quiet pew for undisturbed meditation is ill
to find.

An old farmer—a genial soul—who passed, informed me that if it was Rob Roy's grave I sought,
the kirkyard where he lay was about a mile or so
farther on.

He spoke with that charming West Highland
accent, and was so obviously anxious to be helpful,
that thanking him for his courtesy, I walked towards
the MacGregor's last resting-place.

In the shadow of an old ruined church, looking
down on Loch Voil, the redoubtable outlaw shares
his grave with Mary, his wife, and two of their
five sons, Coll and Robert.

The wind for his watcher, the mist for his shroud,
Where the green and the grey moss will weave their
    wild tartans,
A covering meet for a chieftain so proud.

This is a land with a battle history, where pride
and passion held sway and no man craved stronger
passport than his own right arm.

GLENOGLE TO BALQUHIDDER

MacLarens, MacGregors, Buchanans, Grahams, Stewarts—all have played a part here. Each clan has taken its share in turning the beautiful, smiling country-side into a cockpit, and many a squabble—frequently open conflict—has been enacted in view of the hoary old kirk.

> Often, alas, the fiery cross was sped,
>   And hills resounded the wild battle-cry ;
> Wars of extermination fierce were waged,
>   Most dreadful in their wanton cruelty.

Balquhidder, although so intimately associated with Rob Roy and his family, is Clan MacLaren country.

Not far from this spot took place one of those savage clan battles so often arising out of mere trifles, magnified by the uncompromising clan feeling and native pride.

This affair was no exception, and seen through modern eyes it appears to be a mere trial of savage strength and prowess.

The apparent cause of this bloody conflict appears almost childish to one who digs no deeper than the obvious facts. Clan feeling, of course, explains much, and the wrongs of other days were the basic reason for much that is obscure.

Before the coming of modern Poor Laws almost every village had its " natural," who, because of his affliction, was given more liberty of deed and speech than would be tolerated from a more normal character. Most middle-aged people will recollect the type who, in our less tolerant age, have disappeared from public life. Consanguinity was, perhaps, the root cause for much, but be that as it may, every village had its " Heather Jock " or some such creature ; taken for granted in most cases, occasionally almost public characters. Remember it was the disappearance of Daft Jamie which led to the discovery of the grisly doings of Burke and Hare in a city so large as Edinburgh. Think what the molestation of a mental case would mean if the aggressor was a member of another clan where in any case little love was lost betwixt the tartans.

Here, then, was the stage set and ready.

One of the MacLarens of Balquhidder was of the above type. Attending the annual fair of St Kessaig, held at Kilmahog, not far from Callander, one of the Buchanans of Leny, in passing, knocked off MacLaren's bonnet with a salmon he happened to be carrying. MacLaren told him he would not dare to repeat the act at next St George's fair, held in Balquhidder, and the matter apparently ended there. When the Balquhidder fair came round the Buchanans attended in force, fully armed and determined to prove their strength and daring.

Then, for the first time, the insulted MacLaren told his friends how he had been treated at Kilmahog. At once the Fiery Cross was sent round, and every able-bodied MacLaren hastened to obey.

The rage and impatience of the insulted clansmen was such that they impetuously attacked the Buchanans ere their muster was complete or their forces in order. As a result they were driven from the field in disorder. Victory seemed to lie with the Buchanans until a MacLaren clansman, observing his son being cut down by an opponent, caught the " madness of battle," and shouting the war-cry of his clan, rushed again to the attack. The MacLarens rallied, advanced once more upon their seemingly victorious enemy, and by sheer desperation carried the day. Only two Buchanans escaped from the carnage, later to be slain by their implacable clan foes.

The MacLaren were an old clan and a proud, and many and deadly were their feuds with neighbouring septs. But they went even further than most, insomuch that no man was allowed to enter the Balquhidder church on Sabbath until the last MacLaren was seated !

Naturally, this attitude was bitterly resented by those of a different name, and many fierce quarrels and scuffles took place at the church door.

To-day all names are alike in value, and in the little modern church no man has a prescriptive right in his worship.

The afternoon was waning as I left the old kirkyard, but I decided there was still time to traverse the loch-side to Inverlochlarig and see the house where Rob Roy died.

Narrow the road is, too restricted for the modern speed merchant, and fairly embowered in trees.

I had not gone more than a few yards when a something, which at first glance I mistook for a brown and withered fern, suddenly came to life, scampered along the bank and shot up a tree, so incredibly quick were its movements. A squirrel it was, not the lazy pampered animal of the South, but a denizen of the wild, quick as a flash in its

H

movements and immersed in pre-winter arrangements.

The road wound on in its undisturbed beauty, sloping braes on the right, on the left the loch. No sign of man and his handiwork unless a huge square mound of cut bracken in an open space amongst the trees, the work of someone preparing bedding against the time when winter's snows demanded a warm byre for his bestial.

After I passed Craigruie House, silent and deserted amongst the trees, the character of the scenery gradually changed.

Sunshine, greenery and the bloom of wild flowers gave place to a stage amongst the most rugged and lonely of the West.

Bog-myrtle and ferns in profusion, wet peaty soil, a long strath hemmed round by towering bens. The mist came down again, creeping almost to the loch-side, sheets of rain swept across the water, and a more desolate, lonely spot I have not yet traversed. Not so much as a water-hen amongst the reeds; no wailing cry of peesweep or whaup; just rain, mist and silence.

On the left I caught a glimpse of a square stone wall enclosing a few yards of hill-side, almost enveloped by an old rowan tree.

Surmising its purpose I scrambled through the peat bog—for it was little more—and sure enough it was an old-time burial-place. The iron gate was locked, but the wall had fallen in at one part, and soon I stood amongst the long wet grass.

Only one stone was visible, old and weather-beaten, the arms at the head undecipherable. So far as I could make out, the last tenant died in 1744. Under the overflowing branches of the rowan borne down with the weight of unripe green berries was another stone, but so draped in the moss of years that its message to the living must have disappeared several generations ago.

I squelched back again through the bog and peat to the narrow roadway, but by now the spectral mist had shrouded even the near-by hills and the place was lonely and silence-stricken.

The hard road surface (and it was surprisingly good) gave place to a muddy path which at once led to a fast-flowing brown stream. Farm-carts cross here by a ford, too deep to-day for safety, but a swinging wooden bridge took charge of pedestrians.

And so I reached the house where Rob Roy died. Not facing his foes, claymore in hand as would appear a suitable end for such as he, but in his bed like any peaceful dweller in the glen.

When Rob Roy was on his death-bed, indeed in his last hours, he was told that one of his enemies wished to visit him, and was indeed without.

" Raise me from my bed," was his response, " throw me my plaid around me, and bring me my claymore, dirk and pistols—it shall never be said that a foeman saw Rob Roy MacGregor defenceless and unarmed."

Implacable to the last, during the brief interview, we are told, he maintained a " cold and haughty civility," and when his one-time enemy left he ordered the pipes to play " ha til mi tulidh," and expired before the dirge was finished. So passed a figure to live in memory as long as tales of strife and daring hold hearts in thrall—an outlaw, but like Robin Hood, a friend of the poor.

> They were suited well to their own rude times,
>   And ours will not let them go,
> Till the last of Scotland's sons shall say—
>   'Mid the final wrecks below—
>   " Ha til, ha til me tulidh ! "

To-day, of course, hardly any part of the original house remains. It is inhabited by some half-dozen shepherds, who live their lonely lives remote on the hill-sides.

A woman from the modern farm-house adjacent looks after their meals, but she was no historian. She had heard of Rob Roy, but he was before her time, and so was only of passing interest. " The men knew," she said ; but the men were not about, and the day was rapidly giving place to evening.

From here a good hill-man would find it not too difficult to make over the hills to Crianlarich, Ardlui or Stronachlachar, as he thought best. They are almost equidistant and are really not far as miles go, although some good hills intervene.

Every crag, every mountain-side hereabouts must have been familiar ground to Rob Roy. Isolated, free from the harrying blades of his enemies, well-nigh an inviolable sanctuary. If his eager spirit and sense of oppression had been less dominant he might have lived a happier life—who knows—but even so, Scotland had lost a page of her romance, the glamour of which shall last as long as his native hills and glens.

IN GLENOGLE—NOTE THE THREE BRIDGES—ON LEFT, SAID TO BE THE ROMAN ROAD ;

THE NARROW ROAD BY LOCH VOIL, BALQUHIDDER

GLENOGLE TO BALQUHIDDER

For, free as the eagle, these rocks were his eyrie,
   And free as the eagle, his spirit shall soar.

But by now it was more than grey in the glen,
indeed darkness did not seem far away, and so I
turned for home by the way I had come, nine long
hill-miles towards Ben Vorlich.

VIII

BY LOCHEARN TO ARDVORLICH

O it's up in the morn and awa' to the hill,
Where the lang simmer days are sae warm and sae still,
Till the peak o' Ben Vorlich is girdled wi' fire,
And the evenin' fa's gently in bonnie Strathyre.

HAROLD BOULTON

No wonder Scotland has a plenitude of lochs and running waters. Doubtless it makes for beauty and luxuriant growth—tall trees and lovely ferns nestled amidst their tender mosses—but sometimes it palls to find rain morning after morning, with no respite.

Here in Lochearnhead they laid full responsibility on the Lammas floods, and looked grieved when I passed an obvious retort.

But rain or no rain, it certainly looked enchanting as I paused for a moment before taking the road. The colour scheme, the whole vista, was exquisite.

The hotel was embowered in roses—the long oval loch spread out in front, on either hand high green hills, wrapped in their cloaks of mist. One or two imposing laburnum trees, heavy with seed-pods, formed a near-by background to the rose hedge, and indeed the world looked very beautiful to-day.

The swallows were flying low, hundreds of them it seemed, and every moment I expected one at least to immolate itself on the telegraph wires, but just as disaster appeared imminent, a graceful swerve to safety, at express speed, and then the grand circle once more in seemingly endless procession.

As I took the ambling, twisting road by the loch-side, one after another the little white cottages, perched on a slightly higher level than the turnpike, were veritable bowers of roses and nasturtiums.

Loch Earn is almost on the path here so close is it, but so abundant is the vegetation that only an occasional glimpse reveals its shimmer.

The wayside bushes are weighed down with luscious rasps that no one seems to gather. Last summer when wandering amongst the by-roads near Forfar and Kirriemuir I noticed the same thing. Literally miles of bushes almost at the breaking-point so heavy was the fruit, dropping to rot on the ground.

A winding, turning road this, as loch-side roads should be, each bend disclosing new glories, each turn a different charm.

Off to the left is the gash called Glen Beich, and up on the rocky hill-side I spied a shepherd and three dogs. He was moving at surprising speed, a heavy bag on his back, and the dogs were the embodiment of energy. Suddenly one would detach himself from the moving group, obeying a command, and bound up the rocky side, in and out amongst the boulders, now lost to my vision, anon appearing a black moving dot on the green patch, and then a trickle of sheep descended at his will. It was wonderful work, and even at the distance formed a most interesting picture.

The setting on the right was now very beautiful —trees, heather and ferns, giving a colourful background of almost enchanting loveliness.

To botanist, naturalist, fisherman or mere lover of scenic beauty, here was a very paradise.

The sun was coming out again, and on the other side of the loch hills and glens were appearing as if by enchantment, while the background of mist, slowly rolling eastward, once again gave proof that Nature can stage-manage in the grand style !

I wanted a root of heather for my garden, and high above on a sandy bank was the ideal bush. As I gently inserted the spatula out it came—and then I found it to be literally alive with ants. But these were not its only tenants. A small, beautifully marked snake, some ten inches in length and in girth equal to an ordinary lead pencil, was nestling amongst the roots. It was too bad to dislodge so many citizens of the wild, so I gently replaced the root in its former position and left them, I trust, none the worse for my interference.

Once again Nature stage-managed a transformation. The hills disappear, hidden by a forest of larch, oak and fir. The road was almost dark in parts, adding a new beauty and charm to the way.

The larches here are conspicuously beautiful, and it set me wondering how to-day they form such an outstanding feature on so many western roadways, their introduction to our land being so recent.

Now, the little township of St Fillans, living on the outer edge of high, rocky hills, rugged and bare, to-day's mist adding infinity to the scene.

Opposite is the island where the Neishes thought they were secure, until " the lads were the lads," and a dire fate befell them.

In front lies the road to Crieff and the far North ; to bens which dwarf these hills, and glens whose loneliness is like an ache in the heart, so desolate and forsaken are they ; but here too is peace and solitude, and to cross the narrow, hunchbacked bridge which spans the Earn at St Fillans is to leave the world behind for a space, so silent and deserted seems the path.

Busy motors may rush past on the high road to Crieff and the North—but here was a pedestrian's sanctuary, a care-free walking road.

Few motorists trouble one, and buses are forbidden. Here was indeed a haven where one could hold the crown of the road undisturbed.

Cool trees, green moss for a carpet, and the singing burn, crooning away to itself in an undertone, while just a few yards away (and by the same token some miles distant !) the rushing cars on the main road. But soon the burn is gone and the loch glitters and shimmers on the right.

The path is of surpassing beauty now, the bracken almost as tall as the high deer-fence which in parts guards the narrow roadway.

Trees meet overhead, and the loch is lost below as the road climbs upwards.

This is Ardvorlich country—what a setting for deeds of clan daring, and many a black act found its birth here.

Over there is Glenartney, where Drummond-

Ernoch was so foully used by the Children of the Mist, and this narrow, beauteous pathway leads past Ardvorlich, dark amidst a setting of trees as if seeking seclusion so that again such fearful visitants may be strangers to her door.

At the highest part of the roadway the trees fell away, and below stretched miles of loch, a huge plain of silver without a ripple or movement, or so it appeared from this vantage point. Down and round the bend, easy walking now, over a narrow bridge and once again the loch keeps company with the roadside. A musical lapping of the water, the faint rustle of trees accompanied a silence that was almost eerie.

Again the road mounts, but by such easy gradients as to be almost imperceptible until the loch appears sheer below, the steep bank a festoon of fern, oak and rowan. The rowans are early here, and the red berries add an extra splash of beauty to the canvas. Inland were trees, how far they travelled back before joining the hills I cannot say, but only here and there was a background visible, and an almost perpendicular wall of rock, moss-covered and hoar, veils a wider view. The hills I saw from the other side are lost now that I walk almost at their feet !

Just where the oak and rowan give place to a fragrant larch wood with a brown and inviting carpet, where one could idle and smoke but for the long miles ahead, a small weather-beaten stone stands alone and isolated by the loch-side.

It marks the place of interment of Major James Stewart, whose bones were afterwards removed to the family vault at Dundurn, and who "died about 1660."

I wove quite a romance for my own satisfaction as I slowly proceeded along this larch-lined path, as I take it this is the Major Stewart who slew Kilpont, and whose birth was preceded by such a fearful tragedy.

There are one or two varying accounts of the Kilpont murder.

Wishart (according to Sir Walter Scott no very reliable authority) describes how, early one dawn, "before the drums had beat to march, the whole camp was in an uproar, the men all running to arms, shouting and storming like madmen in their rage and indignation."

Montrose hurried to the spot, fearing trouble between the Irish and Highlanders, when he found Lord Kilpont's body lying on the ground, several wounds providing full evidence that he had been dirked. Kilpont was not the only victim, as Ardvorlich had also stabbed the sentinel and made his escape into the night.

Some said Stewart had been bribed by the Covenanters to kill Montrose, and that on voicing his intention to Kilpont, upon whose assistance he relied, that officer was so horrified that Stewart murdered him to close his mouth. Another theory was that the murder was committed merely in hope of reward. Probably both are wrong, but the fact that Stewart made his way to the Whig army and was given a high command by Argyle probably gave rise to many stories.

The most likely version is that when Alaster

Macdonald, with some Irish auxiliaries, was on his way to join Montrose, they crossed Ardvorlich's lands and committed some outrage which he naturally resented. In addition to lodging complaint with Montrose he also had a violent scene with Macdonald, so much so that both were placed under arrest, it is said on instructions of Lord Kilpont.

To a man of Stewart's hot temper this was insufferable, and to avoid trouble and feud in his camp Montrose brought Ardvorlich and Macdonald together and forced them to shake hands and become, outwardly at least, once more on friendly terms. Stewart was such a powerful man that when he grasped Macdonald's hand he crushed it so as to make the blood start.

After the Battle of Tippermuir, when the army was encamped at Collace, Montrose entertained his officers, and naturally Ardvorlich and Kilpont were of the company! There is an old rhyme which says " Grace and peace cam' by Collace," but it was far wrong on this occasion.

Excited by drink, Stewart apparently upbraided Kilpont for his former action, and to men of their type words led to blows, and Ardvorlich in his anger stabbed his friend and then made good his escape. That he joined the Covenanting army means little. To a fighting man, fierce and resentful, continuance with the Montrose forces was impossible, and under the circumstances nothing was more natural than to put his services at the disposal of the other faction or alternatively be outlawed by both.

LOCH EARN

ST FILLANS AND LOCH EARN

BY LOCHEARN TO ARDVORLICH

Afterwards in Lochearnhead they told me the tradition of the Major Stewart stone by the roadside—but I cannot vouch for it although it is likely to be founded on fact, as are so many of these old-time, bygone tales.

Major Stewart had an inveterate hatred of the MacGregors, and considering how he and his forbears had suffered at the hands of that unruly clan, his animosity is not to be altogether wondered at !

In life he was a strong, virile, indeed ruthless man—quick to anger and ready to avenge insult, real or imaginary, to the full.

He had many opportunities of wreaking vengeance on his hereditary enemies, and hanged and slew not a few MacGregors in his day.

That the Clan Gregor was not composed of weaklings history proves ; however, they were generally worsted by the redoubtable Ardvorlich warriors.

When death—the one implacable enemy he could not resist—claimed Major Stewart, as the cortege was proceeding slowly by the loch-side, word was whispered that the MacGregors, robbed of vengeance when their enemy was in life, were gathering to wreak some unspeakable insult on his dead body. An emergency grave was dug by the road-side, and there he lay until, at a later date, his remains were taken up and laid to rest in the family burial-place ; and so in death, as in life, his enemies were foiled.

The story may or may not be true—I give it as it was related to me—but many more unlikely deeds were enacted in these old days when clan feuds were rife and passions carried sway.

But another discovery drove the thoughts of Major Stewart and his stormy life from my mind.

On the inland side of the path, amongst tall rank grasses, was another stone, weather-beaten and obscure. I could just decipher the inscription :

NEAR THIS SPOT WAS
RE-INTERRED THE BODIES OF
7 MACDONALDS OF
GLENCOE KILLED WHEN
ATTEMPTING TO HARRY
ARDVORLICH
ANNO DOMINI 1620

Here was glamour of old clan days with a vengeance. A restless, fighting sept the Glencoe men, but perhaps not much worse than some of their neighbours who dwelt in a greater, or at least more outwardly apparent, odour of sanctity.

Up there lies Ardvorlich itself, and through the trees I glimpsed two ponies, pannier-clad, with some attendants (the one in the kilt fitted into the picture ideally), walking quickly towards the house. They were beaters, and the long day on the grouse moors had apparently left them fresh and strong, because I should not care to go far at the pace they were making.

But if the men of Ardvorlich were not always on such peaceful missions, they lived in a district which was frequently the scene of warlike unrest, and it took strong men to hold their own amongst such neighbours.

At one time a stone called the Clach Dearg, in

the possession of the Ardvorlich family, had a wonderful reputation for the cures it was supposed to effect amongst sick cattle. Unlike modern remedies, each of which is limited in its scope, the Clach Dearg, or red stone, was alike good for all. It was simple too in its application, indeed one had merely to dip it in water, and after drinking, the diseased animal was certain to recover its health and energy. The legendary story of this talisman is, I think, that at one time it was used in some sacred rites by the Druids.

This sort of " charm stone," if I could so call it, was not altogether uncommon in past times.

In Glenlyon House they had also a stone which was even more powerful in its results. As a matter of fact if the water in which it had been immersed was affused over those going to feud or battle, it possessed the valuable merit of making them immune from serious wounds. As lately as the '45 this stone was produced, and the men going off to "fecht for Charlie " underwent its baptism. There was one exception, and he said it was not merely superstitious but actually sinful, and so refused to have the ritual performed on his person. He alone was killed ; all those so protected returned from Culloden unscathed !

No less wonderful was the cure for madness which was invested in a bone, at one time the property of Campbell of Barbreck; or the precious Lee Penny which performed many miracles in its time.

Quaint flotsam and jetsam these upon the troubled sea of Scottish history and superstition, but doubtless effective enough in their own way. Faith, it is said, can move mountains.

Nor was second sight confined to the Highlands, indeed Peden the Prophet was a Lowlander, and is there not a tale of another Ayrshire man who, stranded in London, far from home and loved ones, was told by some supreme agency to go home and dig in a certain spot and there he would find something to advantage him ?   Doing so, he recognised the place spoken of by his spectral assistant, and digging as instructed, found a pot of gold which laid the foundation of a noble family !

This may seem all by the way, but in truth it is not so far from our subject either.   Look back amongst the trees there and you will see the turrets of Ardvorlich " much resembling pepper-boxes," because this is the Darnlinvarach of " A Legend of Montrose," and here it was that Allan had the " cloud upon his mind."

Heather hills again stretch away on the left, and by now the road has deserted the loch, although glints of its sheen are visible through the thick foliage.   On passing the gates of Edinample Castle, a gaunt white house amongst a bower of trees, perfect in its setting and admirable in its taste— the glistening miles of silvery water come into the open with a dramatic gesture.

> In the lone glen the silver lake doth sleep ;
>   Sleeps the white cloud upon the sheer black hills,
> All moorland sounds a solemn silence keep,
>   I only hear the tiny trickling rills.

From here the long vista of hill and glen on the

THE PASS OF LENY, CALLANDER

FALLS OF LENY

western side is majestic. The sun was going down and his dying glory formed such a picture that I stood in the rain—for strangely it was a constant and steady downpour on my side of the loch, but dry and bright on the other—loth to leave it all.

And so, down the short brae, past the little white church, and back to the Balquhidder road again.

KINGSHOUSE TO CALLANDER

This is the road the clansmen trod,
  In the days of the long ago,
When a man was a man—and his own keen blade
  Was the ward of the way he would go ;
    When a man's sword arm
    Was his guard from harm,
And he walked as his own will bade !

IT was hard to believe that just over the hill-side lay the dark and rugged Inverlochlarig. This morning the sun was making amends, and if to-day the beauty of the road was more domestic, it had a full share of witchery and charm.

Yesterday in Rob Roy's glen it was bleak and forbidding ; here near-by bracken runs to meet the tree-clad slopes, splashes of colour relieve the greenery, and altogether it was a blither road to traverse this bright morning.

Even so, I do not know which road was better—it is perhaps a matter of mood. Wooded slopes, tall, nodding foxgloves, far heather stretches, charm the eye and please the senses, but they cannot inspire the heart with that feeling of awe which comes only when one is alone amidst the stillness primeval and desolate, of dark towering bens and tumbling waters.

This fair roadway of to-day is Highland, but it is

domesticated. One instinctively knows that somewhere in front lie houses, shops, tourist hotels—
yesterday led only to the wide-open, ben-ringed
straths pathless and untrodden, where the red deer
live, and the whirr of the grouse or the bleat of
a sheep is all that ever breaks the silence. An
occasional isolated cairn, its purpose forgotten ere
its sentinel rowan was a sapling, was the only sign
that foot had passed that way.

Here man has taken his place and wrestled with
Nature until he has forced his will in parts. Hay-
fields cropped, but sodden in the August sun where
the rains of yesterday form pools in the hollows.
Some green, unhealthy-looking corn, poor fruit for
such heavy ploughing, the eager bracken waiting a
chance to overrun and claim once more its ancient
birthright.

For a moment I paused to see if by chance old
Ben More showed up against the waiting hills, and
there, a yard or two in front, I spied a hill-sheep
and a rabbit, noses almost rubbing, feeding off one
small patch of green grass! It formed an amus-
ing picture, and one I wanted. Silently—or at least
so I thought—the camera was adjusted, but when
I looked up the rabbit had disappeared! It was
running no risks!

The day was hot now, bees humming about their
duties, but not a bird note could be heard. August
is the silent month amongst the feathered songsters,
and but for a little brown wren which mysteriously
flitted in and out of the hedgerow, of bird life there
was no other sign.

Over on the right somewhere lay the old Balquhidder Church of yesterday, but I could not trace it amongst the wood-clad hills. It was a wonderful morning for day-dreams in the quiet heat, where but for a passing car the busy world might be non-existent.

The years cannot have brought many changes to these hills—and down the far-lying braes it would be no difficult thing to imagine the flash of a red tartan as Rob Roy or one of his sons adventured forth in peace or war.

Gone are the days when " to gang into Rob Roy's country was a mere tempting o' Providence." Time has long since broken that entail of evil which seemed fated to heir these hills and glens to sorrow and bloodshed.

Rob Roy was not by any means alone in the depredations of that day, but his name has come down to us, outstandingly because of the glamour Scott spread over him like a mantle, and of the times in which he lived—

> When tooming faulds or sweeping of a glen,
> Had still been held the deeds of gallant men.

The popular impression of a man who does deeds of prowess is of a great giant, upstanding amongst his fellows, but Rob Roy was not that. In fact he was not particularly tall, but he was gifted with two outstanding features which fitted him specially for his wayward, challenging life. These were his breadth of shoulder, which gave him power, and his extraordinary length of arm.

Think of the wonderful advantage a swordsman could claim whose arms were so long that he could tie his hose-garters below the knee without stooping.

Red as his name denotes (Red Robert) he was in many ways a braggart, but nevertheless a brave, valiant character to strive and survive as he did, his hand against so many implacable enemies. And in his wife he had a fitting mate, and Rob Roy on one occasion accused her of having caused most of his strife ! After all it is good that he lived ; his exploits and escapades have given an added interest to the grandeur of the hills and the beauty of the lochs and glens amid which his stormy days were spent.

It was difficult to believe that these serene and quiet uplands had resounded to the tumult of battle, and that hunted men had skulked from avenging blades amongst the rocks and bracken.

And now across the hump-backed bridge and through Strathyre, gay with scarlet geraniums and rambler roses, over the outward guardian bridge—and so again to the silent road.

Overhead the tall trees meet and the sunshine is lost for a space. Dark and sombre, but deliciously cool after the glare, the mossy banks are laden with ferns and the inevitable foxgloves range high amongst the bracken and tall grasses—and then the open road again, Loch Lubnaig shining and rippling in front, a sparkling silver sheet.

The mountains rise sheer from the loch-side carved from the solid rock, each with its banner of cloud, and a solitary angler plying his craft from a slowly moving boat is the only sign of life.

Here lived Bruce, the celebrated traveller, and

here he wrote his ponderous work on Abyssinia, running to five volumes no less, published towards the latter end of the eighteenth century. Near-by, the world first greeted Alexander Campbell, a poet and staunch Jacobite, who numbered Burns, Scott and Hogg amongst his distinguished friends. Not far away lie the mortal remains of Dugald Buchanan, the Gaelic poet mentioned elsewhere. The world has passed on, and they are forgotten by most, over-shadowed by a more modern school, but mayhap they laboured not in vain !

Scott has, of course, overwhelmed all other associations with his " Lady of the Lake," and a setting of wondrous charm it is ! The winding road holds by Lubnaig with its varied facets. On the left a garden of wild flowers is displaced by dense bracken, which in turn gives way to wood, here and there a patch of purple heather, amid which rocks and boulders add a sterner beauty.

I was told of a white wild cat which made its home somewhere near-by, and if true it probably by now adorns some " sportman's " smoke-room ! Like the magpie and other so-called vermin, the wild cat, far from being extinct, would seem to be increasing in some districts. Owning no game preserves may account for my views, but I should be sorry to hear that the wild cat, badger and golden eagle had been finally exterminated and banished from their native haunts.

If Scott may be claimed as the literary giant of this district, Ben Ledi dominates it physically, raising his gaunt old head three thousand feet into the clouds, and peering over his neighbours from some uncanny angles. The name Ben Ledi signifies the Hill of God; and I sometimes think his huge bulk is more appreciated at a distance, for then he towers above the smaller bens like a Saul amongst the people !

In far back, forgotten days Ben Ledi was the stage of strange Druidical rites. There is no stone circle or monument to mark the occasions, but from its heights the people worshipped the sun, and this Beltane sacrament, if I may so term it, commenced on May Day and lasted for three days. Here was kindled the sacred fire, and doubtless many strange cantrips were indulged in by the priests.

When Campbell, in his wandering tour, visited this place, the boys still kept up the old Beltane-day customs.

He describes how these lads, gathered from the surrounding hamlets, met in some sequestered spot amongst the hills where the turf was thick and green. Here they lit a fire and cut a deep trench round it so that the inside formed a table; they then consumed a meal consisting of milk and eggs beaten into a custard. A thick oaten cake was then baked on the embers of the fire and divided into pieces equal to the number of persons. One part of the cake was bedaubed with ash or charcoal and then all the pieces were put into a bonnet. Each lad drew his cake, and he to whose lot fell the blackened section was deemed the victim or sacrifice to Baal's fire. Instead of being immolated, however, he was forced to jump three times through the embers of the fire, and that finished the ceremony.

Probably it is a relic of the old pagan days,

and perhaps by some such drawing of lots were the priests provided with human victims for their Beltane sacrifices.

Like the old Hallowe'en customs of a past generation, these things will soon be mere memories, so Anglicised are we becoming even in the country villages.

There is one dark legend associated with this grim old mountain, a tale more modern than its fire-worshipping devotees, awful if true, as I believe it is.

One winter's day a funeral party from the neighbouring Glenfinlas, numbering some two hundred mourners, was slowly wending its way to the graveyard of St Bride. They were crossing the mountain shoulder, white with snow, and under the belief that the ice was strong enough to carry them, or whether deceived by the snow, they proceeded across the small loch which graces the hill-side. When fairly upon its bosom the ice gave way and the whole company perished in the icy waters, Lochan-nan-corp, or the Small Loch of the Dead Bodies it is named to this day!

Dark thoughts these this bright noon, but in keeping with the rugged, cruel-looking hills hereabouts—and then the Pass of Leny took me and the mountains were for the moment obscured.

The Falls of Leny are amongst the show places of our land, and grand they doubtless are—but give me the Falloch in spate; dashing amongst the rocks, foaming from the glen, the rowans red above and the nearest township a clachan!

You may not share my view, but be that as it

may, the wild free braes on the left are more
interesting to me. Their untrammelled, natural
beauty is portrayed in one of Scott's stanzas, and
line for line they comport to it like a word
painting :

> Boon nature scattered, free and wild,
> Each plant or flower, the mountain's child.
> Here eglantine embalmed the air,
> Hawthorn and hazel mingled there ;
> The primrose pale, the violet flower,
> Found in each cliff a narrow bower ;
> Foxglove and night-shade, side by side,
> Emblems of punishment and pride,
> Grouped their dark hues with every stain
> The weather-beaten crags retain.
> With boughs that quaked at every breath,
> Grey birch and aspen wept beneath ;
> Aloft the ash and warrior oak,
> Cast anchor in the rifted rock,
> And, higher yet, the pine-tree hung
> His shattered trunk, and frequent flung,
> Where seemed the cliffs to meet on high,
> Its boughs athwart the narrowed sky.

An old castle stood somewhere hereabouts, but
in 1737 the stones were removed to build a mill
and form a damhead ! It was a stronghold of the
Buchanans, and probably was at that time a mere
tumble-down ruin, as the Charter of the family
dates back to 1247 in the reign of Alexander II.

This same Pass of Leny has been the scene of
many an exciting incident, and here at Kilmahog
one outstanding deed of prowess was performed.

It is an old traditional story that one Shaimis
Beg, or Little James, so designated for his lack of

inches, had a stronghold on the West of Loch Achray, where he was wont to retreat in times of danger or emergency.

This Shaimis Beg was keeper of the King's deer forests of Glenartney and Glenfinglas, and one day a band of Argyllshire Campbells, on some marauding excursion, made a descent on the royal preserves and killed a goodly number of deer, without so much as asking Little James's permission !

As the Campbells were returning from the chase, carrying the choicest parts of their spoil and on the outlook for somewhere to pass the night, they met Little James.

Strong in their numbers, and misjudging the royal warden because of his lack of inches, one of the marauders, pointing to the hut or stronghold on the loch, asked what magpie had built its nest on the island ?

Little James, no whit abashed, retorted it was the nest of one that scorned all greedy hawks, no matter from which quarter they came !

" Tell the magpie from us," returned the Campbell, " that we shall return and harry his nest ; tell him also that we shall return soon, and perhaps he will find that our hawks are good at taking their prey."

" Then," said Little James, not to be outdone in badinage, " it may so happen that the magpie whose nest you would molest may have power over many hawks which inhabit these mountains and glens, and when the strange hawks arrive it may be for their discomfort."

With that the Campbells resumed their journey,

taking their booty with them, as the warden without aid was powerless.

In due course the Campbells kept their promise, but Little James was on his guard, and calling out the men over whom he had authority, they put up such a stout defence that few of the invaders were allowed to return to their homes.

Amongst those who distinguished themselves in this scrap was one of little James's henchmen, by name Broilan Beg Macintyre, so named because of his diminutive size but vast fighting qualities.

The Campbells who escaped from the affray vowed to be avenged on Little James and all who swore fealty to him, but more particularly on Broilan Beg Macintyre, whose blade had inflicted such punishment.

Accordingly, five picked men of the clan set out to waylay Macintyre, and having crossed the Teith somewhere in the Pass of Leny they met the man himself, busy with his cattle, near the old bridge of Kilmahog.

Macintyre was alone and without arms, whereas the Campbells had bows and arrows on their backs and broadswords at their sides.

Evidently they did not recognise Macintyre, and one of them asked, civilly enough, if he knew of such a man and where he was to be found ?

Their victim replied that he did know Broilan Beg Macintyre and thought he could put them on his track, but feigning to be simple-minded, pointing to their bows and arrows, he asked what they were and for what purpose did they use them ?

The Campbells jeered and laughed at him, and

one of the party, handing him his bow told him to shoot. Macintyre, who in reality was a skilled bowman, acted so clumsily that his arrow merely travelled a few yards in wavering flight to the infinite amusement of the Campbells, who thought him a buffoon. But Broilan Beg was no fool, and picking the arrows one by one from his foeman's quivers, he was content to thole their loud laughter so long as he was gaining his point.

Only too late the mockers found their last arrow sped. Then Macintyre suddenly ran swiftly to the spot where he had directed the greater number of arrows.

Quick as the Campbells were to follow and rectify their error, Macintyre was faster, and ere they could come up to him three of the party were transfixed with their own shafts.

The surviving couple made off and left Broilan Beg Macintyre to tend his kyloes in peace!

To the right leads the road to the Trossachs, beautiful and worthy of a visit of exploration, but to-day it was not my road, cool and tempting as it appeared.

Above, the sky was like sapphire, broken here and there by white translucent clouds, and the smell of peat-reek from a near-by cottage lent an added charm. Indeed the whole atmosphere was delightful and vaguely unreal.

> All in the Trossachs glen was still,
> Noontide was sleeping on the hill.

Many years ago the Loch Katrine district charmed me—to-day I leave it unvisited. Last time I ventured it was in the hands of vandals—a cement pier or something of the sort was under construction and the beautiful loch-side was lacerated and dishevelled. Now I fear to go back, preferring to carry the memory of an enchanted spot, once opulent in its finery, and, beautiful as it still may be, defaced and pillaged by those who forgot their sacred duty to posterity.

The Highland temperament is complex, and an example is to be found in one, Malise Graham, who dwelt and had his habitation near Loch Katrine many generations ago.

In the early days of the seventeenth century a gentle name was no guarantee of wealth, and the precincts of Holyrood House were a debtor's sanctuary.

Somewhere about the year 1680 the Earl of Menteith betook himself to the capital to escape from a dunning creditor, until in despair he sent a messenger to Malise Graham beseeching his financial assistance.

Prompt to the call, Graham put the required amount in a roe-skin purse and set off on foot to the relief of his chief. Arriving at his lordship's residence, dusty and travel-stained, the lowland retainer who answered his summons, mistaking Graham for a beggar, was handing him a copper when the Earl, who happened to observe the incident, hastened to chide the man for perhaps giving offence to his kinsman, but Graham, far from being angry, drew the purse from his bosom and handed it to Menteith, at the same time observing that while he hoped the money would relieve his lordship's embarrassment, on his part he was never above taking a bawbee, and indeed would not object to take as many as the man cared to give him !

Over there at Loch Vennacher there is a tradition of a Kelpie. The Kelpie is a mythical demon in the form of a water-horse, and many are the Highland tales which surround the breed. In this incident the demon ingratiated itself with some children playing near-by, until one, more hazardous than his companions, mounted the horse's back. Soon the bolder spirits followed their companion's example, until one by one they were all astride. The artful Kelpie, with diabolical cunning, elongated his body to accommodate them all, but they, poor innocents, did not apparently observe the phenomenon ! Once they were all aboard as it were, the Kelpie suddenly plunged into the loch, where in a far cavern it devoured them at its leisure !

The story, so far as I can gather, was vouched for by one little boy who managed to escape just as the fearsome steed was on the point of plunging into the dark waters.

The water-bull was firmly believed in at one time in the North, and I think it was sometimes angled for, the bait being a sheep and the rope which served as a fishing-line was attached to a tree for security. Dr MacCulloch once came across a farmer actively engaged in pursuit of one which he believed tenanted a certain pool. His two sons were stirring the water with hay-forks while the farmer stood by with his gun, ready to shoot. As the water-bull was impervious to anything other than silver, the gun was loaded with a silver sixpence !

But here we are at Callander with its trim villas and colourful gardens, so well watered under its weeping skies.

The old Dreadnought Inn, at one time a notable landmark, has lately been demolished. The name originated from the MacNabs, whose motto it is. The stage from Stirling had its headquarters here, until railways were instituted, and even in the days of Scott, Wordsworth, Southey, and other celebrities who lodged at varying times in the old hostel, access to the wild country by the Pass of Leny was a hazardous journey. To-day the motor-buses splash one with mud as they pass, and if the Buchanan clan dared send round the Fiery Cross and appear accoutred with targe and claymore, the local constable at Kilmahog would fearlessly beard them armed with only notebook and pencil, and they would be lucky to get off with a caution for committing a breach of the peace !

X

CALLANDER
AND A GALLANT COMPANY

Quoth he, " If men had only tails,
They're near as guid as dogs, O."
DR NORMAN MACLEOD

ALL night it had poured incessantly, but this morning the sun, if a trifle wan and clouded, was doing
its best to make amends and brighten things up a
bit.   Even so it did not look too full of promise.

Not merely had it rained during the sleep hours,
but all the previous evening a weary, steady drip
had saturated the country-side and made hills and
crops alike sodden.

Out-of-doors it had been too uncomfortable and
depressing for exploration, and so my only venture
was to cross the street in search of newspapers and
a book.

Newspapers there were aplenty, but of books
the selection was not one which appealed to me,
until I found a popular edition of an old favourite,
one I had read and re-read several times.   It may
have been coincidence, perhaps I was on the verge
of second sight, through wandering so much of late
among the glens,—whatever tempted me I cannot
say, but the book I bought was " Owd Bob," that
epic of sheep dog trials.   And so the evening

PENNING THE SHEEP, CALLANDER

172

DOUNE CASTLE AND RIVER TEITH

173

became a pleasure as once again I entered into the rivalry of these two canine wonders, the proud, debonair Gray Bob of Kenmure and Adam M'Adam's outlawed, relentless Red Wull.

As I say, what tempted me to buy this book I do not know, but this morning, filling a pipe, I sauntered towards the hotel door, suddenly to become conscious that unusual doings were afoot.

The normally quiet, almost sleepy station yard was abustle with life. Farmers, shepherds, men of the hills and open spaces, were passing singly and in groups, and every man seemed to have at least one dog following closely at heel!

Never was the quiet street so thronged, and obviously something of importance was brewing.

And then the hall-porter told me all about it! The National Sheep Dog Trials were to be decided, and to-day so many dogs would qualify to represent their country at the International Meeting in the autumn.

No wonder there was an air of repressed excitement, and I hoped for the sake of these fine dogs that the threatened rain would hold off. But no— down it came with hurricane force, although well I knew that no deluge could damp the ardour of such a gathering.

Rain or no rain the contest would go on; and come wet or shine I too was determined to witness the sport.

We had not far to go, as the arena was a large field on the immediate outskirts of the town. The clouds were doing their worst now in a continuous heavy downpour; underfoot was little better than

K

a swamp, while a miniature loch in the centre of the field was visibly widening, yet everyone, contestants and spectators alike, appeared happy and unconcerned!

Than Callander there is no more appropriate arena for sheep dog trials, for it was in this district that the first South Country breed of sheep was introduced to the Highlands. The experiment was successful beyond all expectations, others followed the example, and the old breed was gradually superseded.

In 1759 an Alloa shepherd named James Yule had been unfortunate in respect to disease amongst his flocks, and anxious to try what a change of pasture would do, he sent twenty score of year-old lambs—hogs, I believe, is the proper term—to winter on the lands of a Mr Buchanan near Callander.

Two men, each answering to the name of Murray, introduced flocks, one in Glen Falloch, the other in Glendochart. Later, one Lindsay came to Lochearnhead, and so the system spread, the advent of the sheep tending to break down old customs and in great measure cause depopulation, with all the heartburnings and sadness caused by the clearances.

Writing somewhere about the last years of the eighteenth century, one of those old peregrinating journal-makers whose works are so interesting to-day, writing of the Western Highlands says:

" The spirit of speculation has spread rapidly from valley to valley. An epidemic of madness for sheep-grazing seems to rage with unabating fury. Rents within the last ten years have advanced beyond all former calculation ; most parts of the

Highlands are under sheep; and the country has become desolate, and almost drained of its native inhabitants."

But the story of the clearances and the heartless dispersal of the moral owners of the glens is too sad a tale for this late day, and in any case here was gathered as cheerful an assembly as any man could wish to meet, Highland and Lowland in friendly contest.

A shepherd was working his dog when I arrived at the ringside. Blinding rain was lashing across the field, but his oilskin was lying on the grass at his side, and he was apparently too engrossed even to throw it over his shoulders.

And then followed a wonderful exhibition of man's training allied to canine sagacity.

It is all a matter of haste without flurry; the man's pent-up emotion and excitement are not obvious, but are there nevertheless, as every moment counts.

Command and style are awarded valuable points, and the secret of success lies in quick understanding between man and dog.

A whistle—and the sheep are heading straight down the course. Another whistle—on a different note—and Mirk or Rover sinks to the ground so that the speed of the five sheep is checked. It was all very wonderful—the pages of " Owd Bob " come to life !

Listen to this : " At the pen it was a sight to see shepherd and dog working together—the master, his face stern and a little whiter than its wont, casting forward with both hands, herding the sheep in ; the grey dog, eyes big and bright, dropping to hand, crawling and creeping, closer and closer.

" ' They're in ! Nay—ay—dang me ! Stop 'er ! —good Owd Un ! Ah-h-h, they're in ! ' and the last sheep reluctantly passed through on the stroke of time."

Change the idiom and there you have it, be it in Yorkshire dales or amongst West Highland hills.

What made it even more noteworthy, to me at least, was the fine work done under such distressing conditions. The rain was torrential with but few fair intervals, and the fairway was now quite under water. Time and again the sheep balked at the water, but the dog forced them on in a marvellous way.

I admired the men—hearty, open-air, good fellows—but I take off my hat to the dogs ! It was a competition—and a keen one at that, every man anxious to have the honour of representing his country at the even sterner trial in September— but never was rivalry conducted under more friendly conditions.

Dogs were here from all quarters of Scotland— from Campbeltown in the west, Berwick in the south, St Andrews upheld the honour of the east, and from Inverness a champion came to represent the north.

As for the men, widespread as were their homes, every farmer greeted his fellow as Tom, Sandy or James. It was an outstanding example of big, clean, open-air methods, and a joy to be in such company. In Doric or Gaelic it was all the same —broad humour, kindly jest—a handshake and a

" hard luck " for the man who failed to pen his sheep in the stipulated time, or a hearty clap when the work was done in smart, business-like style.

If the shepherds concealed their anxiety under a show of indifference, not so the dogs! They quivered with excitement when a rival was working its trial, and their eyes never left the sheep, as if each awaited the signal to " away bye " and show the other fellow how to control his charges!

In front as I stood, the Leny was gradually rising—a rushing, dark-brown flood. On the right towered Ben Ledi, a black, broken mass amidst the clouds, one moment clear and dominant, soon again screened and indistinct behind the mist and rain.

Slightly to the left of the great ben, and I hope discernible on the photograph reproduced, is a huge boulder which goes by the name of Samson's Putting Stone.

Perhaps you do not know, but Samson at one time lived with his mother in a hut on the hillside, and naturally his amusements were of a type befitting his herculean strength.

One morning he lifted this great stone with the intention of throwing it into the valley below, but either he had not sufficient breakfast (which, as a slur on his mother, I discard) or the stone slipped from his hand and came to rest in its present, and rather precarious, situation.

We are to-day puny mortals, but even Samson's feat was child's play compared with that of Old Nick, who once took a huge rock in each hand and threw them at St Patrick. One is to-day Dumbarton Rock, on which stands one of Scotland's four

" official " castles, and the other is named Dumbuck, so that his missiles were no light pebbles. Fortunately St Patrick escaped between the two, and sought a more serene haven in Erin.

All that, of course, is by the way, and has nothing to do with sheep dogs and their more modern tasks.

By now everyone was thoroughly drenched, but such was their ardour that, like Tam o' Shanter —although from a vastly different reason—they

Didna mind the storm a whistle.

For my part, I decided to take to the road again before I was thoroughly water-logged.

On my way back to Callander I passed a hayfield now quite under water, only the tops of the haycocks showing, and what before had been bare and comparatively featureless hill-side was now alive with churning mountain burns.

XI

ON TO STIRLING

The day is cold, and dark and dreary,
It rains, and the wind is never weary.

IT was still raining, and in no uncertain manner, when I left Callander by the Doune road. Everything seemed water-logged, and the passing cars were splashing and adding to the already overgreat discomfort.

Scotland is a beautiful country, but on a wet spell such as this its beauties are apt to be lost in the mists and haars, and it takes a very plenitude of beauty to atone for floods and spates.

However, I was on the road, rain had done its worst, and I was determined to keep to my programme, come what would.

The road was uninteresting until I came to a ruined cottage on the left. A small furry animal on the roadway was behaving in a curious manner. It would run about a third part of the way across, raise its head in a peculiar, peering attitude, reminding me of a miniature sea-lion, then turn and scurry back to cover. I halted a few yards off to watch what was brewing. It was, of course, a weasel, and was quite oblivious of my presence. After one or two attempts it ran to the camber of the road, lifted its young one and bore it towards the old cottage. The poor little one had been run

over by a passing car and was crushed and lifeless.
I am not an admirer of the weasel tribe, but I felt
sorry for the hapless mother, cruel, blood-thirsty
little beastie though she is !

I wonder when wild life will adapt itself to the
swift-moving motor traffic. Between Callander and
Doune I counted four small birds—all chaffinches,
I think—and one dead rabbit on the roadway.
Next time you happen along a country road keep
a sharp look out, and the mortality will surprise
you. It is, I suppose, unavoidable under modern
conditions, but anyone who tramps the open roads
must often regret the seemingly inevitable destruction of so much innocent bird life. Everyone
knows how foolishly a dog behaves towards motor
traffic, and there is some lack of understanding
amongst even the most intelligent of animals in
this respect. Still :

> I'm truly sorry man's dominion
> Has broken nature's social union,
> And justifies that ill opinion
>   Which makes thee startle
> At me, thy poor earth-born companion,
>   And fellow-mortal !

The road had been commonplace so far ; pretty
in parts with its green braes and wooded parks,
until after passing Burn-of-Cambus, when it rapidly
changed in character.

The outlook was now altogether different. Away
in front were great hills, and while the rain was still
as persistent as ever, the sun was shining upon their
peaks, and as I plodded through the mire they

reminded me of the fabled house with the golden windows.

I marvelled at the number of magpies to be met with on the road. It is a beautiful bird, and appears to me to be developing into a larger creature than formerly. With the selling of estates and the reduction in gamekeepers and wardens, vermin—for in such category is this graceful bird classed—is not being kept in check, and hawks and weasels are on the increase. Anyone who frequents the open spaces will have noticed this.

These magpies were not scared, and kept about their business on the roadside until I was almost upon them, when they sailed rather than flew into the near-by branches and returned to the roadway ere I was well passed.

Fortunately for me there were five in the group I particularly noticed, because there is an old freit associated with the magpie, or the pyet as I knew it in my boyhood's days, which tells us :

> Ane is ane, twa is grief,
> Three's a wedding, four's death.

Skirting Doune the promise of beauty was rich. The woods were verdant and checkered with varying tones of green, and at the bridge spanning the Teith the spell of romance lay over all.

In front stands a white church and manse as if built to grace the spot, as indeed it does ; while on the left the castle of Doune made a picture too exquisite to pass without lingering over and for a time dreaming of other days.

The village of Doune was at one time a noted

centre for the making of pistols, and was indeed a warlike district in more senses than one.

Charles Mackie tells that when Prince Charlie reached Doune he was hospitably entertained by the family of Newton. Colonel Edmonston's sisters, dreading discovery of their guests by treacherous servants, personally waited on the Prince.

Their relations, the Edmonstons of Cambuswallace, were also present, and when the Prince was about to depart, having graciously held out his hand, after all the other ladies had kissed it, Miss Robina Edmonston of Cambuswallace, anxious to have a more special mark of favour, asked that she might " pree his Royal Highness' mou'." Charles, nothing loth, took her in his arms and kissed her "from ear to ear," to the envy and mortification of the other ladies present ! It is only fair to say that Chambers gives a slightly different version of this incident.

They were staunch Jacobites, the Edmonstons. One of the family carried the standard at Sheriffmuir, and the same gentleman once overawed Rob Roy.

James Ramsay of Ochtertyre recounted the incident to Sir Walter Scott in person, and so we may accept it as authentic.

There was some public celebration or occasion on foot at Doune, and amongst other festivities it was marked by a bonfire. James Edmonston of Newton was present, as was also Rob Roy. The famous outlaw had said or done something to give offence to Newton, and that gentleman ordered him to leave the scene or he would throw the MacGregor into the fire !

" I broke ane of your ribs on a former occasion," said he, " and now, Rob, if you provoke me further, I will break your neck."

Rob Roy is said to have suffered in prestige for taking the threat so quietly, but as Edmonston was an important man in the Jacobite party, and was doubtless surrounded by powerful friends, the MacGregor was probably wise in retiring.

It is unlikely that unless some such circumstances weighed the balance strongly against him that he who would not barter

> The wild deer's franchise for the heifer's thrall,

and whose whole life was a battle against superior odds, would slink off like a whipped dog.

A nephew of Rob Roy, Gregor MacGregor of Glengyle, or as he was known to the Highlanders, Ghlun Dhu, held Doune Castle for the Prince in '45. Although situated in such close proximity to Stirling with its Hanoverian Garrison, MacGregor occupied Doune for the insurgents until their return from England. The prisoners taken at the Battle of Falkirk were sent here, amongst them John Home, the author of "Douglas," who made his escape and afterwards wrote a "History of the Rebellion."

Here is an apposite verse from his pen :

War I detest ; but war with foreign foes,
Whose manners, language, and whose looks are strange,
Is not so horrid, nor to me so hateful
As that which with our neighbours oft we wage.

The verse, of course, has no connection with his own incarceration in Doune Castle.

As was to be expected, Scott knew this district well, and the castle figures in "Waverley," and to most its associations with Fitz-James are well known.

Romance and chivalry, fell deed and daring, have all played their part hereabouts, but the most intriguing tale of all was the revenge of an insulted tailor !

Doune was a favourite residence of Margaret, widow of James IV, and her tailor was one James Spittal. In his day the only way to get across the Teith was by means of a ferry, and the boatman was a thrawn type of Scot who, apparently, was a law unto himself. Arriving on the bank one morning the Queen's tailor found that he had no money on his person, and the ferryman refused to let him across. Notwithstanding his lack of small change Mr Spittal was in reality a wealthy man, and so by way of poetic justice he built the bridge and the ferryman was ruined !

The bridge was widened and repaired by the Road Trustees in 1866, but the stone bearing an inscription from the old bridge still survives. I could not properly decipher it, but in the centre there appears to be a pair of scissors, insignia and proof of the bold tailor's art !

Trudging along in the rain, it was a never-ending source of wonder to me how Nature orders her affairs during the seasons.

From experience I know that green and varied as the journey is to-day, it can claim no thrill of outstanding beauty, and yet in a month or two it will be transformed into a vista of enchantment. The hills will appear behind the quick shedding trees and will vie with each other in their shades of bronze, brown, russet and crimson. The dying bracken, blood-red in the distance, will run to meet the snow cap, and the whole will form an autumn scene I do not care to miss. The roadway will be carpeted in a deep, richly coloured mast, edged curiously with yellow pine needles. Unflinching old mansions, with an aura of romance about them, will appear where a month before no thought of such was apparent, giving an added interest to the scene.

The brilliant old cock pheasant, so startling amongst the green to-day, will merge with the tawny hues and become part of the colour scheme. That robin which is now so noticeable on the fern-covered dyke will be practically indistinguishable amongst the fallen leaves. As Fitz-Gerald sings :

> 'Tis a dull sight
>   To see the year dying
> When winter winds
>   Set the yellow wood sighing.

Fine thoughts these on this rain-sodden road, but prompted and presaged by the ripening hips and haws of the hedgerows.

Day dreams, however, were poor shelter from the persistent downpour, and even the leafy branches above were adding their drips now, their resistance having been sorely tried.

The hills on the left were dark and angry-looking,

as if they too were being tormented by their weight of cloud, and then I saw standing high and proud Stirling Castle. Presently the rain was, if anything, worse, but the grey old citadel appeared as if bathed in the evening sun. The trees concealed it again, and now was disclosed the Wallace Monument, stark and straight amongst its woods on Abbey Craig.

A good samaritan offered me a lift, but I was too wet to sit in comfort, and preferred to finish the last mile or two on foot.

Entering Stirling from this part is picturesque and impressive.

On the right the castle is strong and dominating, a landmark which can hold its own with every challenge ; but couple it with the Wallace Monument on Abbey Craig upstanding against its background of hills—and then you have an entrance with which few towns can vie !

Look back now along the road you have come, until then rather restricted by the wayside trees and hedgerows, and you will find a serried row of massive bens, fantastic they looked in the half light, but overpowering in their bulk and majesty.

The great ponderous slopes tower to the skies and form a guard to the Western Highlands, and these same hills were not without their danger to the Lowland farmers in the old days when the restless clansmen were on the move. There is no little truth in the saying,

> Forth bridles the wild Highlanders,

and old Stirling has withstood many shocks from

every airt and was deserving of all the natural protection she could possess. But if the heart is old, the branches are young and vigorous, and I know of no town where the suburbs are finer.

Every moment brought the grey old town a step nearer, and when I arrived it was to find the streets dry, the late sun strong and warm, everything bright and genial, until I could scarce believe that only a mile or so behind me the rainstorm had lasted all day, probably still raged, while here conditions were delightful.

As I passed beneath the solid rock, above, in the courtyard, I could see the kilted soldiers standing in groups on the scene of so many stirring incidents in the history of our land, and I fell to day-dreaming again and passed down the narrow street with a light step.

XII

STIRLING—
SCOTLAND'S BATTLE-GROUND

Old faces look upon me,
Old forms go trooping past.

W. E. AYTOUN

NEXT morning I was up and out of doors before
sunrise.

Everything seemed grey and lonely. The streets
were muffled in a thin early autumn haar which
lay over and about the town and completely altered
its appearance.

It had been my intention to explore the old-
world spots before the douce citizens were out o'
bed and about their daily business, but there was
no one about to guide or direct.

It is a strange sensation to walk about the streets
of a busy town and find all quiet and deserted.

The streets seem altered ; houses assume a new
and unusual character, while the shops and business
premises, with their drawn blinds and barred door-
ways, have a strangely desolate air.

Gradually the curtain of night was raised. The
first audible sound was the note of a thrush. Then
a sparrow chirped, and another, until the bird-world
became clamorous and alive.

The white spectral mist gradually lifted, or rather

faded out, and from somewhere behind the hills an opalescent, pearl-pink sheen appeared and gradually increased in beauty.

Another day was born—just such a morning as most likely ushered in the days of long ago when the Roman Legions camped here, or the wild clansmen arose from their repose amongst the bracken.

Stirling looked very enticing in the early dawn. An occasional grey wisp of smoke from a chimney-pot, the sun glinting on a window-pane, spires and buildings emerging beneath the dominant old castle, clean-cut and strong, and behind, old ere man knew them, the mighty silent hills.

And now I knew that last night when I came to Stirling by the Doune road in the rain—to a town bathed in evening sunshine—beautiful as was the setting, I came by the wrong gate !

The proper way to approach this fascinating old town for the first time is by the South road. Come as you will, it presents a charming exterior, but come by the Glasgow road, and as you round the bend some three miles distant, the castle suddenly looms ahead, stark and dauntless, and in a moment you find your mind harking back to old warlike days when strong men in the pride of arms contested the road you tread.

But even so, and high and proud as the fortress stands, it is dwarfed by the bens which form its background. Away there dwelt the restless kilted warriors, ever ready to hold their own, and not averse to sampling the richer plains of the Lowlander, for Forth, notwithstanding its proverbial application, did not always " bridle the wild Highlander."

L

If you are fortunate, in that the bens are snow-capped and the forenoon sun is up and strong when you come, then you will see a panorama you are not likely to forget !

Still, come as you will, at once you realise that this is a town with a pedigree. Something tells you that here in the years gone by was hung the calendar of great days.

As in most county towns, there is a subdued atmosphere of assured position, hard to define but germane to the place. You sense that where to-day motor-cars park and buses ply, at one time clattered mounted men who rode on a king's business.

If I were to write a history of Scotland, I should take Stirling as my fulcrum.

History generally is a record of war, or the results of war, linked with selfish and scheming diplomacy, and those clustering old buildings were a hot-bed of such intrigues.

Centuries before the exploits of Wallace and the Bruce, the Romans knew this place. Queen Mary spent some infant years in the castle which cradled James II, James IV, and James V, and here, too, was crowned James VI.

An unfortunate name for a Scottish monarch—James. What tragedy overhangs the line—a fell black cloud of misery and woe !

Later, Bonnie Prince Charlie, with the hand of fate as always, turned against the Stuart race, played cantrips here on his way north to that fatal day on Drummossie Moor.

Yes : I would take Stirling as my centre, and from

there gather the threads of history and so trace my heroes down the troubled years of the past.

Bannockburn; Sauchieburn; Stirling Brig; Sheriffmuir; Kilsyth; Falkirk — I do not write them in chronological order but simply as they crowd on the memory, and in these few, plucked at random from the sheaf of time, is material for many thrilling chapters.

Bannockburn forms a glorious chapter in our national story, and on its battle-field was forged the charter of our race, but to me the daring ruthless day at Stirling Brig holds greater fascination. Moreover, had there never been a Stirling Brig, there would have been no Bannockburn, but in any case both were epic, and the two famous fields are almost within sight of each other. Above all, I love the fearless message Wallace sent to Warenne when that English leader sent two clergymen to offer terms if the little army of patriots would lay down their arms. "Let the English come on," replied Wallace, "we defy them to their very beards."

No room for doubt or misunderstanding there, and when the invaders' men-at-arms heard the defiant reply, they insisted on being led to the attack.

The fighting leader of the English forces, a Scotsman, Sir Richard Lundy by name, and a skilful general, realised the strong position of the Scots, and hesitated to join the issue. The invaders occupied the southern bank of the Forth, the Scots army were on the north, and a narrow wooden bridge was the only means of crossing.

Cressingham, the treasurer of the forces and a churchman, insisted that Lundy should advance at once, and, to do him justice, took his place in the van.

The English army then moved to the attack, and when about half were over and the other divisions were crowding on the south bank, impatient to cross the narrow bridge, Wallace gave the order, and the Scottish spearmen rushed headlong on the foe. The utmost confusion now prevailed, but soon the result was beyond doubt. Great numbers were slain by Scottish spears, and many were driven into the Forth to drown before their comrades' eyes. The invading army fled after destroying the bridge by fire to prevent pursuit.

Then followed one of those acts which, if true, reflects little credit on the victors. The proud and haughty Cressingham was slain in the first encounter, and so much was he detested by the Scots that it is said they flayed the skin from his body and made it into pouches.

Still, the Battle of Stirling Brig "was a famous victory," and as we look back, its true significance as the key-stroke to peace and freedom is at once apparent.

> High praise, ye gallant band,
> Who in the face of day,
> With daring hearts and fearless hands,
> Have cast your chains away.

The story of Sauchieburn is to me equally fascinating. Here father and son were in opposing camps, and it ended in the death of James III and the accession of his youthful heir, James IV.

James III was never a fighting man, and although mounted on a wonderful charger, which it was said by the giver would carry him to victory or take him swiftly to safety, and armed with the famous sword of Robert Bruce, his heart failed him and he fled from the field.

The Bruce's sword, which in the hands of its original owner never failed or shrank from a contest, was afterwards found lying on the battle-ground, dropped in his haste or discarded in flight.

The craven monarch was riding for safety for the Forth, where lay the fleet under the gallant and loyal Sir Andrew Wood. He was unaccompanied, his friends and supporters being still engaged on the fateful field.

On passing a house, or mill, his spirited horse took fright at a woman who was carrying a pitcher of water, and threw its royal burden.

Stunned and shaken by the fall, clad in the cumbersome armour of the times, the King was unable to rise, and was carried indoors by the miller and his wife.

Feeling that his time was near, a condition perhaps more occasioned by nervous dread than physical disability, he asked his rude host to send for a priest.

" Who are you ? " questioned the miller.

" This morning I was your King," replied James, conscious that the day was lost and his reign at an end.

Rushing forth to find aid, the miller's wife spied some mounted men, unknown to her, in pursuit of the fleeing James. Accosting them, she explained her anxiety for the monarch and his wish for a priest.

"I will confess him," said one of the warriors; "lead me to his bedside."

When taken to the spot where James was lying, he approached with reverent air and questioned His Majesty if he could recover if immediate aid was forthcoming ? The King expressed the thought that he would, and the stranger, drawing his poinard, stabbed him to the heart.

The name or title of the regicide has never been revealed, and so this old-time battle of Sauchieburn, staged more than four hundred years ago, still cloaks its baffling historical mystery, now never likely to be solved.

Every chapter of Scottish history has its tale of stricken field or martial glory, and here is a cluster of such episodes.

In the old battle days Stirling must have formed a strong rallying point. Apart from the central fortress, Stirling Castle, there were within easy distance, indeed almost adjacent, amongst other keeps and strongholds, those at Doune, Robert the Bruce's at Clackmannan, Mar's Tower at Alloa, and Castle Campbell, the lowland seat of Argyll, which was ultimately razed by his implacable enemy, Montrose.

Romance states that the real name of Castle Campbell was Castle Gloom—that the Glen of Care flanked it on one side and the Burn of Sorrow on the other ; and that the castle looked down on the village of Dolour. Chambers was very wroth with Dr MacCulloch for accepting this story unquestioningly, and points out that Caer is not a Gaelic word and really means castle or camp; Dollor is merely *Dol or*, a high field; and the old Gaelic name for the stronghold was Coch Lleum or the Mad Leap, because of its precipitous position.

However, the old romantic description fits it admirably, even though "facts are chiels that winna ding," and so we must let it go at that!

Over there stands the Mote Hill :—

> . . . O sad and fatal mound,
>   That oft has heard the death-axe sound,
> As on the noblest of the land
>   Fell the stern headsman's bloody hand!

And some of his work would repay investigation too, as his was sometimes a busy profession in the days when a king's frown was a dangerous omen!

Almost five hundred years ago—in 1449 to be exact—James II acted as umpire when three chosen Scots tilted with three champions of France before an assembly of nobles and their ladies. To-day the motor-buses run near-by the tilting ground, and Stirling has a football team named King's Park.

It is all for the best, I have no doubt, and motor-buses and grand-stands are much more comfortable than accoutred chargers, or the pastime of the youth and beauty in the old dark days of sliding down a hill-side using an ox-skull for sledge.

As I stood at the wide corner place for a moment, the streets now busy with traffic, above the other sounds rose the peculiar drone of an aeroplane. It passed outwith my vision in a moment or two, swift and graceful, and as an every-day occurrence attracted little attention. And yet in Stirling, a stone's throw from where I stood, was made one of the world's first attempts to conquer the air.

The story goes back to the days of James IV, and was not a very successful affair for the braggart who made the effort.

The chief actor was an Italian friar who professed to be an alchemist, and so impressed the King that he had him created Abbot of Tungland.

Anxious still further to impress his royal master, he made it known that he had discovered the secret of flying, and a date being appointed for the display of his prowess, the King and his Court attended to witness the exhibition.

The Italian impostor did not lack courage, and fixing a huge pair of wings to his arms, he jumped boldly from one of the castle battlements. He fell heavily upon the rocks below, and was fortunate in that he broke only his thigh-bone!

If lacking in balance, his ingenuity was fertile, and as an excuse for this misadventure he gravely informed the amused spectators that his failure was entirely due to the fact that he had created his wings from the feathers of common barn-fowls, whereas he now saw that he ought to have selected only those of the eagle!

What is probably a deed of treachery and broken faith without a parallel was committed in Stirling Castle by James II.

That he was flouted by a section of his nobles who counted their station as above the law must be admitted, but the stain on his kingly honour is one which can never be erased.

STIRLING

Amongst the ruling families of Scotland, that of Douglas had always held high estate ; they were a sept feared by virtue not merely of their following, but also of the prestige of their fighting name.

In the reign of James II, when the fifteenth century was half run, Douglas had entered into a pact with two other powerful houses, represented in the east by the Earl of Crawford, and in the north by the Earl of Ross.

It was obvious to the King and his adherents that this triangular compact made the conspirators greater than the crown, and unless something was done to split them, the result might shake, if not destroy, the throne.

The Earl of Douglas was invited to meet the King in Stirling, and attended the conference with only a few of his followers, secure in the safe conduct given under the King's hand.

The Black Earl was received with every outward sign of friendship, and after supping with James and his chosen councillors, the King introduced the subject of the league Douglas had entered into with the Earls Crawford and Ross.

But the Douglas was not a man to be either bullied or cajoled, and he point-blank refused to repudiate the compact as his monarch wished.

To be bearded in his own council-chamber was more than the King's temper could support, and drawing his dagger he suddenly stabbed Douglas twice, exclaiming, " If you will not break this league, I shall ! "

Sir Patrick Gray and his fellow-courtiers soon completed the work, and the reeking body was thrown out of the window of what is to this day known as " the Douglas Room."

It was an unpardonable and an unkingly act, and was followed by bloodshed and war, which lasted for three years, until the King's forces triumphed over the rebel Douglases at Arkinholm in 1455.

A few weeks after the Douglas murder the new Earl, accompanied by six hundred fighting men, marched on Stirling and openly defied the King.

The letter of safe conduct which should have protected the slain Douglas was dragged at a horse's tail through the streets, and the town was pillaged and set on fire.

Stirling town has been plundered and sacked more than once since that date, but the last time it suffered in this manner was when the Highland army helped themselves to anything they fancied on their way north before the advance of Butcher Cumberland.

Never again is the old citadel likely to fire a gun in anger or be called upon to stand the rigour of a siege, but indeed it has played its part in the history of a nation, and so is entitled to rest and brood on the storied past, rich in a dowry of song and tradition, story and romance.

Lennox, while Regent of Scotland when the King was a child of five years, held a Parliament in Stirling. It is a striking commentary on the times that this callow laddie, King as he might be, was compelled to attend the proceedings, and a not uninteresting fact that there was a hole in the roof of the building in which the Parliament sat !

Naturally, the royal child was bored and restless,

more given to looking about him than listening to the heavy oratory.

His wandering eye soon spied the vent in the roof which held his attention, so that when Lennox, who, by the way, was his paternal grandfather, resumed his seat on the conclusion of a doubtless ponderous and lengthy speech, the child-monarch innocently remarked, "I think there is ane hole in this Parliament."

His prattling remark was prophetic. Some days later, ere the parliamentary session was concluded, the town was in the hands of the Queen's party, Lennox was dead, and the Earl of Mar was Regent in his stead!

But kings and princelings do not have it all their own way in the annals of this old town. John Knox, that dauntless theologian, preached in Stirling, I think at the coronation of James VI, then an infant, and many another great divine has expounded his doctrine to the citizens since that great reformer's day.

Not the least interesting wearer of the cloth was the Rev. John Russell, who "got his kale through the reek" so richly from the pen of Robert Burns.

While a slightly older man than the poet, Russell survived him by several years, indeed was still in the flesh when Waterloo was won, and he must frequently have had cause to regret the hall-mark stamped upon him by the invective of the Bard.

"Black Jock" was one name he would never escape, and generations yet to follow will know him by the title. As Russell was amongst the most bigoted and intolerant of the " Auld Lichts," his castigations were doubtless more than earned.

Professor Wilson recalls that he was one day walking in the vicinity of Stirling Castle. Unknown to the Professor " it happened to be a fast day," which in those times was given over to preaching and meditation, when he heard a noise which, to quote his own words, was " to be likened to nothing imaginable in this earth but the bellowing of a buffalo fallen into a trap upon a tiger, which, as we came within half a mile of the castle *we discovered to be the voice of a pastor engaged in public prayer*." The italics are mine. Professor Wilson adds that " his physiognomy was little less alarming than his voice, and his sermon corresponded with his looks and his lungs, the whole being, indeed, an extraordinary exhibition of divine worship."

That was " Black Jock " at his daily avocation, and by all accounts well might Burns write of him :

> But now the Lord's ain trumpet touts,
>   Till a' the hills are rairin',
> An' echoes back return the shouts,
>   Black Russell is na sparin' ;
> His piercing words, like Highlan' swords,
>   Divide the joints an' marrow ;
> His talk o' Hell, whare devils dwell,
>   Our vera " sauls does harrow,"
>   Wi' fright that day.

Kilmarnock, indeed, must have been a quieter and better town to reside in when the Rev. John Russell decided to leave the " wabster lads " and remove his bull's voice and frenzied personality to Stirling.

STIRLING

A hundred years before Russell's time Stirling boasted another quaint theologian, by name Hunter, who appears to have been minister of the second charge. At least the first minister, a Mr Munro, along with the provost of the town, charged Mr Hunter with drunkenness, indeed in the outspoken manner of the times there was no beating about the bush, and they plainly stated that he had already consumed so much liquor that " at the sacrament he was under the influence of drink." The Bishop suspended him, and his subsequent doings are unknown save that in his old age he married a girl, daughter of a gardener.

From ministers to " grace before meat " is an easy transition, and Cheviot, that industrious collector of proverbs and out-of-the-way lore, is sponsor for the following :

It appears that at a dinner held in Stirling Castle no one present was able or willing to " ask a blessing " on the meat, and so the Earl of Airlie's footman was ordered to perform the office. At once the man, who obviously was a witty fellow and was doubtless called upon for that reason, without hesitation recited :

> God bless King William and Queen Mary,
> Lord Strathmore and the Earl o' Airlie,
> The Laird o' Bamff and little Charlie.

There is another version of the grace given by the same authority, which reads : " Bless these benefits, and a' them who are to eat them ; keep them from chokin', worrying, or overeating themselves ; and whatever their hearts covet, let their hands trail to them."

As I write, Stirling is in the throes of a ghost scare, one of those silly experiences none too uncommon of late years in various districts.

Last night the ghost appeared in the backyards of Middle Craigs, a white, spectral figure with outstretched arms, but before the civilian watchers and the police had gained entrance to the yard, with a distinct shuffling of feet—an unusual accompaniment for spectres and apparitions—the ghost had eluded the pursuers and completely disappeared.

But the whole of the old town is haunted. You can feel it in the atmosphere, the ancient buildings and the black battlements of the castle above, and it would never surprise me to see a gallant figure, in strange garb of other days, come down the crown of the causeway, sword in hand.

The playing children have gone indoors now, and the streets are surprisingly quiet and deserted. Stand here at the castle foot and let your imagination run riot for a spell as the sun goes down and a bat flutters past. What a motley procession to conjure with—kings, queens and princelings—all the royal blood of Scotland, grave or gay, have passed along here at some time in their checkered career.

The figure slipping by in the half light is a King, James V no less, but known to-night as the Guidman of Ballangeich, off in search of illicit pleasure and amatory joys amongst the peasant-folk outby. An English warden goes his rounds, anxious to see that all is safe ere retiring for the night. The skulking figure in the shadow is a spy from the desperate band of the lion-hearted Wallace, who is determined to drive the invaders forth across the border or die in the attempt. A gay cavalcade of knights and ladies fair passes on prancing steeds or caparisoned jennets making for the jousting; Knox with his fanatical bearded face and warnings of evil and woe; a Prince, the last of his race to seek a throne, shot at from a stronghold by rights his own. The history of our land unrolls in pageant form, because here is the old heart of centuries gone, the anvil on which Scottish deeds were forged.

The white silent haar of the morning was creeping back again, blurring the hills and enfolding the carse, and gathering round the castle hill it enshrouded the old historic stage where deeds were done which will live while Scotland breathes, and with a last look at the staunch old relic I made for the busy main streets where blue-clad policemen regulate the bus traffic, and the modern world thrives.

XIII

AN INCONCLUSIVE JOURNEY

There's some say that we wan,
  And some say that they wan,
And some say that nane wan at a', man ;
  But one thing I'm sure,
  That at Sherra-muir,
A battle there was, that I saw, man.

It all came through a chat with a fine old gentle-man who was sleeping in the Stirling hotel on his way north. Who or what he was I do not know, but he was a genial soul, garrulous to a fault, and I was glad to foregather with him !

We sat at the fire and smoked, and he told me how, many years before, he had explored the Sheriffmuir district while spending a holiday in Dunblane, and found it fascinating and teeming with interest.

I had, of course, read about the Battle of Sheriff-muir, pondering how the Stuart faction, had they possessed one lion-hearted, resolute leader, might easily have altered the history of our land. I had many times passed the road leading to the battle-field, but it looked so uninviting that I had never been tempted to explore the place.

The '45 and the personality of Bonnie Prince Charlie so dominate the Stuart cause and overshadow the preceding Jacobite risings and intrigues, that I had taken this battle for granted.

Now, sitting here chatting about it with an elderly English wayfarer, my interest was whetted by his tales and experiences, and I decided to devote my last free day for some time to come to this high-lying battle-field.

We sat late, and he told me of some ancient stones, each with its story, and none of which, according to his theory, should be missed by any man who wants to know something of his native lore!

The stones did it. I determined, come what might, fair weather or foul, to see those ancient landmarks, and to see them next day!

The sun was high as I left Stirling by the North road. The old bridge across the Forth—cousin-germane to that other and more famous brig which spans the Ayr—was a reminder of other days, and it pleased me to fancy that Argyll might have led his red-coats by this crossing to their camp at Dunblane, where they lay, before the clash of arms, that November day more than two hundred years ago.

Immediately in front rose the Abbey Craig with its great shelf-like broken side, once the vantage ground of mighty Wallace, and now crowned with his monument.

Across another narrow bridge at Bridge of Allan and the roadway climbs north. Pause for a moment at the summit and the Carse of Stirling is spread beneath like a great arena, pent by hills and mountains, with the castle rising straight

M

from the plain and dwarfing the clustering town into insignificance.

So under the tree-hemmed roadway to Dunblane, a town of great antiquity, which has played no unimportant part in historical and ecclesiastical directions.

It dates from Culdee times, and boasts a cathedral which was founded about 1140 by King David I. Like other sacred edifices it suffered in its time from the vandals, and a mob from Perth, under the leadership of Argyll and others, overthrew the altars in 1559.

Tannahill has made the name widely known to many, and given it a niche in poetic fame with his beautiful song, " Jessie, the Flower o' Dunblane."

> The sun has gone down o'er the lofty Ben Lomond,
>   And left the red clouds to preside o'er the scene ;
> While lonely I stray in the calm simmer gloamin',
>   To muse on sweet Jessie, the flow'r o' Dunblane.

Some authorities claim that the original Jessie is buried in the churchyard here, while others say that she existed only in the poet's fancy.

In the time of the '45 an Amazon of a heroic mould lived here, a servant-maid whose affections were all for the " King o' the Highland hearts." She was so incensed when Cumberland's troops passed through the village on their way north that, from an upper window, she emptied a pot of boiling water over their heads !

Tradition has it that it took some persuasion to prevent the red-coats from setting fire to the town in reprisal !

AN INCONCLUSIVE JOURNEY

There are two or three interesting roads to Sheriffmuir—one a mere path—but my friend of last night mapped this adventure, so I followed his plan.

At once the broad North road, with its rush of .motor traffic, was behind me, and the rutted, undulating country lane—for it is little more—led direct to the hills beyond.

The moss-covered stone dykes were a-cluster with hartstongue ferns, and notwithstanding the bright sunshine, everything looked damp and water-logged. After the first dip from the main highway the heavy path seemed to climb interminably, until suddenly the moor spread out in front and on every side the dying heather stubbornly contested the pathway. So quick indeed was the transformation that the wild desolation of the place was abrupt and unexpected.

In front stretched the heathery waste, in places jet black against the farther greens and browns. Here and there dark clumps of fir added a more sombre note to the whole, lent a strangely mournful beauty which somehow seemed in keeping with the atmosphere and the all-pervading silence.

Back towards the west by the road I had travelled ranged mountain behind mountain ; each white-topped ben seeming mightier than his fellows until clouds and earthly giants merged—the farther hills towards the north cloaked in snow.

Now for the first time I was conscious of a biting wind carrying an occasional sudden blash of rain, and was fain to shelter for a moment behind one of the butts which ran across the moor as far as vision carried. Anxiously I scanned in every direction—but no sign of fabled stones I had come to inspect, and by now the brightest of the day was behind.

A heron winged clumsily past, and I followed towards a struggling pine wood which guarded the sloping moorland, hoping that there, might be concealed the giant boulders so graphically described overnight.

The place seemed alive with game birds. A cock-pheasant rocketed away from almost under my feet; grouse were more than abundant, but the few isolated farm-houses were too distant to afford guidance, and of man there was no sign.

Last night it had all appeared too easy—you went by such and such a farm and took a certain path to the right or left and the treasure was there for the taking, but somewhere I had gone wrong, and now the position seemed absurdly confused.

There was one stone in particular I had really wanted to see, because there a terrible deed was committed, almost pagan in its rites, shortly before the Argyll and Mar forces joined in battle.

My story of it was that one of the clans, anxious to propitiate the fates, insisted that their claymores should be blooded ere going into battle.

As there were no prisoners in the Mar camp, a man who was believed to sympathise with the Argyll whigs was taken from a near-by cottage, and the band in turn transfixed his body with their weapons, and then, satisfied that all would now go well, marched off to their allotted position in the battle-line!

AN INCONCLUSIVE JOURNEY

A "Muckle Stane" marks the spot where this atrocious deed was committed, but I had missed my bearings, and the ghastly landmark was not apparent.

Somewhere, too, are "Seven Stanes" which might well be mistaken for the scene of no less noteworthy incidents in Druidical times, but really marking the scene of a "great battle" fought between William Wallace and the English invaders generations before the more modern affair which takes its name from Sheriffmuir.

Somewhere here on this lonely, dark moor, Wallace, learning that his Southron foes, to the number of 10,000 men, were marching from Stirling, divided his force into three divisions and hid them in the moss holes and gashes with which the terrain abounded.

Unaware that the Scots were even in the district, the English army straggled along without serious formation, and were surprised and furiously attacked from three sides. There followed a dreadful scene of carnage. The hatred between the countries was such that no quarter was given, and the invading forces were butchered to a man, with trifling loss to the Scots.

To mark the occasion Wallace had the "Seven Stanes" erected, a grisly monument to his prowess.

Well, here was I, standing on this desolate winterbound moor, dreaming of old-time battles and looking for stones that marked their site, while the sun was gradually sliding down behind the hills and the sky was taking the colour of lead.

And then came one of those things which " just happen."

Where he came from, or who he was, I do not know, but a man stepped out of the old fir wood just like some knight of old. The two features which impressed me were his hawk-like face and the monocle which dangled from a black ribbon. Still, he was my last hope, and I strode across the pine-needles and cones and told him my troubles and doubts.

" Stones," he said, and I wish you had been there to see his flashing eye and the sarcastic turn of his lip. " Stones—certainly there are stones, as you say, but what you call tradition is all trash and nonsense.

" There is no truth in the stories we are told to-day, sir—none ! If you are an Englishman go down there," and he pointed along the road I had part-way come, " go down there to the inn and buy a half-bottle of whisky, and you can have any number of tales told so long as it lasts ! If you are a Scot leave all that alone—it is worthless and traditional only."

Never have I met such an irascible man—and yet so kindly in his anger ! One thing anyhow emerged—there was an inn " down there," and so, thanking him, I made off, realising that I had taken the wrong airt at the cross-roads !

Everything seemed strangely silent. Now and again a lonely fir nodded as I passed—the empty butts spoke of life of an intermittent sort, but animate things had bedded for the night and only the flaming, lambent lights in the west broke the leaden gray.

AN INCONCLUSIVE JOURNEY

When at last I reached the inn it was getting dark—that quiet, shadowy lack of light which steals across a moor—not the jet blackness of a town.

The stones were there—vouched for—not standing as the old strong men had left them in the long ago, but still marking the place where the conflict had been waged.

No : it would not be wise to go over the moor and see them. They were there all right, and their shadowy silhouettes were pointed out in the gathering darkness, but the moor was soaking and it would be better to come another day.

This was wisdom—the knowledge of the local which no sane man flouts, and so but for the recumbent shadowy outlines the " Seven Stanes " still eluded me !

Here was fought Sheriffmuir, a battle which surely stands out as one of the most remarkable episodes in British history.

Both sides claimed the victory, both leaders were unsoldierlike in the handling of their forces, and as someone said, if Dundee had been alive and in command of the clansmen the Whig army might have been annihilated. As it was, the right wing of each army crushed the opposing left wing, but the victory really rested with Argyll, bad as his leadership was.

As always when fight or foray was afoot, the MacGregors were in the affair too.

Rob Roy was in command of a considerable band composed of his own clan and the M'Phersons.

By inclination and sympathy the redoubtable

outlaw was all for Mar, and he took his place amongst the kilted faction. On the other hand, loyalty to his patron, Argyll, forbade that he should draw steel against him, and so here we had the peculiar incident of a body of armed fighting men ready to take their place in the battle-line, and yet inactive because their leader would not give the word.

It is said both Mar and Argyll sent urgent messages to Rob Roy asking him to do his part for them, but he coolly responded that if neither side could win without his aid, they could not gain victory by it. His hot-blooded followers were anxious to rush into the fray, but Rob forbade them, and indeed the M'Pherson leader, although under MacGregor's orders, had a heated altercation and nearly came to blows on the point.

When the battle was over Rob and his men, with great impartiality, gathered the spoil from both sides and returned to their native fastness, probably well satisfied with the part they had played !

Rob Roy there stood watch on a hill, for to catch
  The booty, for aught that I saw, man :
For he ne'er advanced from the place he was stanced,
  Till no more was to do there at a', man.

It is well that the MacGregor's reputation can stand even such a lapse as that ; his conduct on this occasion may be condemned, but his courage was undoubted, and it was an understood thing that spoils went to those who could take them !

A Highland army going into battle must have

been a terrifying sight. Here, as on other fields, the claymores advanced so quickly that the cavalry were put to it to keep pace with them. And the blades bit deep, giving no quarter.

Some onlookers who watched the battle from a hill-top remarked a band of red-coats surrounded by clansmen. From their eminence it resembled a red diamond with a dark struggling border. Gradually the diamond became smaller, until not one soldier was left alive.

Amongst those killed in the Highland troops were the Chief of Clan Ranald and the Earl of Strathmore.

Scott recounts that when the Clan Ranald men saw their chief fall mortally wounded, they were inclined to waver until Glengarry rushed forward crying : " Revenge—to-day for vengeance—to-morrow for mourning! "

You may slay men like those—but you cannot subdue them !

Still the heather grows and a clean wind blows over the moor where men fought and died, many, perhaps, never really knowing why, and through the pines the sighing of the breeze is unceasing coronach for those men who died well.

A few yards, and I came upon a cairn—erected by the Clan Macrae exactly two hundred years after the Battle of Sheriffmuir to witness and speak of the deeds their tartan had accomplished !

It was erected to the memory of the Kintail and Lochalsh companies of the clan, who formed part of the left wing of the Jacobite army and fell almost to a man.

A solitary cyclist was leaning against the stone dyke, anxious to know if I had seen his friends. He did not know much about the place, but hazarded the view that the " gathering stone " was somewhere up the path on the right.

It was almost dark now, but I wanted to see one stone—anything at all rather than home unappeased, and so I climbed the dyke and kept along the dank wet path.

There may be a stone there—indeed there is little doubt there is, but I have not seen it. Squelching through heather holes, amongst recumbent wire, over a burn with soft, treacherous banks in the half-dark, and always in front more heather-clad wastes.

The stone eluded me. The moon came up, white and beautiful, the hills were suddenly bathed in silver, and the scene was one I shall never forget, but through it all I had a pang in my heart. The stones had eluded me in a land I want to know and take to my heart ; I had ventured my last free day amongst the age-old traditions of this wonderful westland, and in giving my last I had lost.

XIV

GLENARTNEY

Come when the moon is high
And see the reivers' ghosts go by !

MANY times have I passed through Crieff on my way north, and the clean attractive little town always held its appeal. It is a delightful place to explore, full of romance and tales of other days, with a literary flavour too, as here was born David Mallet who, with James Thomson, wrote " Alfred," in which appeared " Rule Britannia," while not far from the town is laid the scene of Ian M'Laren's " Drumtochty," but the world of to-day, forgetting the " kailyard school," in its reading shows a preference for stronger meat. But this morning I had no time to loiter—a long day was in front, a long road to traverse.

The " Highland Line " runs through the town, so that it stands, as it were, a buttress between Highland and Lowland, and for many years was the centre of a great cattle Tryst when the dwellers of the hills brought down their black cattle, and buyers from the lowlands and even south of the border attended in great numbers. Tumultuous scenes were sometimes enacted, the men of the North, proud, haughty and quick of temper, and the lowlander—who had not been by then altogether tamed and softened by law and custom—equally ready to hold his own. Indeed the gallows—" the kind Gallows of Crieff "—was never long without its hideous ornaments. Law-giving was strict here, as it had to be! The town lay too close to the wild hills and glens to run undue risks, and self-preservation demanded a strong hand when dealing with marauding or quick-handed gentry.

Sir Walter Scott mentions a quaint custom amongst the Highland drovers who, when passing the gallows on their way to or from the town, used to touch their bonnets and mutter, " God bless her nainsel, and the Tiel tamn you."

Whatever indignities or stringent laws Crieff forced on the clansmen, they got it all back with full measure when, in 1715, they burned the town and practically wiped it out. A like fate was narrowly averted when the army of Bonnie Prince Charlie were retreating from Stirling in the '45, but better councils prevailed.

Heart-rending as were the scenes when the whole populace were left without a shelter to their heads, many with hardly a rag to cover them, the new town which gradually sprang from the ashes of the old is certainly a most delectable spot, and forms a delightful starting-point from which to " plunge into that most paradisaical part of all the paradise of Strathearn, the seven miles between Crieff and Comrie," as Chambers has it !

To-day there was no sign of anything but peace and goodwill as I came down the hilly streets bathed in glorious sunshine, but in a moment the hills had me in their grip again !

Far on the left, high above the intervening trees,

stood the Baird Monument, as if to guard wild Glenartney and its dark secrets.

It's a roundabout way the road out of Crieff by the west, as if half-hearted about crossing the Highland line, and anxious to delay the adventure as long as possible! And certainly the hills look daunting enough—wild and menacing, indeed, in their frowning strength.

Over the Turret water, crooning away to itself as if singing the praises of the scenic beauties it had passed on its journey through the hidden glens beyond.

The road dips, and in a moment the hills are gone—everything is lowland and domestic, an anti-climax to the view of a hundred yards back. But only for a moment, and soon again the hills and pine-clad slopes dominate the view, their stern beauty softened by a plenitude of silver birch; an added grace to the rugged outlook.

The road was good, the sun genial and warm, a lark was trilling, and on every side were bowers of trees flanked by hills. Truly it was a fine start for a day which bade well and fair.

And then on my right appeared a vista of lake and wood so compelling in its beauty that my measured miles were forgotten, and for long I lingered. A swan was gliding on the calm surface of the lake, and its reflection in the water, this perfect morning, added a quaint touch to the scene. No matter how often or at which season, Ochter-tyre can never be passed by anyone who seeks perfection in landscape.

Here Robert Burns visited Sir William Murray

and saw beauty which, in his eyes, even surpassed that of Nature, in the person of Miss Euphemia Murray of Lintrose, the niece of his host. A girl of eighteen, she was already known as " The Flower of Strathmore," and the poet in his tribute to her charms bestowed upon her undying fame.

> Blythe, blythe, and merry was she,
> Blythe was she but and ben ;
> Blythe by the banks of Earn,
> And blythe in Glenturit glen.
>
> The Highland hills I've wander'd wide,
> And o'er the lawlands I hae been ;
> But Phemie was the blythest lass,
> That ever trode the dewy green.

Miss Murray afterwards became the wife of a Court of Session Judge, and was doubtless forgotten by the bard, whose wandering fancy created so many immortals.

Not the least picturesque feature hereabouts are the wonderful old beeches, and I found myself wondering if Burns had passed beneath their spreading branches in days long gone by.

The hedgerow bank was equally beautiful if in a less conspicuous manner, a perfect carpet of harts-tongue ferns with here and there a nestling strawberry plant. The little starry flowers which earlier had lent an extra feature to the greenery had by now given place to the delicate miniature fruit so neglected because of its modest self-effacement, but too luscious and sweet to be ignored.

The road was a succession of winding bends, each in turn adding a new beauty to the view.

GLENARTNEY

In a field I surprised a gathering of rooks, a parliament in session, only there was no official speaker. Even had there been, every individual was too busy airing his own views to pay much attention to rules of debate.

There were hundreds of them, possibly thousands, at least the whole field was glossy with their black coats.

A car passed, and the sable cohorts rose into the air and circled and gyrated in a most bewildering manner ere settling down again to discuss the obviously weighty problems which had convened the meeting.

For a mile or two the dominant note on the landscape had been the tall commanding pillar of the Baird Monument, occupying a high wooded eminence. Somehow it reminded me of Cleopatra's Needle as it stood, dark and straight, overtopping the attendant trees; I found later, when standing alongside, that it was built of granite, almost white, and sparkling in the sun.

Soon I was climbing the narrow winding path to the summit, an effort well worth the labour and bringing an abundant reward.

Underfoot was dark and moss-grown, and so rarely is the pathway frequented that on several occasions I had to brush aside the overhanging branches or literally break through rank under-growth. The very birds seemed to resent my intrusion, and every now and then a blackbird—self-appointed guardian of the country-side—gave hurried warning of my approach.

From time to time I passed huge iron rings

attached to great sunken blocks, presumably used in hauling up the mighty stones of which the monument is built. Some of the stones which form the base appeared to my inexperienced eye to weigh many tons, and it must have been a Herculean task getting them to the summit of the steep, broken hill-side.

From the top, where the trees allow, the view is magnificent—Crieff below looking in the rarefied atmosphere like a model town built by some lad.

Robert Chambers tells us that " seen from the south Crieff looks like a troop of men hurrying up out of the low country into the Highlands," but I could not get that aspect of it, although, of course, the Crieff of to-day must be a vastly different place from that which he knew.

The monument, you may know, was erected to Sir David Baird, hero of Seringapatam. The original edifice was struck by lightning some forty odd years ago, and almost destroyed, but it was rebuilt—and an imposing landmark it is !

This hill on which it stands is named Tom-a-chastel, and age-old tradition states that at one time a castle occupied the site, and an admirable vantage-point it must have been. The Royal Castle of Earne, no less, and for her part in a conspiracy against Robert the Bruce, the Countess of Strathearn was doomed to perpetual imprisonment in the dungeon.

The vegetation on the hill or mound is luxuriant, indeed the red campion still lingered although by now a mere memory of the hedgeside in most places.

THE OLD BRIDGE, STIRLING

STIRLING CASTLE

Apart from the soft rustle of leaves, there was a Sabbath quiet over the place. The cooling breeze was welcome, and the world of to-day seemed very far away as I sat down on the grassy bank and filled my pipe.

The view commanded every airt—and every quarter has its story. Down there where the highway runs, to-day so peaceful as to be almost lonely in its aspect, was enacted long ago one of those fierce lawless affairs so intermixed with the story of our land.

This is Murray country, and that family had long been at feud with their neighbours, the Drummonds, and on this occasion would appear to have been the aggressors.

As fancy took them, the Murrays from time to time harried the Drummond lands and carried off spoil and cattle, doubtless with counter reprisals on the part of the Drummonds, and so things went on, just as was happening in many other parts of the land, between warring factions. These were mere raids and excursions, and, considering the times, not really serious !

Ultimately the rival clans met in pitched battle, and the Drummonds were defeated.

The victors had gone off with the spoils of war once again, when Campbell of Dunstaffnage, with a large body of his clansmen, arrived on the scene.

Dunstaffnage had come on a mission of vengeance on the Murrays, as that clan had murdered his father-in-law, and so joining forces with the defeated Drummonds, instantly followed the Murrays into their stronghold.

N

With the odds now heavily against them, and fatigued by their recent battle exertions, the Murrays, with their wives and children, took refuge in the church of Monzievaird.

This sanctuary was unknown to their enemies, and might have remained undiscovered had not a Drummond, on passing near-by the place of concealment, so incited one of the hidden Murrays that, unable to restrain his passion, he seized a bow and shot the man from a window.

Now, of course, the secret was out, and the church immediately surrounded. The Murrays were called upon to surrender, but refused to do so.

The building, which was thatched with heather, was set alight, and the inmates, some hundred and sixty men, women and children, perished in the flames.

Sorrowful old memories these to hang over such a smiling country-side as this to-day, but many dark tales are associated with these same hills, and it was not always the deer or grouse that men hunted as quarry over the heather wastes or amongst the rocks.

Over there amongst the dark hills lies wild Glenartney, but it does not show to greatest advantage from this elevation. Indeed, it is a glen that takes some knowing—lonely, forbidding, almost unapproachable in its demeanour. Somehow to me it looks as if brooding over the past, regretful of the days when the royal house claimed its deer as a right; of its departed glories, when men strove for its possessions and nameless deeds found their stage in its bosom.

GLENARTNEY

Down there on the plain of Lochlane, near-by Strowan House, Prince Charlie is said to have reviewed his troops ere retreating to the fatal North by way of the Sma' Glen. There is a local story, too, that Queen Anne spent some time at Lochlane House, so the place has many royal traditions.

To-day the glen proper is for the pedestrian only—its associations still immune from all who cannot woo it gently and unhurried. Unless you care for solitude, for the free wind which blows from the hills, keep to the King's highway—the glen's secrets are not for you!

But—if you love the tales of old: to dwell on the days when rival factions strove and no man was protected by other than his own right arm, when even the King's rights were flouted and the royal venison a perquisite of all who had the courage to take what they coveted—if that you love, then here you will find a plenty!

The glen will always be associated with an atrocious deed of blood, the onus of which is, rightly or wrongly, laid at the door of the MacGregors. There may be a doubt about the actual perpetrators of the act—one of the blackest in Highland blood feud, not because of the actual deed but for the incidents which clothed it; but as the MacGregors have many gruesome outrages placed to their record, their shoulders are broad enough to carry this one also, although the Glencoe Macdonalds may not be altogether innocent. The Privy Council, at least, had no hesitation in placing the crime to the Clan Gregor!

The tale goes that the King—James VI—had

his deer-forest in Glenartney, and, to celebrate his nuptial feast, instructions were issued to Drummond-Ernoch, the warden of these hills, to secure a supply of venison for the royal table.

When about his lawful business in the deer-forest, Drummond-Ernoch and his men came upon a band of MacGregors helping themselves to the royal venison.

The King's forester executed summary punishment on the outlaws by cropping their ears as a warning that the royal estates must be free of such vagrants, and then let them go.

Better for him had his work been more complete, as ere long the MacGregors were on his track, roused to their very depths at the insult put upon their tartan and bitter for vengeance.

Soon their chance came, and one day, meeting Drummond-Ernoch in Glenartney, they slew him and cut off his head, which, wrapped in a plaid, they took along with them as proof of their bloody work.

On their way home by Loch Earn, they passed the old mansion-house of Ardvorlich, and reading by the signs that the men-folk were absent on some business of their own, they entered the house and demanded food.

The lady of the house, a sister of the slain Drummond-Ernoch, knowing there was blood feud between them, was glad to get off so easily. At once she placed bread and cheese before the Mac-Gregors, saying that this might stay their pangs until she prepared something more substantial.

One of the uninvited guests demanded a cup of

water, and when she returned from the well, there on the table, the mouth stuffed with bread and cheese, was the gory head of her brother !

With a shriek she fled from the house, and for some days wandered about the hill-sides like a mad woman. Ultimately she was found and brought home to Ardvorlich, where shortly she gave birth to a son, James Stewart, referred to elsewhere, who became notable for his physical strength and uncontrolled passions.

Meanwhile the MacGregors departed for their native glens, taking the ghastly trophy along with them.

On the following Sabbath the head of Drummond-Ernoch was laid on the altar of Balquhidder Church and the MacGregors, one by one, placed their hands on the head and swore to protect the perpetrators of the deed and share in the consequences, whatever they might be !

The Government took a very serious view of the business, and letters of fire and sword were issued against the clan. Neighbouring chiefs and lairds drove against the MacGregors, and much blood was spilt, and doubtless opportunity was seized to pay off many outstanding scores on either side.

There is an air of deep mystery about Glenartney, making it easy to weave romantic tales, and here many broken men have sought sanctuary in the days of reif, providing as it does easy escape to the western hills and seas.

James IV spent some happy days " a-chasing the deer " in Glenartney, and unlike the modern stalker, who will spend fruitless hours on the hill only to find his wary quarry too alert and elusive and the heavy trail vain, he went forth with all the panoply of majesty. Surrounded by nobles and courtiers, with numerous ghillies and attendants, a goodly company and a brave, they doubtless accomplished considerable execution amongst the native royalty of the glen.

A minor fight, but serious enough in its own way, took place in the glen one October evening in the days of Rob Roy.

The MacGregors were the aggressors, and having *lifted* a huge drove of cattle, they were making for home when they were overtaken by the irate owners. The ensuing battle was a brisk enough affair, the pursuers determined to recover their property, the reivers just as stubborn to retain their ill-gotten spoil, and a number of men paid the penalty ere the issue was decided in favour of the rightful owners. Farming or cattle-breeding was a business fraught with considerable risk near-by the Highland Line!

Fights and skirmishes amongst wild clansmen— desperate sallies after the protected deer make good reading, and moreover one can fully understand them because of the times—but the cloud of a darker tragedy hangs over the glen—one which even now it is hard to forgive.

Indeed one of the most vindictive deeds ever committed by a Government was the arrest and execution of Dr Archibald Cameron, brother of Lochiel, in 1753, for the part he had played in the rising under Prince Charles Edward Stuart. It is true that he was specifically mentioned in the Act of Attainder of high treason, but by the date of his arrest the country was sick of the butchery which followed Culloden.

Lochiel having died in France, Dr Cameron is thought to have been actuated by a desire to offer advice and assistance to his fatherless nephews, so he returned to his native land and spent some time in hiding in Glenartney.

How his presence in the West was conveyed to the Government is not now material, although there is a strong suspicion that some spy, afraid that Dr Cameron was home to make inquiry as to the whereabouts of a large sum of money, remitted by the French Government to aid the clans in their insurrection, and which had mysteriously disappeared, did so to protect himself.

Be that as it may, a party of soldiers from the garrison at Inversnaid, advised of his whereabouts, effected his arrest, and he was at once sent under escort to Stirling. From there he was transferred to Edinburgh and then to the Tower of London.

He was put on trial in May, and although seven years of exile had intervened, the court found him guilty and he was sentenced to death.

One favour only was granted—the execution date was put forward by a week to enable his wife to return from Flanders and see him for the last time.

When lying under sentence, the use of pens and paper was refused, but Cameron secured some stray scraps of paper and wrote some pencil notes for his wife recounting some of the occasions on which he had been enabled during the rising to prevent reprisals and save much bloodshed. One of these deeds was when, by his personal exertions, he prevented the whole town of Kirkintilloch from being given to the flames and the inhabitants put to the sword.

It is a commentary on the barbarous Government of the day that Dr Cameron was conveyed to Tyburn, suspended for some twenty minutes, when he was taken down, his head cut off, his heart torn out, and burnt!

Fear and sycophancy made cowardly judges!

Back to the main road again, I set my face towards Comrie—a road which could tell of strange untoward happenings ere it became a public highway free to all.

Montrose lay one night at Crieff almost three hundred years ago, and must have retreated this way before the superior forces of Baillie, who had marched against him from Perth in the hope of a daybreak surprise.

But Montrose was too good a soldier, too experienced a tactician to be caught napping. Outnumbered by horse and foot, he made his way along the Earn to Comrie, crossed the stream and went by way of Ardvorlich's lands to Lochearnhead. Next day the Highlanders marched to Balquhidder, where Montrose was joined by Lord Aboyne, and doubtless more than one fighting man of Clan Gregor found the warlike Montrose too fascinating to resist and threw in his lot with that gallant leader, to do his part, a month later, in Auldearn, never again perhaps to see his native braes.

Still winding in its leisurely way, but now tree-lined, the leafy branches meeting overhead, the road was restful and enchanting.

The massive pile of Lawers House, seat of an old Scottish family, is a notable feature on the landscape.

Some two hundred years ago the cloud of tragedy was cast over this stately old home. Sir James Campbell of Lawers had a close friend and confidant, one Duncan Campbell of Edramurkle. Sir James and this false companion had gone to visit a young lady to whom the former was shortly to be married. On their way home they spent a day or two together in Greenock, and being short of cash but anxious to buy a pistol when in a town, Edramurkle borrowed a sum from his trusting friend of Lawers.

That night, when Sir James was fast asleep, Edramurkle requited his kindness by shooting him twice through the head, and absconding before the deed was discovered. Robbery was said to be the motive, and although the—in those days—large reward of one hundred guineas was offered for information which would lead to the arrest of the murderer, I do not think he was ever brought to trial.

Soon now I passed over the bridge which spans the Lednock Water and entered the quiet little town of Comrie.

Samson, as we know, amused himself by tossing a huge boulder about on Ben Ledi's side, indeed all the world knows, because the stone as proof still lies where he threw it, to the wonder of all lesser mortals. But Callander had not a monopoly of these exuberant displays of thew and sinew. Here, too, Samson visited in his wanderings, and by way of physical exercise, or maybe only from mere joy of living, he flung some huge stones from the neighbouring hills, and later those mysterious Druids made use of them for their pagan rites.

Comrie appears to have spent its early years under rather trying circumstances. If it is true that Galgacus and Agricola fought their great battle here, other notable occurrences must appear as mere incidents, but the series of earthquakes which it has undergone lend it an unchancy reputation.

To-day it is a smiling, sunlit town, benign and happy-looking, as if it at least found the modern world treating it well, and was endeavouring to atone for its somewhat noisy past.

No one should pass Comrie without climbing the hill road and viewing the Devil's Cauldron—a sight well worth the exertion, even if it does " gie ye a pech," as an old man predicted when first I ventured there.

Up you go—up until you wonder if the labour entailed is worth while—but it always is on these hill-roads, and the clear free air is a tonic and a delight.

I have traversed this road in all weathers—when wind was blowing and whistling down the glens— rain lashing and biting, and mist enveloping the hills like angry smoke. Again when all was white beneath a mantle of deep snow and the bens stood out with an added beauty. Then you can trace the hare and the fox. Here a rabbit made its useless effort to escape the feral weasel: under there you know some game birds slept—the shepherd's footprints are clear—the spot where he stopped to examine something and his collie circled round. It is all there clear to the discerning eye —the story of the wild told by their loitering or hurrying feet.

Climb up some day and see it for yourself—the carpet of hartstongue ferns, the tormented battling water—these alone will fill your eye with a beauty you are not likely to forget.

From Comrie to St Fillans is the most beautiful part of the road. On the left for quite a stretch a guard of pine, fir and larch—green all the year round and fitting into their setting most admirably, while on the right heavy dark hills, broken and rugged.

A mile or so, and the Earn comes close to the roadside and sings a cheery chorus to the wayfarer. Across the railway and opposite a conical hill, which always appears to remain green no matter how its neighbours change their shades, is a sight to instil terror to the more timid. This is a wild-looking monster rushing down the hill-side, huge fangs gleaming, withal a frenzied-looking creature.

In truth it is merely a stone, carved by nature into the form of a huge crocodile, and a paint-pot in an idle hand has completed the likeness. It is "tethered" to the hill-side by a rope, and legend states that the monster has been chained up in this way since one memorable New Year morning when it chased Rob Roy across the hills!

And then St Fillans. With the evening sun

glinting on the loch, every cottage embowered in blossom, the shadow of Ben Vorlich almost at its feet, it would be difficult to choose a more delight-ful halting-place. Over there where the Neishes paid such a dire penalty to the outraged Macnabs, a man and a girl were fishing in the cool of the evening, an occasional plop and the widening rings on the placid loch sure proof that a cunning hand need not lack sport enough and to spare. And then the sun went down behind the hills in a wonderful glory of colour, and but for an occasional mysterious woodland sound from the other side of the loch, the world seemed asleep.

XV

OVER THE REST TO INVERARAY, LOCH FYNE AND THE CAMPBELL COUNTRY

Over the hills to the setting sun,
 (Hark to the song of the burn)
By the cloud-kissed ben and the winding glen,
 (A road that your heart will travel again)
And the peace that your heart will earn.

THE road to the Campbell country is well guarded. If you go by Loch Long-side the deep sea loch is there as a foil, and if your way lie from Tarbet as did mine this day, the old Cobbler stands sentinel, keeping a weather-beaten eye on you as if ready to flash the tidings from his lofty perch far across the intervening hills to the watch-tower on Duniquaich Hill guarding the clanship in Inveraray.

Once through Arrochar and round the top of Loch Long you cross the narrow bridge which spans the burn, "the brown grey river," as it is named, past Ardgarten, and then you are fairly on the highway to adventure, mist and mountains.

The *highway* to adventure is a proper term, because almost before you realise it Rest-and-be-thankful has you in her toils, and you are mounting up and up with no seeming respite until the very mountain caps appear to await your coming. The

Rest, as they call it for short, is a long pull and a sore.

Almost at the summit there is a hairpin bend which haunts the nervous motorist, and if now no great ordeal to the modern high-power car, it is not exactly the sort of place one wants to chance every day.

As always in these parts we are in the wake of armed forces. Long before Bruce climbed up this rugged path it was a battle-ground for King Arthur away back in the sixth century, and was doubtless the scene of many an ambush and foray down the intervening years.

The Dutchmen are said to have had a camp on Loch Long and to have brought wine here to trade with the Highlanders; and generations ago, as we know, the Norsemen harried and laid waste its shores with fire and sword.

If it no longer echoes to the slogan of the clansman or the fierce shouts of the invaders, this morning I had an experience exciting enough of its kind. Two-thirds up and going strong ere changing down to negotiate the bend, a flock of sheep spilled round the corner and came slowly down the hill to meet me.

It is not a nice place to stop at any time, but to jam on brakes and hold up until the baaing creatures meandered past was more than I had bargained for. Behind them the shepherd was beckoning me to come on, and then I sensed, rather than heard, his whistle. Two dogs seemed to spring from nowhere, and the sheep were off the road and on the hill-side in less time than it takes to write the words, and with a shouted, but I fear unheard, thanks, I was safely round the bend and at the summit.

Here stands a stone admonishing all travellers to " Rest and be thankful," and filling a pipe I stood on a rock and followed with my eyes my shepherd and his flock, now far below. It is only from this vantage with the long winding road and far valley that one fully realises what a climb this is, or how :

> Now wound the path its dizzy ledge,
> Around a precipice's edge.

Once again my soul is filled with admiration for old General Wade, the wonder-worker, for this, too, is part of his living handiwork. "The incontrovertible general," Robert Chambers styled him for his manner of making roads " as straight as his person, as undeviating as his mind, and as indifferent to steep braes as he himself was to difficulties in the execution of his duty "—surely an epitaph eulogistic enough for any man, yet one richly deserved.

There is a strange fascination in standing on some high, wind-swept place, and here the glorious white-capped hills behind, dark Loch Restal in front, the far-winding descent and the deep glen form a picture not likely to fade from the mind.

On the way up to this vantage spot dark Glencroe is apt to be missed by the man at the wheel, but to appreciate its fearsome beauty one should do it on foot, as I have on many occasions, and then its lovely ruggedness is almost overawing. Whenever I find outstanding characteristics in the topography of my country, I always refer to Robert Chambers, that wonderful man whose every minute must have brought its task, so indefatigable was he in his writings.

Sure enough he had been here, and his description of Glencroe would stand to-day as then : no word need be altered, so perfect is his picture.

Let me quote him, and if you know the road, at once you will recognise how true he is : " In lonely magnificence, and all the attributes of Highland valley scenery, Glencroe can only be considered inferior to the vale which so nearly resembles its name. Its sides are covered with rude fragments of rock ; and a little stream runs wildly along the bottom, as if anxious to escape from its terrible solitudes."

The long, narrow road is now more track than highway, huge rocks and boulders strew the path, while right and left the mountain-sides reach up to meet the blue,

And heath-bells bud in deep Glencroe.

To-day there are no heath-bells, either here or in the glen which is now just behind, only withered bracken, and it appears lonely and desolate ; indeed, one almost awaits to hear a shout of " Cruachan " or " Loch Sloy " and to see the green tartan, or the red, bar the way, but only a whaup calls or a sheep bleats, for the clansmen warriors of other days are gone.

Leave the pathway for a little and one is almost lost to time. A well-known Glasgow man told me of his two young nieces who had fallen victims to the prevailing sun-bathing habit.

INVERARAY

ARROCHAR—ON THE WAY TO INVERARAY

TO THE CAMPBELL COUNTRY

One glorious summer evening, on passing through this glen, so quiet and travel-free was the road, they changed into their bright-hued bathing costumes.

On climbing the hill-side they started playing hide-and-seek among the rocks, when they espied an old shepherd coming slowly towards them. Full of pranks and high spirits, they danced gracefully towards the old man, when, to their astonishment, he stood for a moment terror-stricken and then turned and ran as for dear life !

Some lonely shieling would that night hear of the fairies he had seen on the mountain-side—who knows ?

Leaving "Rest and be thankful" we soon come to cross-roads, the first break in our journey. The quick turn on the left across the bridge goes by St Catherine's, through far Glen Branter to the Cowal shore, but our quest takes us to the right.

A beautiful road indeed, but for us a short, sharp descent requiring wary going, past Kilmorich Church, round by Cairndow Inn, and Loch Fyne bursts into view. There is a tang of sea-wrack and the clear, strong air is a tonic for jaded nerves like the fairy wind which blows from " Seven glens and seven bens and seven mountain moors," as no doubt it does and to spare.

Loch Fyne herrings have been a delicacy for many generations of gourmets. Long ago the Frenchmen used to steer their barques here and exchange ankers of wine for the fish, and so valuable was the traffic that the name Loch Fyne was derived from the French rendering of " the loch of wine."

o

242

A beautiful countryside this — hill - encircled, wooded, yet open to the sea, what more suitable environment for the great MacCailein and his Campbell henchmen ?

If it appears calm and tranquil to-day it was not always so, and most of the neighbouring clans were ready—not, perhaps, without due cause—to drop their hunting or pastoral pursuits and take up the claymore against these Argyllshire men.

The history of our country is full of references to Argyll and the Campbell Clan, but their real story will never be written, and perhaps it is well that much should be forgotten.

Many travellers have followed this beautiful lochside road we are traversing to-day, but there is one whose story interests me particularly.

Nearly two hundred years ago—in the year 1751 —two fair beauties burst upon London " and turned the West End almost mad." They were sisters, " the two fair Gunnings," as they were called, and on one occasion there was an unprecedented scene at a Court drawing-room, the gentlemen present climbing upon chairs and tables to look at them. In any case, the Duke of Argyll married the elder when she was left a widow by the Duke of Hamilton, and as she had two sons by each of her ducal husbands she was thus wife of two Dukes and mother of four !

If she came this road which to-day is ours alone, driving in her heavy coach across the bridge at the loch head, with its fragrant pine woods, in summer days heavy with the scent of honeysuckle, I wonder, sophisticated as she must have been, what were her

thoughts when she turned her back on it all once
more to seek the far-away London Court ?

Soon, too soon, so wondrous is the Highland
roadway, we are passing Inveraray Castle, home of
the Argylls, and the little town is upon us.

It has changed its position now, for in the old
days the houses clustered near the Chief's ducal
home, but as it is, the setting is perfect, and a trim
and beautiful little township it is.

When Burns visited Inveraray, the inn was full
to overflowing, guests and retainers of the Duke
occupying every available corner, and in the hubbub
and excitement the poet was ignored and slighted,
and gave vent to his feelings in a bitter verse :

> There's nothing here but Highland pride,
> And Highland cauld and hunger ;
> If Providence has sent me here,
> 'Twas surely in His anger.

Perhaps, however, he who knew so much of
Scottish life and character was prejudiced against
the Loch Fyne people, for many a tale would he
hear of their ruthless methods when an overweight
of numbers gave them security. Burns had a
wonderful admiration for Glencairn, and mayhap
knew of how an ancestor of the Earl he so revered
was tricked and deserted in his hour of need by an
Argyll and his clansmen.

The occasion was that known in Scottish history
as Glencairn's Expedition to the Highlands, and
this army, commanded by the Cunningham chief,
who had with him Lochiel, Atholl, Glengarry,
Graham of Duchray, MacGregor, and several

others, was joined by Argyll with one thousand foot and some fifty horse. Argyll had apparently become faint-hearted and decided to withdraw with all his personal forces.

Glencairn despatched Lochiel and Glengarry to compel the Campbells to return to their positions, and they were overtaken somewhere in the vicinity of Castle Ruthven, then in the hands of the English, but Argyll escaped with a remnant of his mounted retainers.

The Campbell clansmen, thus deserted by their leader, offered to return and again join issue with Glencairn, but Glengarry would have none of it, and was on the point of attacking them when the timely arrival of his general, Glencairn, prevented what would doubtless have been a massacre.

They were ordered to lay down their arms before any treaty could be entertained, and on their declared willingness again to take the field and loyally stand by their leader, they were bound by oath to keep word and faith. All ranks subscribed —and within a fortnight every single man among them had deserted! The Glencairn rising was ultimately quelled by General Monk, and several of the officers were hanged.

But that is an old story now, and to-day Inveraray was a-bustle with men and beasts ; for there was a cattle sale on hand ; most interesting, not to say exciting, affairs were in progress.

The green in front of the hotel was fenced in to form one huge enclosure, and as droves of shaggy, wild-eyed cattle or flocks of sheep and rams arrived, they were driven into this common arena to mix indiscriminately.

Many a fierce combat was being waged by the young bulls. Now and again a sharp clap told of two rams " hurtling " at each other, while all unconcerned, groups or odd couples of shepherds, farmers, and drovers stood smoking and chatting, awaiting the all-important personality, the auctioneer, now and again administering an admonitory whack on a too bold or inquisitive animal.

It was like a scene from another country. Gaelic was the speech, the gentry in their Campbell tartans, while in the midst stood the beautiful war memorial to the Lochfyneside lads who would know it no more.

I do not know how old Inveraray is in the annals of men, but Bruce fought here; but an older memory than even that of the Bruce adorns the place in the form of a stone cross, said to have been removed from Iona.

Apart from the short summer season when tourists pay fleeting visits, they live in a world of their own in this Campbell quarter. Easily enough got at to-day, perhaps, but it is interesting to note that in 1691 an Act was passed by the Convention of Royal Burghs exempting Inveraray from certain taxes because of the difficulty of access to the place !

Gilpin, the Prebendary of Salisbury, toured Scotland in the closing years of the eighteenth century and left an interesting record of much that he saw.

Amongst other places, his wanderings took him to Inveraray, and he records that at certain seasons the natives declare Loch Fyne to be one part water and two parts herring! In one bay of the loch there were sometimes to be seen six hundred boats engaged in fishing.

He relates that amongst the implements on board each boat the bagpipes were rarely forgotten, and the "shrill melody" could be heard resounding from every part.

On Sunday evenings the crews put away their bagpipes and the shore echoed to their singing of Psalms!

But more stirring deeds have found their setting here in the days when might was right and a chief's word law.

To me, the seventeenth century holds a rare fascination.

In many aspects it marked the parting of the ways.

If manners were uncouth, bloodshed not by any means uncommon, torture and horrible sentences meted out by the law, nevertheless the right hand was groping towards culture and the arts while the left still firmly held to mere savagery.

It is true the peasant of the Lowlands was illiterate and credulous; the clansman of the North barbaric, and asked for nothing other than to carry out the will of his chief—but a new spirit was abroad.

The clergy, coarse and outspoken as they may now appear, were leading, blindly it may have been, to a spiritual freedom which was ultimately to spell emancipation for the whole land. Many of the Highland chiefs were, even if only in trust, great landowners. Several of them acquainted with courts, sending their sons into the outer world to be educated, were yet cruel and high-handed.

In a century which recognised Shakespeare, Courts of Justice were a misnomer, and in Scotland more often than not the colour of a man's tartan did more to condemn him than the deeds for which he was arraigned.

On a spring evening in the year 1671, a number of Highland gentlemen met in Inveraray in the house of a certain John Rowat. Why they were assembled there, what they were plotting or discussing I do not know, but the sequel proves them to have been an ill-assorted fellowship.

Apparently differences had arisen, the exchanges were heated, *and the candle having gone out,* some one shot the Laird of Lochnell, a near kinsman to the Duke of Argyll. A dangerous position for all concerned !

Argyll was not the man to allow this to pass, and although one Duncan MacGregor admitted that he had fired the fatal pistol, James Menzies of Culdares was imprisoned and charged with the crime.

To be tried in Inveraray before a Campbell jury for the murder of one sib to their clan allowed of only one verdict. Menzies contrived to petition the Privy Council to be allowed to "thole his assize" in Edinburgh, and Argyll was ordered to appear before that body to show reason why the prayer should not be granted.

I do not know the result, or what action was taken—influence rather than justice or charity would doubtless be the deciding factor—but my point is to emphasise the autocratic power, the eagerness to grasp every opportunity to pay off old scores, to avenge past clan wrongs even on an innocent man !

This incident is not an isolated one, nor was it peculiar to one territorial magnate or chief, but was unhappily too frequently a recognised procedure, as one finds if the annals of the times are sifted.

One of Scotland's historic mysteries is intimately connected with this town and is known as " the Appin murder." The tale has been told many times, and is part of our Scottish lore to-day.

In the days of the '45 the Campbells took the Hanoverian side, while the Stewarts of Appin were " out " with the Prince. The Stewart estates were, as a result, forfeited to the Crown, and Campbell of Glenure was entrusted with them.

One day, as Campbell was returning from Fort William, a shot rang out on the hill-side, and he dropped mortally wounded.

One James Stewart was arrested, taken to Inveraray, tried before a Campbell jury, and hanged for a murder he probably did not commit. Indeed, the secret of who actually fired the shot was well guarded, but there is little doubt, indeed, that an innocent man was made to suffer.

R. L. Stevenson has made the tale his own, and there you can read it for yourself.

Many tales are told, but of all the romances woven round this old Gaelic stronghold give me Neil Munro's " John Splendid." He has written more than one book centred round Inveraray, but no other haunts my memory like that fascinating romance.

Up one of these Inveraray streets rode John Splendid without a turn of the head—and left me wishing that I could hear more about him, where he disported his gallant figure, and what strange adventures befell him on the road.

I wonder which way he turned—if he came round the loch side by Cairndow and the road we have just left, or if he struck out toward the setting sun in the direction of Loch Awe.

All stories of this district enthral; many of them may not be true, but they fit their setting and the wild blood of the days that are gone.

Montrose harried the Campbell country in December 1644. For leadership and valour this campaign must take high rank. The passes, difficult at any time, were snowbound and almost impassable, but the spirit of feud and hate, combined with indomitable pluck, accomplished the seeming impossible.

The invaders swept across Argyll and spared no man fit to carry arms, putting all to the sword, burning, ravaging and houghing or driving the cattle before them. Villages, farmhouses, cottages, all were given to the flames, and Inveraray was sacked. Montrose then retired north and in the following January, at Inverlochy, surprised and routed an army four times his strength.

The Campbells fought with great courage, but their defeat was decisive. Argyll watched the fight from his galley, when his presence as an active leader might have been more useful to his men.

Time has softened much of the old clan feeling, but it is not yet dead. Men are not so open in their loves and hates to-day, but now and again the old fires spring to life, splutter for a little, and die out again.

Only a year or two ago a most spirited encounter took place between the Duke of Argyll and the parish minister of Inverchaolain over a font missing from Cairndow Church. There was a lengthy and bitter correspondence between them, and the Duke of Argyll dated one of his letters " On the Feast of St Patrick the Apostle, 1925," while the minister headed his reply, " On or about the Anniversary of the Lamont Murders, 1925," this being in reference to a massacre of the Lamonts by the Campbells on the Cowal shore, on which occasion, I think, the Provost of Dunoon was hanged for passing a too free criticism on the deeds then committed.

It's an old story now, but clan feelings die hard, and even in this year of grace I know otherwise peaceful citizens who can work themselves into a mild passion over wrongs committed many generations ago.

The Campbells were not always on the losing side, however. They were a great and powerful fighting clan, capable of putting many warriors in the field, and loyal to their chief.

They suffered much in the old lawless days, but Argyll was powerful in the councils of the nation and generally managed to protect his people in the raids and counter-raids which were a feature of the times.

They were ruthless in their vengeance when opportunity gave them power, but in that they were, mayhap, no worse than their neighbours.

TO THE CAMPBELL COUNTRY

The siege of Dunaverty Castle is a striking example of how clan wrongs were righted and of the strong feelings engendered by present and past offences.

The Macdonalds had been laying waste Argyll, harrying with fire and sword, and doubtless many black deeds had been committed in field and clachan.

The Campbells, who were accompanied by Sir David Leslie, pressed on their marauding enemies, and the Macdonalds retreated to Dunaverty Castle, no great distance from the present-day Machrihanish Golf Course, so well known to many holiday-makers.

The position was supposed to be almost impregnable, but the Campbells cut off the supply of water, and so the Macdonalds were ultimately compelled to ask for terms.

"Would their lives be spared?" Sir David Leslie in reply told them : " I shall not see you die." On this answer the Macdonalds laid down their arms and surrendered the castle. The next proceeding was to tie the prisoners two by two, back to back, and cast them from the castle wall on to the rocks beneath.

A minister of the gospel stood and counted them as they fell, and it is said his boot tops were covered with blood. Sir David Leslie, who had promised not to see them die, left the camp until it was all over, so that by his absence he might keep his word!

Horrible they seem, these old tales of other days, but they are not peculiar to any one district, not alone to the fierce clansmen. Across the Clyde on the Ayrshire coast the family feuds were conducted in a manner just as thorough, and if the Inveraray gallows carried a rich crop, that in the capital itself was not long idle.

To-day the gulls are wheeling over the fishing boats and the drums of war are, let us hope, for ever silenced in our land.

Somewhere from the other side of the loch come the strains of the bagpipes, and here in this perfect setting is the wild music most appropriate.

The heavy hand of the past is forgotten in the witchery of this beauty: the blue atmosphere so peculiar to the mountain country, the still woods, the colouring which simply must be seen because it cannot truthfully be described or depicted, form natural charms enough for most, but coupled with the lore and legend of the old fighting days, who, knowing it, can resist the call of the land where loyalty to one's chief and tartan was stronger than death itself ?

TOWARDS THE BLACK MOUNT

There's a road that pulls my heart-strings
   As it winds towards the ben,
There's a song the joyous burn sings
   As it hurries through the glen
Where the bracken waves her banners,
   And the red deer roam,
The road that calls me ever,
    Calls me home !

FOR days the country had been mantled in white. Road reports were bad, many highways altogether blocked and quite impassable. Everywhere it was the same story, and so I decided to see the Black Mount in its winter garments, but how best to get there was the problem.

It was still snowing when we left Glasgow, and the farther we went the more hopeless seemed the outlook, and yet it was not cold. The burns were open, but they somehow had a listless, dead appearance, not the rushing tawny streams of a month past.

And then, almost before I realised it, we were running alongside Loch Lubnaig. Cold and chill it looked, not a ripple on the surface; above, the dark leaden sky and the silent, falling snow. No gay nodding foxgloves among the green bracken this morning ; the beauty of the autumn rowans a thing of the past—only the sturdy firs standing green and defiant of all that Boreas and his crew could send.

A range of hills—a familiar glen—and then below lay Loch Earn, looking strangely shrunk and deserted, Ben Vorlich, wrapped in white from crown to toes, seeming to overbulk the neighbourhood.

But engine-drivers have no time to admire lochs and bens, and almost at once wild Glenogle had us in his grip; and disdainfully we mastered the long walking miles and were soon running up Glen Dochart.

Here winter was master of his own house. Loch Dochart was frozen over, and in addition long white patches of snow were scattered about the ice, giving an extra chill to the view.

Amidst the white, the old ruined castle stood black and defiant, but its sturdy air was merely a pose—its day is long since gone by, and no red tartans hid amongst the firs plotting against its inmates. Not even a bird was visible, although well I knew that when night fell and the moon was all but concealed by the falling snow, what the lonely wayfarer misjudged for the hoot of an owl would really be a ghostly signal for the reacting of the old-time tragedy, and the walls would echo again the fierce warrior slogans and the shrieks of their victims.

Round the bend, the lines almost running over the toes of giant Ben More, and here we are at Crianlarich.

Last time I was here the rowans had painted the place scarlet and green; peat-reek vied with autumn roses, a Highland garron with its game panniers had a sprig of heather on its forelock, and everything was gay and colourful.

This morning the hard snow crunched beneath my tackets as I crossed the station yard, and a whistling errand-boy, a basket over his arm, was sliding on the path where the snow had been brushed clear.

Still it was fine to be back in Crianlarich again, high-lying and cold as it was to-day, indeed its elevated position is overlooked because of the towering bulk of Ben More and Stobinian. The wind was shrewd, but snow and wind were soon forgotten in the hearty welcome awaiting me.

At the hôtel they predicted bad weather and heavy going—and they proved to be no false prophets, indeed it was altogether different from the joyous road I had so lately known, and in place of a kindly sun, above was a sky of slate-grey as if heavy with snow. Still, there was to be no turning back now, and a glance at two passing fishermen, one without an overcoat, renewed my waning faith.

The clan road of the old marauding days came up Glenfalloch and turned west shortly before the site of the Crianlarich we know, and so this morning it was on my left, but too deep in snow to give sign of its presence, although high on the overhanging bank where the old drove road led, stands the oldest house in the village.

At one time it was an inn, frequented by caterans and drovers, passing to or from the glens beyond, and was the scene of a tumultuous episode in the life of Rob Roy.

The Duke of Montrose, discovering that Rob Roy

and his men were living in the inn, and doubtless
fearing this to be the preliminary to some lawless escapade, sent a party of his clansmen, in charge
of a kinsman, Graham, and supported by some
military, probably from Inversnaid, to capture the
outlaw. Ascertaining that Rob Roy was sleeping
in the inn and his clansmen were occupying a
near-by barn, the Grahams attacked the inn at
daybreak. But it is ill to catch a man like the
MacGregor unprepared, and nothing daunted, Rob
defended himself lustily.

Soon the noise brought the MacGregors to his
assistance, but they were too heavily outnumbered
to have any chance of success, and so Rob Roy made
his escape through a back window, and he and his
men got safely away to the wild braes above Loch
Lomond, where they knew every rock and moss-hole
and where pursuit was impracticable.

It was from Strathfillan that the MacGregors,
making rendezvous with some other clans, made
their warlike descent on Inveraray.

Tradition tells us that Macdonald of Glengarry
had charge of this force, and that it numbered some
fifteen hundred claymores.

One would have thought the Clan Gregor had
enough excitement at their own doors without
embarking upon further adventures of that kind,
but they were ever a restless, fighting race, and
about this period, 1715, the whole country was in a
ferment due to Mar's Rising.

And now they were gaily embarking upon a further adventure aware that powerful enemies were
plotting in their rear.

Just shortly before this Inveraray excursion, the MacGregors, numbering some seventy hardy warriors, landed on Inchmurrin, an island in Loch Lomond, used by the Duke of Montrose as a deer preserve.

When darkness fell, they again took to their boats and approached the village of Bonhill, hoping to surprise and plunder the place while the inhabitants were asleep.

Unfortunately for the marauders, their advance was discovered, and at once the alarm was given. The various kirk bells were set a-ringing and an urgent message despatched to the commander of Dumbarton Castle—only a mile or two distant.

That officer fired his guns as a sign that speedy aid was forthcoming, and foiled in their purpose, the MacGregors took to their boats and landed once more on the island of Inchmurrin. There they slaughtered a number of the deer and held a rude feast ere making for their native haunts at daybreak.

But they did not depart quite empty-handed. Every boat and craft on the lochside was their spoil, and they had quite a flotilla when at last they arrived at Inversnaid, having despoiled every owner on their way.

This was more than the authorities and the Lowland citizens could permit to pass unchallenged, and so an expedition was raised to punish the raiders. With so many boats in their possession no one was safe from annoyance and attack from the restless clansmen.

A strange and motley force went forth to punish the Rob Roy faction.

P

Paisley contributed some hundred and twenty volunteers. The Ayrshire towns of Kilmarnock, Ayr and Kilwinning sent roughly four hundred. This force sailed up Loch Lomond in man-o'-war boats from the fleet then lying in the Clyde, commanded by Naval officers, who had with them some three hundred bluejackets supported by some guns with their special crews.

Another force marched along the rough and difficult lochside, and it was comprised of men from Dumbarton, Cardross and the lower reaches of Loch Long. Campbell of Mamore, an uncle of the Duke of Argyll, followed in charge of a well-mounted party of gentlemen and retainers.

In due time this force reached their objective, Inversnaid. There lay the boats, one object of their quest, but no hostile band challenged their approach.

It was a beautiful October morning, the bracken turning from yellow to russet, the bens looking silently down on as motley a crew as had until then startled the deer on their broad shoulders—but of MacGregors there was no sign.

A few deserted turf-roofed huts were visible on the higher banks, but unguarded by their red-tartaned owners.

A shot from one of the guns carried away the roof of a cottage, and one or two old women scrambled through the low doorway and disappeared behind the hill as fast as their aged limbs could bear them, but still no defiant clansmen appeared to protect their heritage.

The forces were landed, and in martial array they

marched stiffly up the hill-path and formed up on the flat summit.

There they stood, drums beating, for some considerable time, but they had the place to themselves. Apart from one or two men who quietly watched them at too great a distance to be molested or interrogated, no living soul was apparently within miles of the intended battleground.

The next morning the gallant force sailed down the loch again, in their turn confiscating every boat they discovered on their journey, and once again the deer were left to browse in peace.

The going was not so bad as I had anticipated. The snow was hard and clean, and bus-tracks made a footpath easy to negotiate. Winding and narrow, round a bend and the village is lost, but now the hills close in on every side of the glen, and if only the sun had come out the picture would have been sublime in its grandeur.

High on the left is a flat stone—" The Place of Shouting" it is called in Gaelic—where a man could stand and give shouted warning of enemy approach from any position, so commanding is the site.

Black too against the brae lie the ruins of St Fillan's Chapel, with its old burial-ground and a more modern God's acre behind.

St Fillan holds high place amongst Scottish saints, and indeed it were meet that he did so, because his deeds were outstanding to a degree !

For a considerable time this sainted man lived in a monastery at Pittenweem, and when engaged in translating the Scriptures, his left hand gleamed so in the darkness that he could carry on his work without the aid of a lamp !

If all stories are true, Scotland owes much to this venerable saint. At one time in the history of our land, holy relics, pieces of the true Cross and so on, were held in high esteem and worked many miracles in their day, but St Fillan's legacy took the form of winning a battle, and no inconsiderable event in the annals of our race at that, indeed no less than the glorious victory of Bannockburn !

King Robert the Bruce spent the evening previous to that great clash of arms in devout contemplation and intercession to God and St Fillan.

In the Bruce's tent reposed a silver case which was supposed to contain a wonderful talisman, forsooth an arm of the saint ! As the King was engaged in his devotions, the case suddenly opened and as mysteriously closed !

The chaplain who was with the Bruce and had observed the untoward happening, immediately approached the altar and, examining the casket, cried out that a miracle had been performed. Afraid lest the day might go against the Scots, and fearful that the holy relic might fall into profane hands, the chaplain had left the saint's arm behind and only the empty casket graced the altar. The sudden and unaccountable opening and closing of the silver case had been to admit the arm, which now reposed within !

The Bruce, realising the good omen, passed the evening in pious devotions and thanksgiving—and with what results on the morrow the whole world is to-day familiar.

IN GLENORCHY, DALMALLY

TYNDRUM—ON THE WAY TO BLACK MOUNT

About a mile farther on and close to the roadside is St Fillan's Holy Pool.

Here a quaint ceremony was at one time indulged in for the cure of lunatics. Part of the ritual was to tie securely the afflicted one and leave him lying on his back all night ! If in the morning the much-tried victim of such heroic measures was found freed of his bondage, the cure was adjudged to be successful and complete. If, on the contrary, the knots were too secure and in the morning he was still bound and helpless, he was considered to be still possessed—but what then took place, or what further measures were enacted, I personally cannot enlighten you.

The old church bell, used in the days of St Fillan, was called into operation during the mystic ceremonies, and for many years it lay open and unprotected upon a flat gravestone. There was a local belief that if anyone dared to lay covetous hands upon it the bell would, because of some unknown power potent within it, return to the spot of its own accord.

A passing Sassenach one day put its power to a practical test, and from that date the bell has not been seen!

But madmen were not the only victims of these dark waters. Witches, or rather those accused of being witches, were here subject to a test, and innocent or guilty, the poor wretches upon whom fell the evil eye of the witch-finder or about whose doings gossip got busy, had not much chance of escape. The milk of human kindness was a very sour commodity in those days, I am afraid.

In any case, the proceedings here were as effective as they were simple.

When an old woman was charged with being a witch she was taken to the Holy Pool, and her thumbs being bound together, she was then thrown into the water. If she at once sank and did not come up again she was adjudged innocent and her name freed from the odium of the charge ; if she did not drown it was conclusive proof of her guilt, and she was fished out and burned ! It was doubtless an interesting experiment to all concerned, with the possible exception of the poor old victims, and was at least delightfully simple in its method and procedure.

Across the white bridge—so named locally, not because of its colour—and under your feet is being enacted a transformation. The stream which flows under on the left is the Connernish, but when it comes out again on the right it has changed its title to the Fillan.

Just hereabouts on the left is what looks to be a pool or mountain tarn cupped amongst some rocks. But it is no pool, at least in name, and flourishes under the proud patronymic of Loch Righ, or the King's Loch.

Tradition derives the name from the fact that at the battle of Dalree, fought here, the Bruce's men, when retreating before the victorious M'Dougalls of Lorn, cast their weapons into the loch to aid their escape.

The smoke in front, rising in a huge grey spiral from amongst a guarding screen of trees, was Tyndrum, and as I drew nearer, on the hills behind

I could note the scars that show where a fortune went in an endeavour to establish lead-mines.

And now good fortune, in the guise of a Ford car, took me by the hand, and right glad was I to accept the proffered lift.

There was a decided change in the temperature, and the wind now had a vicious nip which boded ill for nightfall. A narrow burn, hidden deep in rocky sides, was now keeping us company on the right, and here and there huge icicles had formed. In places they had the semblance of a pipe-organ where they stood, or rather hung, in rows, six or seven feet in length and many thicker than a man's thigh.

The glen got narrower as we bumped along, and almost at the skirt of Ben Doran we left Perthshire behind and entered Argyll.

A wonderful panorama of hill and moor rich in tradition and romance is opening to the view. Argyll—the land of the strangers—has many tales to tell, and the casket of their setting is amongst the most beautiful of our land.

Stretched out in front lay a long white strath, and on the left a camp of wooden huts to house the army at work on the new Glencoe road which ran over on the left, removing hills or filling chasms as need arose. A wonderful feat of engineering, but the hundreds who will travel its macadamised surface towards dark Glencoe may possibly save much sweat, but they will miss the joyous adventure of the old road.

And then Glenorchy and her " proud mountains," an old-time fastness of the ill-fated MacGregors, appeared majestic in her white garments on the left. Now starts the Black Mount, really a serried range of hills, their tenants Breadalbane's deer. Read *The High Tops of the Black Mount* by Lady Breadalbane if you would know more of its denizens.

Over behind these hills was the childhood home of Duncan Ban M'Intyre, but the cottage is now a mere heap of stones and the belling of the stags has displaced the laughter of children.

Up here on the Black Mount was staged another of these hot-blooded incidents with which the West is chequered.

Some MacGregors were hunting in the district, amongst them being the son of Glenstrae, and when seeking rest or refreshment in a house or inn they were joined by young Lamont on his way across the hills from Cowal on some business of his own.

The two young chieftains sat at meat together and everything seemed friendly and well. Later in the evening some discussion arose and the youths quarrelled. Hot-blooded and touchy, weapons were drawn and the MacGregor lay dead on the floor.

Here in the heart of the MacGregor country, unaccompanied as he was, Lamont's position was desperate, and he took to the hills with MacGregor's followers hot on his heels.

Knowing that escape was impossible, he fled in the direction of Glenstrae's stronghold, and outdistancing the avenging clansmen, he craved sanctuary from Glenstrae in person, father of the man he had slain.

Glenstrae, a generous, impulsive man, swore to

protect him, no matter what deed he had perpe-
trated. No sooner was he committed to his oath,
than the pursuing clansmen arrived, explained
what had taken place, and demanded that Lamont
be given over to feudal justice.

Glenstrae, shocked as he must have been at the
loss of his boy, refused to break his word and told
Lamont to have no fear, he was safe under that roof.

Next day, with a picked body of his clansmen,
Glenstrae personally escorted Lamont to the
borders of his own clan-territory. " Now," he
said on parting, " you are safely amongst your own
people and my pledge has been fulfilled. More I
cannot and will not do—but if you value your life
avoid my territory—keep clear of my clansmen—and
may Heaven forgive you for the sorrow you have
laid at my door."

Not long afterwards Glenstrae and his clan were
proscribed; letters of fire and sword were given
against all who wore his tartan, and he was more
homeless than the deer in his corries or the eagle on
Ben Doran.

Then Lamont repaid Glenstrae in kind for his
generous deed, sheltered and protected him amongst
the wild hills of Cowal, and proved a friend to the
Clan Gregor when all men's hands were against
them !

Now over the high-arched bridge which spans
the Orchy and lends its name to the clachan, and
we bump and jolt alongside the stream, while far off
on the right the new road winds towards the sea.

Round the bend we go, bumping amongst the
ruts, sympathising with every agonised protest

from the springs, and Loch Tulla is spread in front, a vision of beauty compensating for the discomforts of the road. The fine old Scotch firs are said to be the lingering heirs of the Caledonian Forest, and one man informed me that when cutting peat he regularly came across giant roots, all that is now left of the great tree-covered tract where the wolf, and not man, was the deer hunter.

Rattling and bumping along over the snow-filled ruts, past the finely situated Shooting Lodge, and so to Inveroran Hotel, where I left my driver-host to continue on his lonely way over the appalling road (for a car) to Glencoe.

In the hotel a casual remark about a golden eagle which graced a corner of the room proved fruitful.

It has been a bad year for snow, and the great birds have been not uncommon in the district of late.

A shepherd coming home across the hills had the unwelcome attendance of a giant specimen for fully an hour. It fluttered—if one can use such an expression about a creature with a wing-spread of some six feet—above his head just out of reach of his crook, its wicked, cruel eyes on his dogs. He kept them close to heel, well knowing the fate of even a fighting collie once these great talons gripped it, and strong man as he is, was not sorry when, approaching his home, his unwelcome escort rose to a great height and was soon a mere speck in the northern sky.

Three splendid specimens have been seen of late more than once, and doubtless the lambs and hill-hares will be having an anxious time.

They told me too that a week or two ago some stalkers near Loch Awe came across a herd of deer running in frenzy with an eagle swooping above them, but on their approach it made off towards the Braemar hills.

After a day on the snow-covered hills, the genial heat of the fire played me a most unfriendly trick, or I might have gleaned some even more interesting facts from the company.

Later as I looked out on the dreary white stretch, the moon breaking through above, I thought of one who loved these hills well and of his word painting :

> The placid moon, the huge sky-cleaving Ben,
>   The moor loch gleaming in the argent ray,
>   The long white mist low-trailing up the glen,
>   The hum of mighty waters far away.

If Professor Blackie's gifts as a poet are open to doubt, as is the fashion to-day with a certain school, his love for his country is never in question.

XVII

BY CRUACHAN AND LOCH AWE

> Land of Campbells and MacDougalls,
>   Where full many a practised hand,
> Nerved with high heroic purpose,
>   Poised the spear, and waved the brand.
>
> PROFESSOR BLACKIE

IN Glenorchy I had a stalker for company to-day, but his mind was too practical to give me any romantic details of the old days when the MacGregor tartan ruled the glen, though on salmon and deer his knowledge was encyclopædic.

Near here, he informed me, was fought one of those dour clan battles which to-day lend an added interest to the glens and straths. In far-off 1463 the Stewarts, aided by the MacLarens, fought a battle-royal with the MacDougalls, Campbells of Lorn and some MacFarlanes, but which side gained the victory, or what it was all about, he did not know.

When Dr Garnett, one of the old-time travellers, passed through Glenorchy, and indeed for many long years to follow, salmon could be had for the taking by any man who cared to exert himself. And so Dr Garnett witnessed a remarkable way of ensnaring the plentiful fish.

At Catnish a rock crossed the bed of the Orchy, reaching almost from side to side. The height of

THE PASS OF AWE

272

KILCHURN, LOCH AWE

this natural dam was such that few salmon could leap over into the pool beyond. A basket was fixed transversely, and the baffled fish fell into the receptacle, and were lifted out at leisure.

The hills of the Black Mount towered above on the right; those of Auch guarded us on the left, but in their driven white they somehow appeared unreal, more resembling cloud effects than towering bens; but when the sun glinted on them for a moment or two, the whole vista was fairylike in its charm.

And then I was brought down to the hard realities of life. To me, at this point, the river took on an added beauty, rippling and shallow amongst a mass of rocks and stones. But to my companion its beauty was lost. "Waste-water," he termed it—no salmon were to be caught in such a stretch! So we tramped ahead, smoking our pipes and agreeing to differ about the real fundamentals of Highland glens.

Christopher North knew the Glenorchy region well, and used to perform wonderful feats of pedestrianism, impossible for the normal man to emulate.

Francis Watt tells how on one occasion the indefatigable Professor called at a farmhouse in the glen at eleven o'clock one night, seeking refreshment. "They brought him a bottle of whisky and a can of milk, which he mixed and consumed in two draughts from a huge bowl." No insignificant feat when one remembers the fiery, full-blooded liquor sold as whisky in some parts of the Highlands in pre-War days!

The hills now fell back, and the long, dreary, white glen reached away in front, bleak and silent. Here and there stood the ruined walls of the old clansmen's crofts, eloquent advertisement of the effect of a deer forest on the old order.

Always when passing through a glen where ruined cottages lie amongst the over-running bracken, there comes to my mind a verse from " Kenneth's Song." I cannot say it holds in this case, but many of the glens in our country are to-day stark and empty, only ruined walls where one time lived the happy clansmen, because the land was necessary for the deer.

> But the big-horned stag and his hinds, we know,
> In the high corries ;
> And the salmon that swirls the pool below
> Where the stream rushes,
> Are more than the hearts of men, and so
> We leave thy green valley.

I was glad when the hills withdrew and the last mile or two changed to a tree-lined path, and so across an old bridge, past a ruined mill, and on to the main highway to Oban and the West, with Dalmally just a short walk ahead, and the crown of the road free of snow !

No part of this road could prove uninteresting for any man with eyes to see, as while now more open than in dark Glenorchy, every step reveals new and ever-changing views in a panorama of hill and glen.

Now we were almost at Dalmally, and from there my guide and travelling companion was taking the bus for somewhere on business of his own, but he accompanied me to the hotel for a moment or two as he was rather before his hour.

Here we met an old man who had lived all his years in a cottage on the hill-side, but his limited knowledge of English made conversation difficult. Indeed even his Gaelic was hard to follow, and it was only by slowly repeating his words that my ghillie friend and another native, sent for to help us to interpret, could with difficulty get his meaning.

When Pennant visited Dalmally many years ago, he made record of a family of smiths, MacNab by name, who had dwelt here, pursuing their avocation without a break in the direct family line since 1440.

There was no MacNab now, the old man said— the last of the line had died or left the place fully fifty years back. But he told us how one afternoon Duncan Ban M'Intyre, having killed a goat possessed of a wonderful horn, he detached it from the skull and brought it to MacNab the blacksmith, with a request that he should fit to it a blade and so make a sgain dhu.

MacNab was a wondrous craftsman, and he put all his skill and cunning into the work, so that the poet was delighted when the finished knife was handed to him.

" How much do I owe you, MacNab ? " queried the poet.

" Money could not buy its like," replied the blacksmith, " and for it money I shall not accept. Make a verse about it, and as masters we shall both be served."

And so Duncan Ban M'Intyre sang of it to the

eager smith, and it was this poem my old Highlander recited to us.

Then the bus arrived and my interpreter friends
bade me a hurried farewell—and so we were alone—
the old man, who was so anxious to tell me all he
knew—and I no less anxious to hear his experiences,
neither of us knowing what the other said! I
wondered how the old-time travellers fared here
more than a century ago, but of course the Parish
Church minister was a ready friend, always glad to
meet wayfarers from the outer world.

An ancient divine who made a tour of this land
in 1803, has left a most interesting record of his
itinerary. He was accompanied by a " Mr S.," who
otherwise remains anonymous throughout.

Amongst other places, they visited Glenorchy,
coming by way of Loch Lomond-side, over the Rest
and by Inveraray and Cladich. A night was spent
at Luss, in hopes of seeing the Rev. Mr Stewart, held
in very high esteem by our author, for his translation
of the Scriptures into Gaelic, for which he received
the " inadequate recompense " of £500.

Mr Stewart was from home, but Mrs Stewart had
remained behind, and invited the tourists to partake
of breakfast. She treated the wanderers in a most
hospitable manner, and now may I quote :

" Leaving the lake, we turned towards Arroquar.
Here we stopped to recruit ourselves and our horse.
From this place I addressed the following letter to
Mrs Stuart :—

" ' MADAM,—As I never had the pleasure of
seeing you before, and perhaps never shall again, I
should be sorry to leave this part of the country

without expressing my sense of your kindness, and that of the other friends whom we parted with at Luss. If you are possessed of a diamond pencil I should be obliged to you if you would inscribe the following lines on one of the windows of the public house at your village:

> 'Whoe'er thou art that travell'st here like us,
> To view the wonders of romantic Luss,
> If mountains, woods, or lakes have charms for thee,
> Here all that's grand or beauteous shalt thou see,
> If manners sweet and kindness please thee more
> Than Lomond's heights, or lake, or wood-crown'd shore,
> Go, seek the manse, and in it thou shalt find,
> Whate'er is lovely in the human mind.'"

When Presbyterianism was established in this district Mr Dugald Lindsay, the Episcopalian minister, refused to conform to the new doctrine, and a probationer was sent to supersede him, but on arriving in his parish he found no house would receive him, and he had perforce to call upon Mr Lindsay for board and bed. That benign man made him welcome, well knowing that every hand was against the incomer.

On Sabbath morning old and young assembled in the churchyard long before the normal hour of worship, and when the new pastor arrived, accompanied by their faithful old minister, signs of annoyance and indignation were at once apparent.

But the murmurs were soon to give place to stronger action, and twelve men, fully armed, stepped forward, led by two pipers playing the march of death, and led the astonished Presbyterian to the boundary of the parish.

There his captors made him swear never again to enter Glenorchy, and furthermore, not to lodge complaints for the acts committed against him that day. The oath was duly fulfilled, and Mr Lindsay remained to minister to his loyal parishioners undisturbed for fully thirty years.

The road was almost clear of snow when I left Dalmally.

A mile or two, and there, on a windswept hill, overlooking the scenes he loved and knew so well, stands the striking monument to Duncan Ban M'Intyre.

He was the Burns of the Gaelic-speaking race and sang to them in a way which stirred their hearts, yet, strange as it may seem, he could neither read nor write !

As a child, " Fair-haired Duncan of the Songs," as he became known to the dwellers in the glens, spent his early years on the hill-sides between Tyndrum and Glencoe.

Although a Jacobite at heart, the poet, because of his fealty to Breadalbane, fought against the Highlanders at the battle of Falkirk, and later, through the influence of his patron, he secured a position in the Edinburgh City Guard.

He died in Edinburgh in his eighty-ninth year, and was buried in the famous Greyfriars' Churchyard, but his heart was ever in his native glens— his fondest memories, of the hills and open spaces.

Duncan Ban M'Intyre was not alone in singing the charms of this rugged country-side.

Hammerton came here in 1852 and fell a victim to its graces. He dipped into its romantic legends and embalmed them in verse, illustrating the pages with his own pencil.

John Stuart Blackie, that modern knight-errant, knew every corrie, loved every stone, took them to his heart, and sang them in his warm, impulsive manner.

His great generous heart still beats amongst these western hills for those attuned to hear it. To read his lays by the fireside of a winter night when the far-off peaks are shrouded in mist, the glens choked with snow, and the wind screaming on the moors, is again to feel the spring of the heather beneath one's feet, to bring to life the sleeping pageant of its beauty.

Over there rises Cruachan, alone with its Arctic-clad companions. Below lies Loch Awe—to-day cold and glassy—no sun glinting on its blue waves.

Loch Awe is the centre-piece, the intimate heart of one of the most exquisite sections of Scottish beauty, crowned with the romance of deeds long past, a land too beautiful to paint with pen or palette.

Above, towers Cruachan—from which is derived the slogan of the Campbells—guarding the Pass, with a scarf of cloud trailing from his head. A noble ben, some twenty miles round the base, but looking more massive and imposing a few miles off.

How these great immutable hills sprang into existence I cannot say—some mighty cataclysm when the world was young; but I can give you the true origin of Loch Awe, where once was a smiling, fertile glen.

Here it is—ascribed to Ossian.

" Bera the Aged dwelt in a cave in the rock. She

was the daughter of a sage. Long was the line of her fathers—and she was the last of her race. Large and fertile were her possessions, hers the beautiful vales below ; hers the cattle which roamed on the hills around.

" To her was left a heritage that she must every night, ere sunset, place a certain stone over a spring on the hill-side. One day, wearied with the chase, she sat down to rest beneath a tree. The sun was strong—and she slept. She slept until morning, and when she arose to go and remove the stone, the spring had burst from its bounds and her inheritance was under water. So was created Loch Awe."

Bera appears to have been a wholly disagreeable person, and no good neighbour for the more industrious section of the folks hereabouts. She dwelt somewhere in the most inaccessible part of the mountains, and, it is claimed, could step from one district to another with consummate ease. When the inhabitants did anything to offend her she sent great floods to spoil their crops and generally kept the district in a ferment.

An ancient philosopher, who inquired into these charges brought against Bera the Aged, exonerated her completely and laid the responsibility on nothing more romantic than water-spouts. Personally, I have an unreasoning antipathy against philosophers and cold-blooded logicians of this sort, and unreservedly acclaim Bera as the true cause of all the mischief.

The island of Fraoch Eilan has its modern romance, but here is one of its old-time legends.

Once in the long ago Fraoch island was an enchanted garden guarded by a dragon, whose duty it was to keep inviolate the luscious golden fruit which flourished there.

There was a gallant warrior named Fraoch, and his beautiful sweetheart, Mego, was, woman-like, consumed by longing for the forbidden fruit. Fraoch, like the fearless heart he was, swam to the island to battle with its guardian if need be, but possess some of the fruit he must.

The dragon saw his approach, and a fearful battle ensued, in which both were slain. Mego the Fair died shortly afterwards of a broken heart.

There is no more strikingly situated fastness of other days in all broad Scotland than Kilchurn Castle. Picturesque to a degree, romance and legend seem in fancy to cling to its broken walls like a mantle of the past.

At one time Kilchurn occupied an island, but the Orchy has been quietly at work for generations silting up the loch.

But that does not matter now. No longer are its stout walls called upon to defend the Campbell owners; never again will axe and spear and claymore flash in the torchlight, or the great ben give back the shouts of struggling warriors. To-day all is peace.

As recently as the '45, Kilchurn was garrisoned by royal troops, but now decay and neglect have played their part well, and only the shell remains, hoary with time and steeped in untold memories.

The very building of the castle is of itself a tale of romance. Sir Colin Campbell of Glenorchy was a Crusader. Ere bidding farewell to his young wife he cut his ring into two parts, one of which he handed to his lady, telling her that if he fell in the wars he would cause his half of the ring to be sent home, but while he was alive, it would never leave his person.

Years passed and there came no word from the Holy Land.

All this time Sir Colin was taking part in many a stricken field, but oftentimes his heart would be in green Glenorchy, and then he would send his lady a message of good cheer by one of his trusty followers. But none of these couriers ever reached his mistress on far Lochawe-side.

Many suitors made advances to the waiting lady, the most persistent of all being Baron Neil Mac-Corquodale, whose lands marched with those of Sir Colin. He it was who had intercepted the returning couriers and slain them so that their good news should not be delivered. And then he bethought him of a still blacker villainy; nothing less than prevailing on a friend in the Holy Land to send home a message that Sir Colin was indeed dead.

Even then the lady hesitated, but at last she gave a halting promise that when the castle was finished, she would wed her neighbour.

Slowly the time passed, but at last the fortress was completed, and, pressed by MacCorquodale, she gave a reluctant consent, and the nuptial arrangements were put in hand.

Meanwhile Sir Colin, as the result of a dream, decided to return to his native land.

On the wedding morn the usual motley crowd was gathered around the castle door, amongst them one man of outstanding person, bearded and bronzed by the sun, who demanded a cup of wine from the hands of the bride. Quaffing it to the dregs, the stranger dropped something into the drinking-cup and handed it back to her with the remark that it was now more valuable than before.

A quick glance disclosed the half ring, and with a glad cry she threw herself into Sir Colin's arms.

The loyal clansmen acclaimed their chief, and as a token of joy and goodwill, MacCorquodale was allowed to depart uninjured and forgiven.

Later, on the death of Sir Colin, his son, Sir Colin Dubh, revenged himself on MacCorquodale, and in just retribution took possession of his lands.

To-day, only some wheeling gulls scream round the decaying towers, and night finds no beacon from its fallen ports.

This must have been a solitary if peaceful spot, when one summer evening in 1755 Campbell of Inverawe was quietly enjoying its beauty. Whatever his thoughts, they were rudely broken by a man, nearly spent, who came running across a shoulder of the great ben and appealed for sanctuary. He had slain a man in anger, and his enemies were hot on his trail.

Inverawe pledged his word to protect him from the avengers, and knowing every rock and crevice on Cruachan-side, he guided the outcast to a lonely cave, and promised to return with food when the pursuers had gone.

On his way down the mountain-side he met one of his clansmen, who explained that he was searching for a murderer who had mysteriously disappeared. The searcher added that the man whose life had been taken was no other than Inverawe's foster-brother, to whom he was particularly attached.

During the night the spirit of his foster-brother appeared to Campbell and demanded blood for blood. A second night the vision appeared demanding vengeance on his murderer, and so wrought on Campbell's mind that next morning he went to the cave and ordered the guilty man to make good his escape.

That evening the ghost again appeared at Inverawe's bedside, bitterly complained at the failure to avenge his wrongs, and ere departing warned his foster-brother that they would meet at Ticonderoga. In the morning Campbell went to the cave determined to avenge his brother and bring peace to his own mind, but the murderer had fled.

The whole circumstance so preyed on Campbell that it was with a feeling of relief he received orders —he was a major in the 42nd Regiment—to proceed overseas.

Do what he would the ghostly threat of Ticonderoga haunted him, until at last he unburdened his mind to his fellow-officers.

In due course the regiment was ordered to advance upon St Louis, when one of the officers discovered that the Indian name for the place was Ticonderoga. The town was stormed, but amongst those who fell, mortally wounded, was Campbell of Inverawe, whose dying words were that the place was not called St Louis, but Ticonderoga, for he had seen his brother!

R. L. Stevenson has made the tale his own and retold it in verse.

It was here, on the side of Cruachan, that Bruce, nobly assisted by his great captain, Douglas, fully revenged himself on M'Dougall of Lorne.

A desperate battle took place amongst the rocks on the steep hill-side, and ultimately the M'Dougalls' defence was broken and they fled before the royal forces. Many were hunted down amongst the rocks and slain, others were drowned in the loch below, and John of Lorne, Chief of the M'Dougalls, only escaped by means of a boat.

The King had now the upper hand in the Westlands, and as a result of this fierce battle he deprived Lorne of a great part of his lands.

The day was drawing late now, and I was thankful for a " lift " from a friendly chauffeur, and soon we were covering the hill miles to Inveraray at a fine pace.

Down through the tree-lined road, wintry looking to-day, where only yesterday, it seemed, the wild flowers and moss had made the way gay for the passer, and then the glint of the loch as we passed through the archway into the town.

XVIII

FROM MY WINDOW AGAIN

The melancholy days are come,
The saddest of the year,
Of wailing winds, and naked woods,
And meadows brown and sere.

W. Cullen Bryant

ALL too soon the pageant of the seasons passes.
Spring with her adolescence and promise, Summer
and her fulfilment, Autumn with her ripe experience, gradually merge and give place to the snows
and desolation of winter.

To-day the burnished browns and russets, crim-
sons and gold are rapidly disappearing before the
windy buffetings, and already the bare skeletons
of once leafy woods are waving gaunt arms above
the withered bracken. Every fresh gust produces
its macabre dance of fluttering leaves, and the moss
is happed beneath a rustling brown coverlet.

Time to draw the curtains again and turn of an
evening to the book-shelves, rovering days behind
us for a spell. The hill-sides and drove roads are
closed for a season—not from choice but of necessity.

Where only a week or two ago the mountain burn
fell down the slopes in a splashing cascade, to-day
a torrent rages. Placid brown streams of yesterday
have suddenly changed their character, and are

rushing through the glens, churned, tormented, and unfordable.

Heather braes are now watery moss-hags, dangerous in places, and every trace of past glories has been lost in the blackened or bleached wastes.

On the lowland fields may be seen vast congregations of stalking rooks, strangely silent and preoccupied. Occasional bands of peesweeps on the marshy places seem lost in contemplation of the changing scene.

One friend has gone completely from my ken in the old tortoise, now snug amongst some hay in the potting-shed, but, as always in this world, another has taken his place. The pert robin has turned up again to haunt the garden and collect his tribute until the dark days pass, as self-contained and sure of his welcome as if he had never basely deserted me in the springtime without a farewell chirp, although well I know he will show the same spirit whenever the bright days return and joy o' living entices him once more to his country seat, his social habits being for all the world like those of some prosperous city magnate.

By now the bens have donned their white night-caps and, tucked beneath their blankets of mist and cloud, will sleep dormant and undisturbed for long, ere adventurous feet bring them back for a period to the living world.

Slush and mud in the city streets, but out there in the silent glens the moon looks down on the white-clad spaces, and the old drove road winds deserted and alone save perhaps when the hill-fox brings home a mountain hare as proof of good hunting or the stags come down in search of better feeding.

The trusty stout shoes are greased and stored away against more likely times. The old ash plant must needs rest content until the burns sing again and the enveloping mists yield to a warmer sun.

> Boughs are daily rifled,
> By the gusty thieves,
> And the Book of Nature
> Getteth short of leaves.

Yesterday morning the field which fronts my home was heavily populated with gulls, and that old-time wisdom and experience which is safely chronicled in our proverbs, told me bad weather was in store.

> Seagull, seagull, sit on the sand,
> It's never guid weather when you're on the land.

True it proved, and by night rain was blattering on the office window and the wind, blowing strongly from the west across the well-loved hills, was making an eerie wailing amongst the chimney-cans.

Pausing from my task for a moment I glanced at the wet, deserted street. A taxi splashed past on its way to theatre or station, and a solitary policeman, mushroom-like under his short glistening cape, was slowly pacing along, head down against the blast.

No night this to be abroad. Better to work an hour longer and hope the weather might abate.

Back to the task in hand then—but somehow the momentary break had cut athwart my thoughts and concentration came slowly.

Only for the wind and blatter of rain the outside world appeared strangely silent. Rain drives the street people under cover quickly of an evening.

And then suddenly there came a loud, high-pitched cry—"hioch, hioch" it sounded, and brought me from my desk to the window again.

Below was a drove of cattle, obviously being driven from Merklands Wharf to the market in High Street, and the men in charge were shouting and occasionally thwacking the laggards in their anxiety to get the job done and be free to shelter from the drenching rain.

Steam was rising in a cloud from the great untidy-looking herd, and occasionally a panic-stricken, or maybe only more enterprising beast, would break from the drove and, inspired by what whim I know not, make a bolt for a side street.

Then would follow a wild race between man and beast, and the great lumbering, wild-eyed brute would be driven back at the run to join his fellows.

Two or three enthusiastic urchins, unpaid but willing workers, ran alongside and helped to guard the passes, and added to the general confusion and hubbub.

And then the houses and cobbled streets fell away from my city eyes, and of a sudden I looked back into the past.

Some one, I think John Buchan, says the old drover race is dead and their place shall know them no more, but I always *sensed* that this was wrong.

Now I know that when all is quiet on the hill-side and in the strath, when the motors have deserted the highways for a space, and the men of affairs, having slaughtered their grouse and fished for their salmon, have gone back to office and bar, the old reivers lurk behind the scattered rocks, wild-eyed cattle are driven at the run, and the road collop is bestowed as toll of clan rights and privileges.

There before my eyes, the rain-dashed window, the street lamps and high buildings, faded into mist and gave place to the dark hill-side where away in front, faintly marked amongst the overgrowing heather and bracken, wound the old-time drove road.

Above, the scudding clouds and a silver-horned moon giving a weird, diffused light. Of stars there were none, and the distant peaks stood black as ebony amidst the silence.

One or two isolated trees were bent towards the east, sure sign of prevailing winds from the Hebridean seas, and a fox barked somewhere in the distance.

And then along the twisting path came a great herd of shaggy cattle! Here and there one paused to nose the runnel of water which died in the heather a yard farther on, but always a guttural shout from behind kept them steadily on the move.

If the kyloe were shaggy and rough and unkempt, how can I describe their owners? Bearded, garbed in mud-stained tartans, armed with claymore and pistol, they looked fit wardens for their charges. Strong and active, inured to hill and weather, ruddy and fearless, they were making for the cattle tryst, and had been some days on the journey. Rain and wind meant nothing to them, and they would sleep, fireless, by their herd.

The moon was glinting on the loch now, and the band was making for water ere rounding up for the night, to be off again with the call of the grouse in the dim morning light.

A hard life—but a man's life—and as I stood from my vantage and watched them pass, envious of their freedom, a beast broke from the herd, and the running drover, with his shout and the thwack of the stick, shattered the spell, and the streets crowded back again to my vision as the drove road faded out.

There in the glistening, rain-swept causeys the cattle were disappearing, the steam cloud rising white above them in the glare of the overhead arc-lamps, and with a distant-shouted "hioch" they were gone.

Never again would they graze in the fresh green pastures or rest by the burn-side when the sun was high : but for me, I knew that over there behind the slates and chimney cans, far beyond the shining lamps and car rails, lay the hills and glens with their glamour and their urge : that some day again I would see in their beauty the early primrose and the flaming gorse—the dog-roses and the purple blanket of heather : that the open road would call me when the bondage of winter was over and past, call with an insistence that I could not resist. Who that knows it can forget the heartening smell of a wood fire ; the corn bowing to the whispering breeze, white clouds against a blue sky,

and the glory of the rowans in their pride ?   Above
the croon of the burn would come the trill of a
lark—and alluring and beckoning, elusive and compelling, the winding lochside road !

A stronger gust of wind, a blash of rain on the
office window, and as I turned to complete my
work it was to leave a vision of deserted street, with
the yellow lamp-light casting dismal shadows over
all.

The solitary policeman with his glistening mush-
room cape at the corner, dreaming perhaps of the
sheiling and surf-tormented rocks of his boyhood,
was alone on his city beat.

THE CALL OF THE HILLS

CHAPTER I

MAKING UP MY MIND

FEW, if any of us, whether born and brought up in town or country, but feel from time to time that the hills are calling, and that we are tired of the conventions and hum-drum life of the City.

To one such as I, having been born in the country this call has often sounded, and has to some extent been gratified by excursions north, south, east or west by steam-boats or motor-car. This spring these services have not appealed to me. They do not take me near enough to the everlasting. One cannot get friendly with the hills while motoring through

A

them, one must walk by their side to get their true companionship, one must sit in their lap to get near to their soul.

For weeks past I have been dropping hints to my wife and family that a tramping tour in, or on the hills would be a great adventure. At first the idea was received as a great joke. Hills on the maps, however, were attracting my attention so much, that they began to enter into the spirit of the search. Routes were proposed, revised and again revised until something like a reasonable round had been arrived at. Three days ago they were asking when I would start on this great wander. I did not know. When pressed with the question again, last night, I said I thought I would go on Saturday and that is to-morrow.

What a commotion! How long would I be away? What would I take with me? Wasn't the weather too cold? What if it rained as it always does in the hills? and a dozen other questions, some to the point and others quite ridiculous, if not embarrassing.

" Let us have a list of what Dad will want on his trip," said my youngest daughter, aged twelve, and straightway she found pencil and paper and shouted, " Pyjamas," " Tooth paste," said another, " Socks," said another ; " Your Flask," suggested my wife and this was received, strange to say, with mingled derision and approval. However, the list went on growing and here I sit in my room with the certain knowledge that to-morrow morning the house will be astir early, and I will be sent, willy-nilly, away to those hills I have talked about so much during recent weeks.

Am I making a mistake ? Will I stay the distance ? Will I have to rough it ? Wouldn't I be more comfortable going by bus ? This speeding of the parting guest or adventurer, makes me think ;

but even as I think, the words of the Highland song keeps sounding in my ears :

" It's a far croonin' that's callin' me away,
   As step I wi' my cromack to the road."

And so to bed.

CHAPTER II

EDINBURGH TO LOCHEARNHEAD

THE first chapter of this book was written in the comforts of my own home, late at night. This chapter is being written in the comforts of a wayside hotel at Lochearnhead, early on Sunday morning.

Yesterday, the first day of my hiking, was a great day for me—not that it was altogether passed in comfort, but rather that I had accomplished the first stage successfully in spite of what were rather depressing conditions.

The morning of yesterday rose clear and bright, but with just that brightness which is indicative of showers, if not of a wet day. The whole morning was a busy time for me—letters, wages, interviews had to be attended to until 11.15, when I had to be literally dragged from my room, and packed off with hurried good-byes to catch the 11.30 a.m. train for Callander.

It was only when ensconsed in the corner of the railway carriage that I realised that I had now started on a new and interesting experiment—that of touring on foot in the Highlands—and all alone too. The thought was, however, quite exhilarating. I felt I could sing; I wanted to shout; but I refrained to try the first, because I never could sing tunefully, and the second, because I might be, and possibly would be, misunderstood. The singing was there all the same, and the shouting, although pent up in my heart and soul.

Arriving at Callander, the gateway to the hills, at 1 o'clock, I decide to fortify myself by lunching here, and a good lunch I get too, at the Crown Hotel, splendid food and service at a very moderate charge. If all hotels would purvey and charge as the Crown does, then hikers would have no cause for complaint.

Lunch finished, I shoulder my kit, including my camera and waterproof, and stroll out of Callander. Speaking to a native, he said it was a grand walk to Lochearnhead—when it's dry weather. I bid him good afternoon, and wander out of the town pondering on the last word of my friend, "When it's dry weather."

By his after-thought it is clear that he was not guaranteeing the day to be fine for long. He was right too, for even as I left him I could see wet spots on the pavement. This wasn't rain surely. I could not feel it, nor see it falling. I take off my cap to test the weather and sure enough with my hiker's hair-cut I can feel too distinctly the tiny drops falling on my head in all too regular and increasing precision. Shall I go on, or return to the hospitable " Crown "? I wonder. I am on the way, however, and each step is taking me nearer to the end of my first fourteen miles, so on I go. Tramp, tramp, tramp. The rain is quite steady now, and is, I must say, rather friendly. With my cap off it is just a little annoying, but wearing my cap it is almost unnoticeable.

After a lot of walking a milestone appeared on the right side of the road. On the side facing me is painted Lochearnhead 13 miles, and on the other side, Callander 1 mile. Only one mile done, thirteen to be done—can I do it ?—and on I go towards the Pass of Leny. Here the wood and the hills close in on me ; just room there appears to be for the road and the river on my left. I take two photographs—will they come out ? I doubt it.

LOCH LUBNAIG, NEAR CALLANDER

THE NEW ROAD, LOCHABER

EDINBURGH TO LOCHEARNHEAD

Through the Pass the hills widen out leaving woods and fields in the wider valley and Loch Lubnaig glistening through the trees. Now for six miles on the banks of the Loch; all is lovely, but still the Scotch mist keeps falling.

Motor-cars keep passing me from both directions, but I go on uninterrogated until a family of tinkers come towards me. I can see I have been selected as a probable contributor to their Romany life. The pipes are blown up. This man cannot play, but he can make the noises horrible all right. I go past them, unsolicited, and congratulate myself. All too soon, however, for there is a red haired, red cheeked Romany lass bringing up the rear. Would I give her a penny? "What do you want a penny for?" I asked. " To buy something at Callander," she said. A straight answer to a straight question got her the coppers. " How old are you?" " Seven, past." " Do you go to school?" "Yes." "Where?" "At Comrie." "What is your name?" "Burke." "Spell it." "B-U-R-K-E"; and on she ran to tell the good news and pitch the coins into the family purse; and so we parted, the one tinker with recent generations of tinkerhood leaping in her heart and myself trying perhaps to catch some of the tinkerhood which had been smouldering for centuries.

Still I go on, my kit weighing twenty pounds is now forgotten. You see you can get used to most things—and here is the village of Strathyre, with the railway station on the left, I go into the hote and 'call for refreshment. Two kit-bags are lying at the foot of a table, while two stalwarts regale themselves. "You are hiking, too," I said. "Oh, no, we are going fishing." Would I come with them? the loch is just ten miles up the glen, and up past the burial place of Rob Roy. This was attractive, but remembering the already wet state I was in, and the probable all-night sederunt of these fishermen, I had to decline.

Saying good-bye to them, I go out into the village street and am made to smile in spite of my dearth of humour, when I hear a man singing from the middle of the road (and looking up to the windows of a boarding-house) these words, "Her heart is warm, her soul is pure, and Oh, she's *dear* to me." I pass round his back in my best mannered way, as I did not feel called upon to subscribe to the upkeep of the *dear lady*.

With Strathyre well behind and Lochearnhead only four miles away I meet another family of gypsies—the Sutherlands this time. Would I give them a copper?—and no less than five young gypsies gather round. Out I bring my small change, with a sixpence showing on top. With one voice they cried:

"Sixpence"—that was a lesson to me. I part with the nimble tanner, but never again will I make a demonstration of my great wealth before a band of gypsies on the open road. That donation is entered in my diary as follows :—

Donation to gypsies	.	2d.
Paying for experience	.	4d.
		—
Total	.	6d.

Now my day's tramp is nearly done. Now I know I can do it. The rain still falls, but one hardly knows it is raining. The road from Strathyre to Balquidder is all up hill—it rises on the shoulders of the hills on either side of me and then drops down into Lochearn. I am past the station, then down past the church, I see the loch in the distance. There is the hotel—and a nice hotel, too. Dinner will be served in a quarter-of-an-hour : of course I'll have dinner, and won't I enjoy it. I have done my stretch and well deserve it.

Not waiting to change I join the party at the meal, and during it I receive nature's warning (in the form of a sneeze) that I am wet and will require a hot bath, an especially warm bed, a hot drink, and my clothes dried. I go direct to the landlord : he understands. A mustard bath, two quilts on my bed, toddy handed me in bed after my bath.

The boots is called, put at my disposal, bath, quilts, toddy; my clothes taken from me—all just as mother would do— and I drop over to sleep with my blood coursing through my veins. The combined effect of walking, fresh air, mustard bath, and toddy.

CHAPTER III

STORM-STAYED

SUNDAY morning. A noise in my room—I open my eyes. I see the close-cropped back neck of the Boots. He raises his head—I see the shaggy black hair which adorns the front of his head. I remember it all so well—these are the last sights I saw last night before falling over—he came in, stooped for my wet clothes and shoes, raised his head with his arms full, said good-night and closed the door. Now he is bringing back the dry clothes and shoes. "What is the time?" "Eight o'clock, sir." "When is breakfast?" "Nine o'clock." "How's the weather?" "No change, sir," and I feel a depression rising in the south of my soul and slowly travelling northwards.

Getting up, my first care is for my clothes. Will they be dry and wearable? They are. Good man this Boots. Shoes dry as well, and polished too, fit for kirk or market, and now to dress and breakfast.

Breakfast is a slow affair at this hotel. You see they are only busy at the week ends at this season, and the staff must be kept small in number. For nine tables we have only one waitress while the Manager, Boots, and other members of the staff do the fetching and carrying for her. The second waitress of the night before, is, for the time, acting as housemaid and getting the rooms tidied up for the visitors who will arrive to-day. When this is known, each one is patient and the breakfast passes off slowly and successfully.

That fine unnoticeable rain I know so well continues to fall during the forenoon, and I decide that Sunday, being a day of rest, I will take full advantage of this fine hotel and the beauties of the district until the rain goes off. None of the other residents, however, make this decision and the weather comes in for a good deal of criticism. Some say they have heard it is always wet in the hills and they have always believed it to be an exaggeration if not a libel, but now they know. I met a party of four from Manchester, who had much to say and were comparing the weather here with Snowden. It has been said that what Manchester says to-day the world says to-morrow. I do hope their sayings of to-day will not be repeated to that extent to-morrow. But who cares, the braes of Balquhidder and the Birks of Aberfeldy are just as "bonnie" to-day as they were in the days of our Fathers and their charm will hold in spite of chance sayings.

Writing in the lounge of the hotel until 11.30 a.m. I suddenly realise that

IN GLEN ORCHY

THE THREE SISTERS OF GLENCOE

311

the house has grown distinctly quiet. I wander out and say to the " Boy in Buttons," " Where is everybody ? " " All gone, sir," he said. " Am I the only one staying on ? " " That's right, sir." And here am I playing the role of the oldest inhabitant, and I have only been sixteen hours in the house. But so it goes and I think we should remember these things when we are tempted to criticise the country hotel.

They have their difficulties in organisation. Travellers are here to-day and gone to-morrow and the management has little hope, and certainly no guarantee that they will have a full house for days ahead.

The Parish Church, I find, is ten minutes walk from the hotel, this is advertised in a neat frame on the wall, and the service opens at twelve. I decide to go, and retrace my steps of yesterday along to the Parish Church.

B

THE CALL OF THE HILLS

Walking along the country road I can hear the church bell tolling. It cannot be termed a silver-toned bell at least it sounds on my ear as being distinctly metallic. But still it is a bell calling the people to prayer to-day as it may have done for centuries. On I go enjoying the call of this bell even as I enjoy and appreciate the bells of St Cuthbert's and St Mary's, Edinburgh.

At the gate of the church grounds I stop, there is the bell swinging in the open belfry as I have often seen in country churches. But — here is something I do not understand—something I have never seen before. It is a long stout rope stretching from the bell into what seems a clump of bushes from where I stand. Let me investigate; and in I go. Here I find the beadle standing out in the grounds with a waterproof coat on steadily pulling the bell. After gazing with unconcealed interest on this find, I walk into church and go to the inmost corner of the back seat. This seat has to me a double advantage, it is a nicely cushioned seat, and, well it is my proper place—a *back* seat.

Looking over the books in the pew I discover I have invaded the Manse seat. It is too late to change, as a lady, who I afterwards know to be the wife of the minister comes in and sits down. She must have read my thoughts as she hands me along a Bible (it was a hymn book I made investigations on) and whispers, " It's quite all right."

The bell stops ringing, the pulpit books are brought in, the minister takes his seat. I become uneasy. I cannot count thirty heads in the church from where I sit and, perhaps, a dozen are children. Can church singing be carried through successfully with such a small congregation drawn once a week

from perhaps six square miles of hill
country.

I need not have worried. The minister,
Rev. Mr Cowie, steps to the desk, and
in an easy, clear, almost conversational
voice gives out the 33rd Psalm. The
organ, played by a young lady, gives the
first verse in full as an introductory.
During the last line four girls rise from
their seats, two from each side of the
pulpit and take their places with their
backs to the pulpit and facing the organ.
Off we go altogether, organ, choir, congregation and then I know my fears are
traitors. Here are the words we sang
to an old tune, I know not the name of it.

"Ye Righteous in the Lord rejoice,
    It comely is and right,
    That upright men with thankful voice
    Should praise the Lord of might."

and so on for five verses. Is our singing
successful? There is no doubt about

it, and we all know it is. It may lack something to the mind of the critic, but to us as a congregation it is the essence of humble, faithful worship. Then come the Prayer—the Bible Lesson—the 60th Paraphrase.

" Father of peace and God of Love,
  We own Thy power to save,
  That power by which our Shepherd rose
  Victorious o'er the grave."

Then an address to children. Another hymn and the sermon on the miracle " Turning Water into Wine." Here the preacher keeps to his quiet, conversational, yet very effective method of delivery, telling of the continuance of this miracle when the tears of sorrow are turned to the wine of joy, and how the Waters of Jordan become the way to wine of everlasting bliss. And then the closing hymn and Benediction. The minister's wife speaks a few words to me. I tell her who I am. I even give her a pencil as my card; on the pencil is printed my business, and my business address. Have I done wrong? will she accuse me of trying to do business within the very walls of the Temple? I don't know! It did not occur to me at the time and I am not worrying now. I do not hurry away. The minister comes through the church and shakes hands with me. I am the last to leave and there towards the gate I follow that flock—some turning to the left, and others like myself to the right. Some will go to the shores of Loch Earn, some to agricultural farms in the valley. Some to get home will have to climb well up the hill sides and I to my hotel in the hills to re-live the joys of a wet Sabbath morning.

I follow them out through the gates, yes, I follow them, and from what angle can I see the picture to greater advantage, or with such appealing force. Here is a new setting for the words of our national poet.

"From scenes like these, Old Scotia's
    grandeur springs
And makes her loved at home—revered
    abroad."

Arriving at the hotel there is no need to ask "where is everybody?" Everybody seems to be here. The lunch is on and every table taken even my engaged corner. I get a seat, however, and enjoy the busy life after the quietness of two hours ago. After lunch, the rain still coming down, I devote the afternoon to reading and to writing, taking dinner in quite a small company at 7.15. Altogether a very pleasant, restful, day. The rain has now stopped. The sky is blue, the loch glistens through the trees as I write, and I, comfortably tired, and happy after my day's activities and experiences will now get up to bed.

CHAPTER IV

LOCHEARNHEAD TO TYNDRUM

I AWAKE. It is Monday morning, it looks dull, but it is early : listening, I hear the wind—not strong, but still a wind. There has been no wind for two days ; the only breezes I have had have been from passing motor-cars. From these I have also had splashes. The day has been when I was the unwilling splasher, now I am the splashed. The law of compensation, I suppose. On looking out I see the trees and shrubs bending to the breeze, and, worst of all, the rain is heavier than ever. Breakfast over, I consider the situation. Monday is not a day of rest, and besides I wont melt. I pay my bill, handing over the usual tips with my innate Scotch careful-

THE GLEN OF WEEPING, GLENCOE

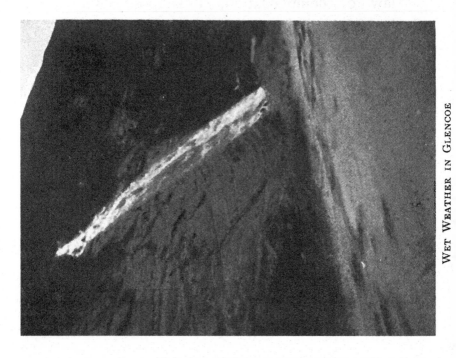

WET WEATHER IN GLENCOE

320

ness ! I then shoulder my kit and camera and out I go into the weather. The rain is not too bad, nor as bad as it looked—how is this?—I turned and got it in the face : the wind was in my back : a southwest wind blowing me due north. From Lochearnhead to Lix Toll it is four and a half miles, three miles uphill over Glenogle and one and a half to the Toll. Three miles is a long pull, but up I go, feeling it much easier than my walk of Saturday, but, of course, the wind is doing most of the climbing for me.

On Glenogle head I get a fine view. Ben More lies straight ahead all patched with snow. He looks tremendous, towering into the heavens with a crown of mist on his head. Here I meet and converse with two cyclists. They are finding it hard going with the wind in their teeth. Two young lady hikers pass, bending their figures to the fury of the wind. For once, I am in luck, the wind is with me, and I inwardly and perhaps selfishly rejoice.

Down the other side of the Glen I **go**, enjoying every step. At a high point on the road near to the Toll, I catch a glimpse of Loch Tay, with Ben Lawers on its side, about twelve miles away, and as usual wearing his cap of mist. I am glad to have had this view of Loch Tay and the Ben, although they bring memories crowding on my mind. It was to Killin and Loch Tay we used to come as a family when we were in the spring-time of our family life and the family circle was still unbroken. For one month in each year we stayed here, and not a single day, so far as I can remember, did we miss boating on the river and loch. This was our afternoon (daily) excursion, piping, fishing, bathing, picnicing, hill climbing ; these exercises became "rites" to us, and we performed them faithfully. These were great days and being so near to our daily round perhaps we could not appreciate them to the full. If ever we row down Loch Tay again, as a family, there will be a vacant seat in the boat, but perhaps he'll be there just as of old. Who knows?

Down the hill I go; I can still see Ben More on the left, and here is Lix Toll. A motor patrolman stands there, we talk a little, and I get my mileages confirmed; and round to the left I go, leaving Killin directly behind me.

Now I am turning towards Ben More, and the going is not so easy; the wind is getting me on the left side, and I have to face up to it carefully to get going straight.

The river Dochart is now on my right, and the valley spreads out beautifully before me. On I go towards Luib, but before reaching there, I find I have lost sight of Ben More. The smaller hills are now intervening. I know Ben

More is over there but, for the time being, I would have difficulty in making many believe it. And such is life, the smaller affairs are continually blanketing us from our greater ideals. On past Luib, and the Ben returns to view. Not in the distance now, but on my left and, so near and friendly like, just makes me think he has come down to meet me, with his ermine trimming decorating his shoulders. On past Luib, and still up Glen Dochart, I meet two boy scouts mending one of their cycles. They had left Glasgow on Saturday, come round by Crianlarich, and were bent on getting to Glasgow to-night. Good stuff; and I believe they will do it.

Facing me now, the hills on both sides seem to come together where I understand Crianlarich lies; just as the hills did as I slowly climbed Glen Ogle earlier in the day. Of course there will be the pass, the County Council has seen to

that. They have also seen to other
things on the road. Coming to an un-
fenced part of the hills I am interested
to read the following notice :

WARNING TO MOTORISTS.

BEWARE OF SHEEP

AND LAMBS

ON THE ROAD.

Here is food for thought: into which
category shall I be placed? and by my
present method of transportation I decide I am a lamb. Crianlarich reached,
I have lunch and am gratified to find that
Tyndrum, my stopping-place for the night,
is only $4\frac{5}{8}$ miles away.

That is an easy afternoon's walk, on
print, but not so easy to walk. About a
mile out of Crianlarich a long hill begins
and I have three miles this afternoon of
the hardest walking I have ever done.
This, all the same, is a beautiful piece of
hill country. Lying in the heather, out of

the wind, I can see hills in all directions, with the river and open valley spread out in its richest beauty. On the eastern side of the valley the clouds play all sorts of tricks with the sun—a wonderful sight on a May afternoon, and well worth coming a long way to see.

Then on again, up the hill, and over the bridge, and Tyndrum, sitting in the pine woods, discovers itself to my view. There is the Royal Hotel. Good enough, I'll try there first. Could I have a room? Of course, I could have number seven. What a room —carpets, chest of drawers, bedroom suite. I look round and then say to the Boots, "Some room!" He smiles; takes the remark as a personal vote of confidence, and straightway begins to practise his vocation on me. Can he get me anything? Of course he can. "You'll have a bath, sir?" Of course I shall. "Shall I have high tea or dinner?" I shall have tea; and yet some say they cannot get decent attention in our country hotels.

And now I have had that something the Boots got me; the bath he prepared for me; the tea he ordered for me; and have written this chapter of my wanderings, while I have watched the pine trees swaying in the wind; the visitors to this hotel, coming and going; and, whether I wanted to or not, listened to a garulous lady at my back, who claims to have inside knowledge of the matrimonial affairs and desires of a great many of the young and even old people in this and other districts.

After all this I think the proper place for me is Blanket Bay.

CHAPTER V

TYNDRUM TO KINGSHOUSE

LAST night when I went to bed I lay listening to the Fillan River rushing its way through the village and down through Strath Fillan, where I had tramped my way up during the day.

This morning I awake and find myself still listening to the river. I had not moved a muscle nor an inch during the night and what wonder—21½ miles ought to make any one sleep soundly. And so I listen to the regular rush. It is not musical like a burn but it is regular and the birds make the music.

I must have wakened just as they, in their community singing sort of way,

In Glen Orchy (i)

In Glen Orchy (ii)

329

had reached a crescendo. You know how they move from pianissimo to crescendo and through all the stages of time and volume just like a grand opera. Then listen on until about eight o'clock and you will find that the fort is being held by a few, a relief band so to speak while the band goes to the fields and river sides for breakfast. And so I listen to the rushing of the river and the birds overhead. Turning over the while, in my mind, the changing scenes I have been part of in the hills during the past three days.

Breakfast over I have again to consider whether or not to brave the storm as it is now raining heavily. I decide to carry on, pack up and am ready for the road. At breakfast an engineer who is superintending the new road from Dalmally to Glencoe offers to take me to Inveroran, but I stoutly refuse. " I must walk it," I say. Could he take my kit?

c

" No, thanks," I reply, " I must do the hike properly." So with the rain falling heavily he and I leave the hotel together. He in his car and I on foot. At the post office along the road I see a shop— " General Merchant "—so here I go in and buy adhesive tape and ointment. I have been warned that this road will certainly make my feet fiery so I say to myself " Be prepared."

A few yards further and I turn to the right up Glenorchy. Up and up I go but still I can see the road rising in front. I stop for breath and look back. There is the smoke rising from the hotel, sitting in the patch of pine trees. I can only see the smoke rising in the rain— the hotel itself is hidden. On I go, and on my left I see the new road which is being made from Dalmally through Glencoe to Ballachulish. A small engine and three miniature trucks carry stones to widen the road at some part. On they go past me, and I trudge on and up. I catch up with the engine and trucks. Of course they have stopped. I am abreast of them when a great clatter makes me jump—stones come rolling just short of my feet, in fact I feel annoyed and look up to suggest that I should have got a warning of this. The man is laughing. "I gave you a fright that time," he said, and I laugh with him. He has staged his joke in the hills and pulled it off too.

We discuss the weather — a handy topic always. "Am I going far?" he asked. "To Kingshouse in Glencoe, to-day," I said. "Eh!" he says, "Rather you than me."

There you are, you see, everyone to his bent, he to his engine and miniature trucks; I to my tramp in the hills, and both are happy in doing just what appeals to us.

Coming to the top of a gradient I see

a notice board with printed notice which reads :—

> "*This road is closed to all traffic, those using the road do so at their own risk, and in case of damage will be prosecuted.*"

So on I go, taking the risk of prosecution in case of my damaging this highway which is under reconstruction at various places.

It is certainly a nasty morning. Mist is on the hills and the rain comes down steadily. Worse still my feet are getting hot with the rough hill roads, and I believe I can locate a blister on the left. Feeling I must investigate I select a fine big boulder at the road side and sitting down take off my shoe. There is a blister sure enough and a big one too. It is an easy matter to apply the boracic ointment but a much more difficult one to apply the adhesive tape. The tape is sticky to cut and when it is cut off to the required length it seems to stick anywhere and everywhere but on the wounded foot. After various tries, however, I get it fixed and with my shoe on I have again comparative foot comfort. Towards mid-day I get into the Bridge of Orchy district and by this time the rain has gone off and the glens are looking quiet and peaceful.

Only five miles now from Inveroran hotel. I do enjoy this part of the day. This glen is lovely to walk in, with the river tumbling towards me on my right. The pasture here, too, seems much better and richer—more grass and less heather. Nearing Inveroran Inn I have Loch Tulla on my right for the last mile and a most pleasant and easy road I find it.

Arriving at Inveroran at about two o'clock I am of course late for lunch but am in time to meet my engineer friend who has left me at Tyndrum in the early morning. He greets me warmly and says I have done a good morning's walk.

Here at this inn I have an excellent lunch and leave about three o'clock to tackle the second and, as I thought, the easier stage of the day's walk. Now I know better and will think twice before I tackle this road on a wet day and late in the afternoon.

Leaving Inveroran I have a splendid start. The rain has stopped at mid-day— the roads are fine — not too dry and hard—just right. On I go, making my way steadily towards the " Black mount." The afternoon is quiet and lovely—hills rising on my left and woods falling away on my right towards Rannoch.

The road soon becomes more difficult, however, the gradient increases, and I soon become aware that I am not on an ordinary " Class A " road. On referring to my guide-book I find what I have to face. At Inveroran I was 500 feet above sea level, and before I reach the highest point near Kingshouse I have to climb to an altitude of 1500 feet.

Here is certainly an afternoon's walk, where every step has to count, and every ounce of my walking power is to be brought into operation. To make matters more difficult the rain comes on again, and a nasty wetting rain it is. Before long my shoes are squelching, but there is nothing for it but to go on as the nearest shelter now is Kingshouse, my inn for the night.

As I reach higher above sea level the woods on my right peter out and in their place there comes up a great wide moor dotted thickly with small lakes, a veritable mountain moss I suppose, in a wet season as this is. Tramping on I am cheered to find that there is another pedestrian coming on behind me. He looks in the distance like a tramp, but one never knows, so I ease up a bit and, whoever he is, I look forward to his company for a part of my way. Along he comes; he has his overcoat over his head and cap, the sleeves are hanging loose in the rain. I can see his black tea can in the outer pocket, still I wonder what he is. Tramp or workman! We talk together as we walk on, and I soon find that he is no tramp but a workman very much in earnest. He tells me, and seems very proud of it—that he has been working on public works since he was a boy. When the West Highland railway was being built over thirty-five years ago he worked on that job. Since then he had been on many contract jobs—all public works jobs he calls them and now he is employed on the new road from Inverness to Dalmally. This morning he was paid off on the section back east, and he is now walking over to another section further West. The road is being

Church and Houses, Glencoe

Old Houses in Glencoe

338

built in four sections and he has a chance of work on one of the other three. He is not a married man he says in answer to my question. The married life is of no use to a man who works on public works and moves all over the country.

So on we walk and talk for several miles. The road still going upwards. His pace I tell you was steady and rather too much for me so I suggest a seat on a bridge. Not for him, however, he has to get on, and on he tramps up the hill, as I sit on the bridge in the rain watching him. Here is a lesson for me ; soon, by his steady going, he is up the hill and round the bend—it's the steady going that does it! He deserves to get a job soon and my good wishes go with him. Sixty-two years of age, he says he can hold his own with the best of them and earn his tenpence an hour.

A little lonely I have to resume my walk again, and worse still I have to "warm-up" again after my rest on the wall of the bridge. However, I have to get on and in another half hour I find myself on the highest point looking down into Glencoe and with only three and a half miles to go to Kingshouse Inn.

The rest of the walk is easy and I take it quietly, arriving at the inn at 7.15 having taken over four hours to cover less than ten miles.

Arriving at Kingshouse Inn I have a hearty welcome. They can see what I need. Tea, my shoes and clothes dried, a comfortable room with a fire. All these without even suggesting them. Kingshouse Inn will long remain in my memory as a long white building on two floors and roofed with slates and inside a veritable house of hospitality in the hills.

CHAPTER VI

KINGSHOUSE TO BALLACHULISH

NEXT morning, it is Wednesday. I awake after a fine night's rest, and am soon out and about. It is a fine May morning, the sun shining, the birds whistling, and everything so quiet and peaceful.

After a walk round I go in to breakfast. What shall I have?—grapefruit? What! can I have grapefruit in Kingshouse; of course I can; and so I have grapefruit, and porridge and cream, and fish, and everything just like a west end city hotel. I tell you I am well looked after and at a charge so moderate that I am almost ashamed of my appetite.

Photographs are taken of the hotel and the hills, and with knapsack on back I reluctantly, at 9.30 a.m., resume my journey down the glen wondering what, if any, adventures I might have that day.

It is a glorious morning for walking, and interest in the beautiful surroundings can never flag. Before I am a mile on the road I come to a team of men widening the road. It is a peaty part, and they have a steam navvy at work (this machine they tell me can lift a ton and a half of material every two minutes), and thus they widen the road where there are no rocks to contend with. Another mile and I come up with another squad : this time preparing to blast rock and to widen the road at a rocky part. In one part they show me where they expect six shots will remove the required rock; in another part they expect over twenty shots will be required, and at another they estimate that one hundred and twenty shots will be needed to blast the rock.

It is interesting to see the men holding the drills to the rock, while they are being driven by compressed air by an oil engine. It is also interesting to find that an Aberdeen firm had one of the contracts.

Walking away from these squads, with all their noises and busy life, one wonders if much of the hills will be left, but as we moralise we see how puny man's efforts are when attacking the great forces in the world.

With all our machinery we can only make pinpricks in the great hills and there they remain, so far as we are concerned, from everlasting to everlasting.

Further on I meet yet another squad, busily working under the eye of an energetic foreman. This foreman (like the others) is very willing to talk, and I ask him how far it is to Ballachulish.

He tells me that by the road it is eighteen miles but if I care to go **over** the shoulder of that hill it is **only** four miles. "Why," I say, "that looks a dangerous hill to me, and I might get lost on it." "Not at all," he says; "the men come over there at all hours of the night and they generally have **a good** drink in them, too." Then I remembered the words in "Tam O' Shanter":—

"Wi' Tupenny we fear nae Evil
Wi' Usqubae we'll face the Devil."

I thank him but say I shall be safer to keep to the highway. Just round the corner I come upon a young man shovelling sand into a barrow. He is working so hard that I go over and say to him, "Are you building this road?" His reply comes at once, and he says, "Well, I'm on the job, anyway." "Jolly good answer," I say; "that's where WE all should be all the time—

on the job." He looks on the job, too, with his shirt sleeves rolled up to his shoulders.

It is now just about twelve o'clock and I have not had my kit off my back all morning. What about a rest. Down I sit and just as I do so a man comes forward with a large black pail, three quarters full of steaming liquid. We talk and I learn he is the cook for the day and this is the lunch hour for the squad over on the hill side some little distance away. I look across the moor and there from various directions are men making a bee line for the pail in front of where I sit. There is no time to retreat, before I can realise what is happening these men walk to the hut, lift a parcel of food and a black tin mug each, come to the man at the pail who fills the mug with tea and then they sit down some on my right others on my left. Some in front

and others at my back on the bank.
Here am I completely ambushed. The
man at the pail having served the lot
now looks at me and says, "What about
a mugful, mister?" "Thanks," I say,
"the very thing." The hotel people gave
me sandwiches this morning; and so I
sit, talking and enjoying my lunch. The
men taking their tea from black tin cans
and I, the guest of the day, having mine
in a white enamel mug. I enjoy this
half hour, and get lots of news of the
road on that section. As they are
leaving I give away two pencils one to
the man on each side of me and invite
all of them to call on me at that address
when in Edinburgh. And so they leave
me sitting on the bank, each taking his
angle through the heather to his job.
I think all have gone and that I am
alone, but no—the man who makes the
tea comes over from behind the hut and
says, "What about a pencil, sir; I can

LOCH BAA, GLENCOE

ROAD BUILDERS AT LUNCH

347

never write home for want of a pencil."
He gets his pencil, and here am I, perhaps
lighting a candle in some dullish home
with a pencil from the Pass of Glencoe.

Loading up again I take the road,
glad of my lunch time experience and
looking forward to fresh adventures.
These are just round the corner—hardly
have I got started than a car goes past.
A shout from the car attracts my attention. It stops—I go back, and here are
my Manchester friends of Sunday morning. They are loud in their praises of
the highlands : they now know all about
it and tell me what not to miss. They
are splendid ; let us have more like
them. What Manchester said that day
let the World say to-morrow.

I now come to a dangerous part of
the road at a point just East of " The
Study" ; the hills rising sheer above the
road are fine, while the deep ravine
on the left is awesome. Here a car is

D

348

parked, its back is towards me—a lady is sitting in it—I can see her hat through the glass. I pass on, and find the owner admiring the ravine below. "A glorious day," say I, but there is no answer to my salutation—and so do the conventions of our time penetrate the hills even to the top of Glencoe. I think of going back and of offering him a pencil by way of an introduction, and then I say, "No, I'm hanged if I will."

From here I now join a finished part of the new road—it runs along the breast of the hill—on the right side of the valley; a fine broad tar Macadam road. From it I can see the old road winding along the valley below. This is the third road through Glencoe. There was first the General Wade road about 1729, then the road in the valley built just over one hundred years ago, and now this road with the date 1930 cut on the stone of the bridges. Already you see out of date. The three hills known as the three sisters — snow topped, and beautiful, towering alone. It was to this part Queen Victoria came in her time, to see Glencoe. All is so quiet to-day and all so beautiful.

On I go and am now nearing the Clachaig Inn, which is within five miles of the Glencoe village. Arriving at this inn, it is nearly three in the afternoon, and I have just time for a refreshment. This refreshment I bring out to the open air and there stretch myself on a summer seat in front of the inn. What a haven of rest. The inn sits in a clump of trees just off the road.

Then the door is being locked behind me—it is three o'clock—I am alone in the hills again. Using my knapsack as a pillow I lie down to rest, my feet on the other end of the seat. A cart passes. I appreciate its passing. Here looking towards my feet I see trees—Plane trees;

they are backed by Larch and Fir further in. Behind me is another clump—a different mixture—this lot has a holly tree and before me rears the hill the foreman on the road advised me to take the shoulder of, this morning. It is all so fine I go on looking for other items of interest. A cairn terrier lies basking in the sun two yards from me — my refreshment lies within easy arm's reach—anything more? Yes one item. I am lying on a 20th century summer-seat with its cast metal ends and two bars of wood for a seat and two for a back. All factory made.

Grape fruit for breakfast. Lunch on the latest of summer-seats. What of Ballachulish? I hope they don't invite me to a night club!

And now on to Glencoe village, five miles distant. A fine shady road wooded all the way. Arriving at Glencoe I find a nice clean old-world village of white-

washed houses, and a comfortable looking church, all of which I take pictures of,
and go back in my mind to the bad old
days and less happy times for the families
of this sometime unhappy community.

And again on through the famous slate
quarry village of Ballachulish.

I am now making for the Ballachulish
Ferry Hotel, two miles further on, and
am directed by a boy along a short cut,
where the hawthorn is in blossom, white
and red, and I again march as Burns
puts it " Beneath the milk white thorn
that scents the evening gale."

Arriving at the hotel I find it a most
palatial and well appointed place. After
supper and post cards are despatched for
home I retire for the night, finding my
room with windows looking on to Loch
Leven.

CHAPTER VII

BALLACHULISH TO FORT WILLIAM

IT is now Thursday morning and again I am up early. The loch is a bit stormy, white caps are on the waves, the wind is from the east and the tide is high. Kinloch Leven Hotel can be seen on the other side, white-washed, and sitting in the shelter of the opposite bank.

On going in to breakfast I meet a party of three—an old lady and old gentleman and their daughter. They have come by motor-car through Glencoe the day before; the ladies are rather unnerved by the trip, and are sure the tyres of the car are in threads and wonder how they arrived without broken springs. They see the ferry and hope they have not a ferry to cross before getting to Oban.

I tell them there is Connell Ferry, but there is now a bridge.

On going out of doors after breakfast they are jubilant at the beauty of the surroundings, and there and then decide to stay for a day. The elder lady says she has a reputation for finding such places, and I think the man very readily agreed as he has had all the driving he wants for the present, and the rest will be welcome after his drive of yesterday through Glencoe.

The boat is at the pier so I bid them goodbye, pay my bill and set off. Going down the pier the boatman begins waving his arm to me, and shouting there will be no boat for an hour. I cannot understand him so I climb on to his boat and get his news that the tide is too strong and that I shall have to wait till it slackens. I climb down into the pit beside him, where the engine is, and ask him if a tide like that can stop him from crossing. "No," he says, "I can cross in any tide and in any weather, but with a tide like that it will not pay me." Knowing that sixpence is the fare I quite understand, and settle down for a talk; a boatman being to me a fine companion. He suggests I am hiking, and I agree, and ask him some questions regarding Inverness-shire where I am going. "Oh!" he says, "don't ask me about the roads of Inverness-shire, but if you want to know anything about the roads in Palestine, I can tell you something." He had been in the East in war-time, but has been boatman at Ballachulish for the past twelve years. After quite a time of talking he thinks he can now get across as the tide is slackening. He sees a car, however, at the hotel door, and leisurely walks up to see if it is coming. It is, and he brings it with him. The car is safely run on to a swivel sort of

KINGSHOUSE HOTEL, GLENCOE

NEAR CLACHAIG INN, GLENCOE

a deck and safely pinned to its place. Meantime I take photographs, and when I see it up there, high and dry, and right in the wind, I cannot help congratulating the lady and gentleman in that saloon car for their courage. The driver admits it is a great experience for him but he is enjoying it thoroughly. Reaching the other pier, I see the car safely away and go to pay my fare. "How much money will I give you?" I ask; and he says, "You'll just give me two pennies. I have enjoyed the talk with you," "No, no," I say; "there you are," and I give him a piece of silver, telling him to drink my health and come and see me in Edinburgh.

The road, my road, now lies down Loch Leven. It is a fine dry morning and the wind is at my back. There is no hurry either, as I have only 12½ miles to do that day. It is easy going and beautiful. The hills rising on my right; and across the loch the hotel I have left two hours ago, with hills on that side as its background. After a few miles the road bears to the right and I am walking up Loch Linnhe. I can taste the salty air on my lips and see white buildings on the other side of the loch. These are the buildings of Ardgour Hotel, etc. Four miles from the ferry I come to a snug little village—Onich. The walls are all white-washed and the gardens are well kept. Several of the houses have neat green painted signs hung out with the one word on them, "Apartments." This I make a note of, and some day, when I am an older man, I may knock at one of these neat cottages and ask for lodgings for the night. What a situation. Hills all round with Loch Linnhe to the right and Loch Leven to the left and within short walking distance too, of the points where I can see the hills that guard Glencoe. On the north of the village several houses are in ruins. They look like crofters' dwellings, the walls are very thick, there are two doors, one for the dwelling-house and the other for the horse and cow; the wooden out-houses, which were required, are all away, and the ruins remain a relic of the good old days.

Further on I come to a road-widening squad. This time it is trees they are removing. The method is to pick the earth away from the roots as much as possible, then put a wire hawser round the tree and pull it over with a heavy road engine. There are several inter-ested onlookers, among them being the Rev. Mr Jamie, an Edinburgh minister who is doing supply work in the dis-trict. After a little talk with Mr Jamie I go on the road to where the engine is; they are just fixing the hawser to a tree. Half-way down the length of the hawser I stop to watch the results but the engineman calls me away at once. "If that cable breaks," he says, "you might be killed." I hurry up beside the engine, and watch for the falling of the tree ; but no use, the cable breaks with a " ping " and flies across the road where I have been standing.

On another two miles and it is lunchtime. Here is a house on the loch side ; a woman working at the door. She is stoutish ; wears old shoes (bauchles) on her feet ; her stockings are loose and make her ankles look thick. I go down the brae to her and ask for milk. Yes, she has milk ; and when she speaks I find she has a beautiful voice and speaks well. I get a big glass of milk, the real creamy milk, and I marvel at its quality. I drink it, losing little time, and eating nothing. I ask her for another glassful and sit down on the grass to wait for it. The second glass is good, but not so rich as the first, and

I then know she has plundered that basin of milk to entertain me, a complete stranger. Sitting on the grass I eat biscuits and drink milk, feasting my eyes on loch and hills.

At my back I hear a voice saying "Ah! this is where you are, is it?" I looked round to see a man with smiling face and eyes coming down the bank towards me. This is the crofter and that his way of salutation.

We talk and he tells me he has as a croft two miles of the loch side, and he says he has to get work away from home to make a living. And so I finish my lunch on Loch Linnhe, pay my score, bid my friends good-bye and step on towards Fort William.

Walking along I can hear four explosions and I know blasting is going on somewhere near. I step out and soon come to a squad clearing the rickle of stone from the road and making a clear passage for traffic. The foreman urges on the men and soon the road has space cleared to allow a single car to pass. He is interested in my tour and suggests that I shall be employing my time more usefully if I take a hand at roadmaking. "What about starting in with us," he said. "I'll give you 1/2 per hour." I consider the proposal, it is tempting as an adventure, but when I look at my hands and think of handling those sharp and heavy lumps of stone I fairly lose courage and refuse the job.

We, however, leave on friendly terms as I soon find out, for, when I have gone round the next bend of the road, I hear one of the men calling me and on he comes running with my cap. I have dropped it from my belt in my stepping about amongst the stones. He, I hope, quenched his thirst at my expense, that night.

The afternoon wears on and I am now on a finished part of the new road. Here is a nice cottage — I shall ask for another glass of milk, so up to the door I go—knock—and hear a pair of slippers flapping towards me. An elderly woman appears. "Could I have a glass of milk?" "Sorry I have just enough for the tea." "Can I have a glass of water then?" I lean on the lintel of the door resting, until I hear the slippers warning me of her re-arrival, and there she has in a glass—a very small glass, all the milk she has in the house. I want to pay her—but no—she will accept nothing either as pay or in a present and I have to go, only thanking her. Walking away I feel I should have asked her name so I take the chance of securing it from a man working in a garden a few hundred yards along the road. Needless to say I have written to Mrs Cumming (that is her name) thanking her again and apologising for drinking the milk she had kept for her tea.

Now I am within a mile and a half of Fort William. The houses are coming at lesser intervals and before long I reach my hotel, after another glorious day not altogether free from mild adventure.

Top
THE VILLAGE OF
ROY BRIDGE

Left
RIVER ROY AT
ROY BRIDGE

CHAPTER VIII

FORT WILLIAM TO ROY BRIDGE

IT is now Friday morning. I go down to breakfast and take the seat at the table I had occupied the evening before. The waitress is a methodical person and evidently has a system of seating, by which one table at a time is filled to its complement before another is opened up. I have, therefore, to move to a table where another couple, man and wife, are seated. This suits me and gives me opportunity for conversation. I find they are on holiday, staying two weeks here and had taken a motor-bus tour to Kinloch Leven the day before. They say they passed me on the road just after I had had a bathe in the loch. They say they could see I had been

E

bathing as I was drying my towels in the wind. The fact is I had washed a couple of handkerchiefs that morning and had tied them to the strap of my bag to dry. One has to do a bit of handy work like that when on the road.

After breakfast I am off again, across the bridge, still farther up Loch Linnhe passing Ben Nevis on my right. On this road I can see the British Aluminium works which get their power from Loch Treig, the water being brought by tunnel through the solid rock for the fifteen miles. Four miles out I come to Banavie where the road branches off to the left to Glenfinnan, Mallaig, and to the Isle of Skye. It is most tempting but I have to resist the temptation and keep to the programme I have sketched.

It has become another lovely day by mid-day, although it had been rather misty in the morning. The sun is hot, comfortably hot, the road quiet and the hills have now receded on both sides of me. Walking up Lochaber I enjoy a perfect morning of peace and joy.

This too is one of the shortest day walks I shall have and so I take time, take pictures, and listen to the silence and to the birds.

On this road there are few workmen, but I pass one squad just at mid-day. Taking time then as I am doing I do not reach Spean Bridge until about two o'clock. Here I see a fine hotel to lunch in, a change from the roadside lunch of yesterday. In I go by the side door, it leads me through the refreshment bar where I stay and converse with the locals who sit around. I do not at the time know who they are but I learn from the waiter afterwards that they are the village joiner, a water bailiff, a working gardener, and the proprietor of the hotel. The proprietor's name is Macdonnel,

a name used by Neil Munro in his book
" The New Road."

The party give me a lot of interesting
information about Lochaber and I appreciate this company and conversation.

After lunch I take pictures of the hotel
and gardens and set off for the afternoon's
walk of four miles to Roy Bridge.

These four miles are distinctly different
from the setting of my walk in the morning. All the way from Spean Bridge to
Roy Bridge there are clumps of trees,
small woods, with, of course, a continual
narrow belt of trees on both sides of the
river.

On the road the trees are not continuous, sometimes a field between me
and the wood on one side, sometimes a
field on both sides, and sometimes the
trees come down to the road side on
both sides. It is a fine and level
stretch of road with few houses and
practically no traffic.

Arriving at Roy Bridge I find it a snug little village on the Roy. Just a church, a hotel, a post office and a few cottages.

The glen seems rocky and rugged and the river looks an attractive water for trout fishing.

Here I have a long evening to write and walk around, going early to bed to prepare for a longer walk on the morrow.

CHAPTER IX

ROY BRIDGE TO LOCH LAGGAN HOTEL

LEAVING Roy Bridge the road leads due east along Glen Tulloch. Its gradients are easy although it must be slightly up-hill, the Spean coming down towards me. For several miles the prospects are just like the last three miles of yesterday's walk, fields and woods. Further on the woods close in, and the road, railway, and river are all running parallel and the three taking up no more breadth than about sixty yards.

At several places the river here runs fast and to-day with the rain of the previous week it has a great flow of water. For several days I have not met any tinkers on the road; but this morning the first to meet me on this quiet road is a family. They say their name is White. The man has a donkey and cart with their furnishings while a woman and three children follow about twenty yards behind. The men as usual are very civil and only say good-morning. The woman, however, stops and asks for help. She explains they are very hard up, they have illness in the family and a girl has died. I ask her what had been the matter and she said the bairn took " *newmonium*." I ask what that is, and again she says " she died of newmonium, she had an *absent* on the jaw too, but that wasna' what she died of." I part with the usual small charge and step on.

A few miles on and the valley again widens ont. I walk on the right of a hill. On my left, away in the distance I can see squads of men working and I am told that this valley will be flooded in a year or two to give additional water for the works at Fort William. At midday I again strike a cottage where I have a pint of very good milk and have difficulty in getting the woman to accept payment for it. She says it is nonsense of me to think of paying for a glass of milk as they have always lots of it. She also invites me to call any time I am passing and I will get a glass. After this lunch I take a seat on a parapet of a bridge to rest and enjoy the scene. A two-seater car comes along driven by a lady. They pass, and just a few yards along a lamb jumps right in front of the wheels and I can hear distinctly the crunch of the ribs. The ladies are upset and come to ask me if I will come and put the beast out of pain. I go along thinking of the various ways I can put their proposal into execution, but when I reach the lamb it is already dead.

SPEAN BRIDGE HOTEL

HOTEL GARDENS, SPEAN BRIDGE

I pull it off the road and advise them to report it at the first police station they come to.

Early in the afternoon I reach Loch Laggan. As the shores are wooded with a narrow belt of fir trees, the view is intriguing. The loch is there shining through the trees, half concealed and half revealed. It seems miles until I come to a point where I can get a good view of it, but then I really do get a view of it both ways. This is at a point which seems to be midway down the loch, there are no trees and I stand on this point and see Loch Laggan to the east and to the west, with the lovely and varying hills on the other side as a back ground.

It is Saturday afternoon, work has stopped on the road, there is little traffic, there is no sound, it is a cool, clear and dry afternoon. The surface of the water is like glass, except in places where I can see the air causing a faint ripple. Can you imagine it? it is lovely!

Leaving this point I wander on and pass a caravan on my left, parked in an old quarry on the road side. There is a pram with a child in it, on the side of the road, in front of the caravan. There is a boy playing at the wheel of the van. The upper half of the door is open and on the lower part a woman is leaning with her arms folded on the door, evidently enjoying, like myself, the peace of the Saturday afternoon. I go past without speaking, it seems as it would be a sacrilege to break the silence of the afternoon.

At six o'clock I reach Loch Laggan Hotel, having wandered by glen, and moor and lake, a distance of nineteen miles during the day.

This hotel is nicely set, just on the roadside above the loch with good views of the hills from the windows. Here I get a good reception, a good room, and a good tea, and decide, the morrow being Sunday, to rest here for the week-end.

CHAPTER X

A SUNDAY'S REST AT LOCH LAGGAN

ON Sunday morning breakfast is served from 9 till 9.15 a.m., so I am told the night before, on making enquiries. I am therefore down soon after nine o'clock, as I do not wish to miss the breakfast. The breakfast-room, not a big one, is filled. The centre table has a party of a dozen; they had been fishing late the night before, and had caught seventy-one trout with four rods. The other guests are more permanent visitors and on Loch Laggan have not had good sport.

The morning is dull; there is no church nearer than seven miles, so I settle down for a restful day. By midday the sun has come out, so I decide on a short walk before lunch. The loch is still and as smooth as glass. Down the loch side I walk, over the road I had come along the day before. I walk along as far as the caravan, and there it is just as I saw it the day before : pram at the front of the caravan, boy playing at the wheel, and the woman with arms folded looking across the loch. This time I stop and talk. They have been there on that road for a year; the man working on the widening and the new bridges. They like staying there and the woman is not looking forward with pleasure to the boy going to school. He is now three, and in two years they will have to go to Spey Bridge to live, and the boy will then go to school. I take pictures of the setting and go back to the hotel to lunch.

The afternoon and evening are spent in complete rest, reading, and the lure of the maps. Tea is served at 4, and a supper at 7.30 p.m. All is peace and quiet on the loch side.

CHAPTER XI

LOCH LAGGAN TO DALWHINNIE

MONDAY morning is damp but fresh, and I am on the road by nine o'clock. I now feel that nothing can stop me—rain, hail, heat or wind. I have found my feet on the road after a week's tramping, and am now enjoying every step of the way. Laggan Loch is soon left behind, and I walk on the road, by the river, with pleasure and with ease. The cuckoo has been my constant friend and companion for the past week, and this morning he is more companionable than ever. First on the right and then on the left I hear him calling, and I rejoice in his friendly salutations, these may not be altogether for me, indeed I take it that they are not, but yet his calls are for me so far as I am concerned, and I register in my soul my appreciation.

Up the river I go passing several small waterfalls—the river-bed being rocky as is usual in the hills. To-day I hope to receive my second batch of letters since I left home, and these are to be at Laggan Bridge, eight miles distant from Laggan Loch. On I go, enjoying the rain which is falling—a sort of Scotch mist it is—and by mid-day I reach the post office, having done eight miles of my nineteen miles for that day. The post office, I discover, is half a mile off my road, but my letters have to be collected and I also expect money to replenish my ever - lightening purse. So there is every reason to call there and get the good news and finances from home. I am not disappointed, letters and cash await me, also good

news of family and business in Edinburgh.

Leaving Laggan Bridge I go back to
the main road, which is to take me over
the north-eastern part of the Moor of
Rannoch. Here I come to a long and
steep hill, perhaps the longest and
steepest since I left Glencoe, but now
hills do not matter so much as they did
a week ago, and on I go enjoying the
climb. It is now time for lunch, and
to-day, as sometimes before, my lunch is
to be of milk, if I can get it.

Seeing a likely cottage, just a little bit
off the road, I go in and enquire if I
may have a pint of milk. The good
lady has plenty of milk, and brings
me out a jugful and also a glassful to
start with. I ask her the price of all
this as I want to pay her, (then, take
the milk sitting on the garden seat, and
wander off when I have finished). She
hesitates, while I fumble for the money,

GLENCOE, KINLOCHLEVEN TO RIGHT

THE FERRY, BALLACHULISH

and says apologetically, " Well, sir, it is very good milk, and we get threepence a pint for it hereabouts, would you grudge that?" I take the glass from her hand, drink half of it, and find it good, and say, "Look here, there's sixpence for the milk, and you've given me good value." Taking then the jug in one hand and the glass in the other, I betake myself to the summer seat in the garden, drink my milk and read the names drawn for the Irish Sweep, which were published that morning. Finishing my milk, and being assured by the newspaper that great wealth will not be mine through the Irish Sweep at least, I take back the glass and jug and give the old lady the paper, asking her if she has anything on the Derby. "Ah, no," she says, " the folks hereabouts ken naething about horse-racing, and I hope they never will." I bid her good-bye, and she fervently wishes me good luck, and

F

invites me to call again when I am in the district.

I now climb up on to the Moor of Rannoch. The hills have again receded, aud I am walking a road with miles of rolling foothills on all sides of me. I know that on my right is the Loch of Rannoch, and on my left lies Newtonmore and the road to Inverness. Up and down, down and up the road goes— it is great, and you may think it is lonely, but nothing of the kind. There is continual change, constant expectation, and constant, shall I say, surprise. About the middle of this moor road, between Laggan Bridge and Dalwhinnie, a two-seater car comes up to me, driven by a lady. She passes me, stops until I come up and asks if I would care to have a lift. I thank her, and explain that I am hiking, and must not break the continuity of the tramp. Her reply is short, "Oh, my goodness"; the clutch goes in, she presses the accelerator, and away she drives across the moor, while I stand and watch and wonder.

Here am I with miles of moor to the right, left, before and behind, and with the hills in the distance. Have I been stupid in refusing a timely lift? Of course I have not; start that sort of thing and hiking is reduced to a farce. On then I go, knowing that after another few miles I must strike the Perth-Inverness road, and get back again to more active life.

By 3.30 in the afternoon the main road is reached, and I am now back again to what is marked as a first-class road on the map. Coming on this road as I do after ten days of secondary roads in the glen, I expect to be glad when I find myself on it. This is not the case, however, and there passes over me a pang of regret that I have left those quiet, friendly roads, which have been so much to me during my inexperience and adventures in hiking in the hills.

The road now is wide and macadamised, quite springy and easy to walk on, but almost too easy and too tame after Glencoe, Glenorchy, Lochaber, and the Moor of Rannoch. In half an hour I am at Dalwhinnie. It is now a dry but cold afternoon, and while I can imagine this a beautiful and pleasant place, I find it, this June afternoon, a very cold and bleak part of the country. Going to the only hotel, the Ericht, I am comfortably accommodated, and have a long and happy evening, reading and resting for the long stretch to Blair Atholl on the morrow.

CHAPTER XII

DALWHINNIE TO BLAIR ATHOLL

TUESDAY morning, 2nd June, I am the first down to breakfast. The morning is fine, the sun shining, the air quiet and still. After breakfast I am soon out on the road and now heading for home. The Highland railway runs north on the other side of the valley. A train for Inverness comes up—the engine jugging away at the heavy passenger train which is seemingly on an up gradient. The dining car is well filled and as I stand looking, handkerchiefs are waved from the windows to me. I wave my stick and wonder at this friendliness and then I remember that we mortals are all friendly, in the distance, and only shrink into our shell through the conventions of our every-day life.

Down the valley I go, passing a few miles on, the stone erected by General Wade when the road was built. It is dated 1729 just over two hundred years ago. The road has been improved several times since and indeed was widened and improved only two years ago but as it still keeps to the old track we can congratulate heartily the engineers of two centuries ago on their skill, in road building. Passing Dalnaspidal, I am now going south " Doon by the Tummel, and Banks of the Garry."

Mid-day brings me to a cottage where I again lunch on milk. This cottage is tenanted by a gamekeper and his wife ; it is on Atholl estate, for I have been most of the morning on the Duke of Atholl's territory, and the Forest of Atholl lies on my left. After lunch I

find the afternoon walk most interesting.
The Garry goes with me now, down to
Struan. At parts I find it running
quietly along meadows, and at other
places cutting its way through gorges
which look to be a hundred feet deep.
At one part near to Struan it comes
right along the road side disporting
itself down a rocky gorge in a series
of waterfalls.

At 4.30 this afternoon I come to the
village of Calvine, where there is a post
and telephone office. I go in here and
phone to Edinburgh, to find that it has
rained there the whole day. They can
hardly believe I have had such glorious
weather.

It is now my turn to be surprised
when I walk out of the telephone office.
Just as I start off, heavy drops of rain
begin to fall and before many minutes I
am tramping in a downpour. There is
nothing for it but to go on, Blair Atholl

is four and a half miles away so you can imagine how wet I must be from the knees down before I reach there. This is my worst wetting since that afternoon in Glencoe, when as I walked, my shoes squelched at every step even as they do now.

Reaching Blair Atholl just after six o'clock I ask a railway man about hotel accommodation and he tells me there are two, the Atholl Arms and a smaller one the Tilt Hotel. I decide on the smaller one although it is the furthest on. Here is the Tilt Hotel. What if they are full up and I have to go back. In I go—am met by the landlady, " Can I have a room for the night ? " " Yes, of course, you can, but my goodness you're wet ! You'll have come o'er Glen Tilt I'm thinking." I have to confess that I am a mere amateur and have, like a coward, come here by the king's highway. "Well, well,"

A Cottage in Lochaber

The New Road, Dalwhinnie

she says, "it doesna' matter how you came, let's get that coat and cap off ye," and she unbuckles the waist band of my mattamac and pulls it off me, taking my cap too. "Now," she says, "just go to the second door on the left and take off your shoes in there." I go. The room is the billiard room, and now being entirely under a spell, and just doing whatever I am told, I take off my shoes and wait for something to happen. Something does happen. In comes a boy in buttons with a pair of knickers, also shoes. "Good gracious," I say, "have I to change my knickers and stockings here?" "No," he says, "You take them to 28, change there, and I'll get them dried." This is too much. I begin to wonder if I might have something I want myself, so I say, "What about a drink?" The reply comes at once, "Yes, sir, a large whisky and a small soda, that's what the gentlemen take, sir." I think I shall better be a gentleman for once, and get on with it. The drink taken, up I go to 28. My hose and knickers on my arm. A nice room, the bathroom next door, electric light, dressing table with side mirrors, etc., etc.

Off come the wet hose and the wet knickers. I pull on the dry ones, I get my braces and try to attach them to the new garments. Good gracious, they have no buttons on the top. I try buttoning them at the waist, and will you believe it they are a perfect fit. On goes the hose, sublime, and here I walk about this hotel a perfect optimist, in shoes, hose, and self - supporting knickers.

After a nice tea I spend a quiet and restful evening with the other guests of the hotel all of whom are loud in the praises of the landlady. They promise me a breakfast I shall never forget and

DALWHINNIE TO BLAIR ATHOLL

I must say their promises are amply fulfilled. If ever I go hiking again and get badly caught in the rain my prayers are that Providence will lead me to another hotel such as the " Tilt " at Blair Atholl.

CHAPTER XIII

BLAIR ATHOLL TO DUNKELD

ON the morning of Wednesday, the
3rd June, I am down to breakfast,
and indeed have breakfasted, before the
other guests put in an appearance. The
promises made to me the night before
regarding breakfast are amply fulfilled,
and the bill presented for all the attention
and board I received was, you will agree,
a moderate one, when I tell you it
amounted to nine shillings. Out again
and southward I go, making now for
Dunkeld. This road leads down the
Tummel, and is on my right beautifully
wooded. The trees here, too, are different to what I have seen on other parts
of the road. There seems to be a great
deal of birch, with a goodly assortment

of oak, beech, larch, and fir. It is certainly a pleasant road, and as the day is fine, and Dunkeld only eighteen miles away, I can afford to take time and enjoy the changing scenes of river and wood and hill.

I soon come to the Pass of Killiecrankie. Here there is a steep, very steep gradient, for what seems to be nearly a mile. Reaching the top of this gradient I see the River Tummel with the hills well wooded stretching out before me. After resting here in the cool of the wood for a little while I take the road again, making my way to Pitlochry, which is now only a few miles distant. These few miles take me down through woods on both sides of the road. I pass the road on the right which strikes westwards to Loch Rannoch and Kinloch Rannoch.

Reaching the outskirts of Pitlochry before mid-day I find it a most attractive highland town, indeed, seeing it as I do this summer morning it strikes me as being the smartest and cleanest town I have struck on the whole journey. The houses here are well built; the gardens well kept; and the whole place has an air of quiet dignity. The shopping part of the town, too, is in keeping with the residential parts, and shops have displays of goods, just as attractively shown, as in the larger cities. Visiting several of the shops I find the shop-keepers most interested and efficient and their stocks large and varied for a town of this size. With the clean streets, smart shops, well dressed windows, and shining sun of that forenoon, I shall long remember my visit to Pitlochry.

Passing on, it is now an easy walk to Ballinluig, where I have a humble and economical lunch of milk and biscuits. Further south I come to the River Tay which is to be my companion now for many miles. Even north here it is a sweeping and noble stream, as it has now been joined by the Garry and the Tummel as well as many smaller tributaries.

It is an easy and pleasant road, well wooded, with the river now concealed from view and now revealed. By four o'clock I have a good view of Birnam Hill which is on the other side of the river, and by five o'clock I am in Dunkeld and fixed at the Waverley Hotel.

Dunkeld is a quiet little town; a stranger might call it sleepy; but I suppose it will have its quiet and constant stream of business to and from the wide country districts around.

After tea I go out and see the town. That does not take long, but I go up the river and see the fine bridge from the river-side. Bridges have a great attraction for me. I am never tired looking at bridges, nor am I ever tired looking for them. To-night I see Dunkeld bridge from the north and again from the south, in both instances at close and at long range, and find it in both cases, combined with the majestic river Tay, a most attractive picture on a summer evening.

Comfortably tired I retire to rest early, looking forward to a day of great adventure on the morrow.

ON THE RIVER TUMMEL

ON THE RIVER TAY

CHAPTER XIV

DUNKELD TO STANLEY

A T the end of the last chapter I promised myself an adventure to-day.
My reason for this statement is that to-day
I am to travel roads which were well
known to me as a boy, and roads I have
not travelled for the past forty - two
years.

My nearest road home would have
been across Dunkeld Bridge, and down
through Bankfoot and on to Perth.
Instead I choose a very round about road,
which leads me through the hills and
by the lakes to Butterstone, then across
the farm lands and on to Caputh and
Murthly. Leaving my hotel, therefore,
I turn right instead of left and make for
the hill road to Blairgowrie. On this
G

road I pass along a line of lochs, namely, Loch of the Lowes, Cluny Loch, Butterstone Loch, and Marlee Loch. It is a quiet and beautiful road, and by it I will reach the village of Butterstone where I was, at thirteen years of age, apprenticed to the clothing business. Every step of the road is known to me, but to-day it looks somewhat different to what it was in the old days. The miles for instance, seem longer, and the gradients certainly feel steeper.

Leaving Dunkeld, I have one steep part to climb which rises one in six. In the old boyhood days I usually ran this hill. I liked doing it that way, and it never gave me more trouble than a shortness of breath. To-day I take it step by step, and am glad indeed when I reach the top. On to the Loch of the Lowes I go, and here I come to an arm of the loch which is a sort of marsh and is overgrown with shrub. In the old days I knew the road across this, and could take every stepping - stone at a jump. To-day I walk round, I cannot trust myself through this, and have no flare for shrubbery and stepping stones.

Past this loch I come to Butterstone Loch, which, in the old days, I knew every bit of. It is glistening to-day through the trees, and I recall the baskets of perch I have hooked in this water. Pike, too; I have had pike out of this loch, which I was afraid of, as I pulled them ashore, and could only carry them home with their tails trailing on the grass.

Now I approach the village of Butterstone. It looks just as it did in the old days. I take photographs, and promise myself a few minutes of interesting conversation with the residents. In the village itself there is little change outwardly. Just the usual tradesmen's houses of such a village; blacksmith, joiner, clothier, shoemaker, post office, and schoolhouse. While taking another picture in the village a man comes up to me, and I have a talk with him, telling him who I am, and that, forty years ago, I had lived here. He gives me lots of news in which he tells me there is neither shoemaker, clothier, nor blacksmith in the village now. The joiner, too, is lying on his death-bed, and nobody is allowed to see him. He also tells me that so far as he knows the blacksmith is the only one of the old residents whois still in business, and I shall pass his house if I am going by Snaigow.

This is my reception this morning in a village where forty years ago I was known, for good or ill, in every house. I finish my picture taking and make my way across country through the Snaigow estate and moor to the Caputh district. Coming to a cottage I ask the old lady if there are still paths across the moor. "Oh, yes," she said. "But with the rain we have had they are terribly wet. You'll be better to go round by the road." So round by the road I go which is a good two miles further than the moor road. Coming to Snaigow I have the pleasure of meeting the blacksmith of Butterstone; he just remembers me faintly, but is glad I have called. His wife is dead and his house is kept by his daughter who produces a goodly supply of milk and biscuits. We talk of old times and the changes which have taken place in recent years in the life of the country districts. Now the village tradesman is little wanted, and most things which he made, can now be got direct from the factories, clothes, sheds, gates, carts, horseshoes, boots, etc., etc., all are being produced by factories in quantities to the extinction of the village tradesman.

Saying good-bye to father and daughter I make my way to Caputh passing the quiet village of Spittalfield on my left. It looks peaceful in the quiet afternoon, backed by the woods of Delvine, and the wooded hills of Gourdie. At Caputh I am in my element, here is a district I know even better than Butterstone, here at least I will have an interesting hour. Here is the church; I try the gate, and find it unlocked. I go into the grounds and there is everything just as I left it. The gravel walk around, the low dyke where we sat until the bell began to toll, the clump of holly bushes in the corner, the ivy on the walls, splendid, I'll go in and sit in the church, for old time's sake. Trying the door it is locked. "Why on earth do they lock up churches on week days?" I find myself saying inwardly, and I pass away to look for other interests. Going west I come to the churchyard, and here indeed is change enough to make me look. In the old days it sat on the top of the mound only, but here it is to-day brought down and fenced by a dyke along the side of the road.

Looking over the dyke I can see the sexton or beadle mowing the grass. I go in by the gate, and go over and speak to him telling him who I am and that I am re-visiting the parish after forty years. He remembers my father well, and says he "You'll be wanting to look round; just a minute until I finish this edge and I'll be with you." And so after finishing his border we walk together among the tombs. He points out the ground and monument of this and that family, and I either know them, or know of them.

We come to the stone erected to J. T.; James, he and I were at school together and in the same class. He was always dux while I was a poor second or third in the class It is recorded that he died in 1891, sixteen years of age. Again the beadle points to the stone of J. S. I am glad to see this, as W. S., the son, was the last to bid me good-bye, when I left the parish. I can remember his words now. "I came to see you, Alec, I wanted to say good-bye to you, and wish you success, and mind we're expecting great things of ye, dinna disappoint us." And so I stand at this grave and hear, as in a dream, Mr D. the sexton read "And of their son William who died May 1st 1895, aged twenty-eight years."

Willie was the model young man of the parish, the friend of young and of old, and now I hear he was called away just four years after I had received his blessing.

The questions now comes strangely upon me—have I come up to expectations? Have I been disappointing? the answers are unmistakeable, they are

RIVER TUMMEL, SOUTH OF PITLOCHRY

BUTTERSTONE LOCH

" No " and " Yes," I have done, and I
have left undone, and that is the truth
of the matter. Passing on we come to
the monuments of my old school master,
my old employer, and many others, I had
known and perhaps, at times, feared.

And so we pass down the braeside to
the gate. Mr D. is proud of his churchyard, it has been extended twice since
he took it over thirty-five years ago, and
he explains now that it is down to the
road side they will have to secure their
next extension on ground to the west.

So we part company at the gate, and
I take my way towards the bridge across
the Tay where in the old days I had
at times helped to work the ferry boat.
Crossing the bridge I stop, and look
back on the scene. There are the houses
of the village, the church on the brae-
head, the Manse up the river, a farm
steading on the hill face, not a house
but is well known to me, both inside and

out, and yet it was in the kirkyard that I got the news of the parish. This morning I promised myself a day of interesting adventure and have had a day of pathetic surprise.

Up the boat brae, as we used to call it, I go. On past Murthly, Ardoch, Luncarty and to Stanley where I am to lodge for the night.

CHAPTER XV

STANLEY TO KINROSS—AND
HOME

L AST evening, after tea at my hotel,
I wandered out to see the village
of Stanley. There is not much to see—
it is a small, clean, little town, standing
on the north bank of the river Tay.
The houses are clean and neat and the
shops are small. After buying post cards
I go down to the river's edge, and this
is well worth doing. The river at this
part comes down round a curve and flows
down round another, in crescent shape.
There are woods on both sides, and on
the Stanley side there is a high bank,
well wooded, and looking south presents
a fine background to this noble river.

To-day, Friday, I am on the road early,

with faint regrets that the Grampians are behind me and that at Perth I must pass out of what is known as the "Scottish Highlands." The road to Perth from here is level and easy, and there are numbers of vehicles on the road, as this is Perth Market Day.

On I go, reaching Perth before mid-day ; on through the South Inch and on to the Bridge of Earn. Leaving Perth by this road I see the river from the Baglie Hill. It must have been from this hill that the Romans looked up the river Tay and saw Birnam Hill in the distance, and many remember the well-known lines of our British poet who writes :—

"Behold the Tiber, the vain Roman cried,
Viewing the Tay from the fair Baglie side,
But where's the Scot who would the
    taunt repay
By likening the Tiber to the Tay."

THE VILLAGE OF BUTTERSTONE

BUTTERSTONE LOCH

This is my last look of the Tay at this time, and on I go to lunch at the beautiful little town of Bridge of Earn. Here I have lunch in a restaurant, and have conversations with two men who are motoring north. I ask them how far away Kinross is, and they look up the road-book to find out for me, asking me at the same time what town this is. One can scarcely believe it, but there you are, men motoring along through the country and towns often do not know exactly where they are.

Now I make my way to Glenfarg. The road is straight and level, and I can see the woods through which I will go. In the distance Glenfarg is most picturesque; the gradient is not steep and the road is shaded with the trees right to the top. There is also a very nice little hotel standing in the wood about half-way up. From here it's an easy afternoon's walk to Milnathort and

Kinross, and I arrive at Kinross at about 6.30 p.m.

The hotel at Kinross is busy with fishermen from Loch Leven. So far as I can hear, no one has got any fish; but they are all optimistic that the fish will move after sunset, but, as it turns out, a storm broke over the district and spoiled fishing for the night.

After tea I enquire for a shoe shop as my shoes need attention, and am directed to a little shop quite near. On going in I can see the shoemaker is a character. He has the sharp features and the nose and eyes of the actor. His hair is long, grey, and curled, and he receives me with almost a theatrical air.

He gets my shoes and sits down to repair the soles, but is soon telling me of his varied shoemaking and theatrical career. He is certainly an enthusiast about the stage, and recites certain parts he has done, or rather, as he says, has put over the footlights. This is a happy addition to my experiences and I will long remember my good friend and actor-shoemaker of Kinross.

And now for home. It is Saturday morning and the rain is falling heavily. At nine o'clock the fishing men are still optimistic, and most of them have gone to Loch Leven, only a few remain waiting for the rain to go off. It is attractive to me to think of going home by rail, especially as I have done all and more than I set out to do. Feeling fit, however, I decide to walk to Burntisland, take the ferry to Granton, and walk home, a distance of eighteen miles. As I go out I realise how wet it is : just as bad as any of the rainy days in the hills. On I go, reaching Cowdenbeath at one o'clock and have lunch there. Still the rain comes down and heavily too, and I arrive at Burntisland at 4.15 p.m. completely soaked.

THE CALL OF THE HILLS

The ferry-boat leaves in about fifteen minutes and in the cold, bleak waiting-room I go walking about to keep warm, so that I may not catch cold. The boat comes to the pier; motor-cars and passengers come ashore, and we are now allowed to go on board. The waiting for this boat to leave, and the crossing of the Firth of Forth, is perhaps the most uncomfortable minutes of this day, and I have quite a difficulty in keeping warm, this cold and wet afternoon. Reaching Granton I walk direct to Ravelston Park, a distance of perhaps two and a half miles. Arriving home, although I have walked nineteen miles under trying conditions, I feel just as fit as I did when I left Kinross this morning. Other days have been as wet, but in no day's walk have I felt as fit at the finish as I do on this, the completion of the journey. There only remains now for me to record my feelings on the trip as I view them

THE RIVER GARRY

THE NEW ROAD, DALNASPIDAL

looking back. I can now remember what the man said to me as I talked with him in Glencoe. " Keep looking back," he said, "as well as forward." "You get some of the best views when you're looking back." And so I suppose it is with many things in life. We enjoy them even more in retrospect than in their actual happening. Should that be so in regard to this trip of mine, to the hills, I will be truly rewarded and enriched, as even now I feel that it is one of the most enjoyable, soul stirring, and strength restoring adventures I have ever had the good fortune to experience.

CHAPTER XVI

AT HOME AGAIN—THE JOURNEY DONE

AND now I am back again in my arm-chair at my own fireside. The map of my tour is spread before me. It is a pan handled map. The tip of the handle is in my library where I now sit. It is an irregular shaped pan with a bent handle, yet to me it is fringed around with unalloyed joy.

I sit here and think of the lochs I have been privileged to glimpse at, Loch Lubnaig, Loch Earn, Loch Tay, Loch Tulla, Loch Laggan. I remember the salt water lochs of Loch Leven and Loch Linnhe, and their kindly salt spray which I have tasted on my lips. Again I think of the rivers which have welcomed me with their singing, their murmuring or their quiet movement. The Leny, the Dochart, the Orchy, the Coe, the Spean, the Roy, the Spey. And then I remember the two days I walked " Doon by the Tummel and Banks of the Garry," coming in due course to that stateliest and most majestic of rivers, the Tay. I think of the day I wandered by those little-heard of lochs, Loch of the Lowes, Butterstone, Cluny and Marlee and feel glad I have been again fortunate to walk by their shores.

Again I think of the men and women I met on the journey and who, by their friendliness did so much to cheer me on the long, and without them, weary road. The man at the street corner at Callander, the Tinkers on the road, the Cyclists, the Boy Scouts, the man with his donkey engine who rolled a truck of stones to my feet. The " public works " labourer I walked with in Glencoe. The ferry man, the foreman and workman building the new road, the men I had lunch with, and who entertained me with talk and a mug of strong tea, the actor - shoemaker, etc. Faster than I can write the moving pictures pass before me and I am thankful for every experience, as it comes up to my remembrance.

Again I think of that day in the district of Butterstone, and the Parish of Caputh, with what hopes I went forth in the morning and with what disappointments I journeyed to my hotel in the evening. I am glad, nevertheless, of each step I took and rejoice in the belief that this day at least I was " Compassed about by a cloud of witnesses."

Again I remember the many cottagers who entertained me with refreshment by the way-side, and whose hospitality and unaffected kindnesses went to my heart. Meeting those folks as I did was well worth the long and sometimes arduous journey, as I now know that the hearts of our people are just as warm and kindly to-day as ever they were.

Yet again I remember those Inns and Hotels at which I called without notice, and received the heartiest of welcomes in every case. Whether I was dry or wet, the welcome was the same, always cordial. In fact it seemed to be my luck to have the most cordial of welcomes just when it was most needed by me, and when I trust I was most appreciative.

And again I remember those beautiful hills and glens through which I wandered for fourteen days. In sunshine, storm or cloud they were kindly to me; and I can remember now how I had to stop from time to time and drink of their beauty.

Will I ever forget that day going up Lochaber, when all was peaceful and still. The sun was shining, but not too hot. The road was level—grazing lands for sheep and cattle were on both sides of the road. A little white-washed house sat on the brae with outhouses on its end. The beauty and quietness of it all gripped me so that I had to stop for a little to understand the picture thoroughly. And then as I gazed on this wonderful setting, which was all mine for the moment, I recited aloud, but quietly—

" When all Thy mercies, oh, my God,
My rising soul surveys,
Transported with the views, I'm lost
In wonder, love and praise,"

And so the pictures come and go, and will, I hope, come and go for many days. I went out on an adventure, and I found, I am glad to say, by Mountain, Loch and Riverside—A Friendly Road.

Living Proof

that cats *do* have nine lives

Living Proof

that cats *do* have nine lives

janet hayward

EXISLE
PUBLISHING

First published 2007
This edition published 2010

Exisle Publishing Limited
'Moonrising', Narone Creek Road, Wollombi, NSW 2325, Australia
P.O. Box 60–490, Titirangi, Auckland 0642, New Zealand
www.exislepublishing.com

National Library of Australia Cataloguing-in-Publication Data:

      Hayward, Janet (Janet Alison)
      Living proof that cats do have nine lives / Janet Hayward.

      2nd ed.

      ISBN 9781921497858 (pbk.).

      Cats–Anecdotes.

      636.8

Designed by Christabella Designs
Typeset in Bembo 12/15
Printed in Singapore by KHL Printing Co Pte Ltd

This book uses paper sourced under ISO 14001 guidelines from well-managed forests and other controlled sources.

10 9 8 7 6 5 4 3 2 1

To my son Charlie

Contents

Introduction

Cats have played a part in human history for at least 4000 years, and have always carried with them an air of mystique. They were first documented in art and sculpture — and possibly also in hieroglyphics — in ancient Eygpt, where they were worshipped as gods and bringers of good fortune. Today many households treat their family pet in much the same way!

Yet life has not always been so indulgent and cosy for our feline friends. As historical survivors of idolatry and hatred, world wars and plagues, it's hardly surprising that cats have been bestowed with the mythical power of nine lives.

THE HISTORY OF THE CAT
It is thought that cats were first domesticated in Egypt, at least 1000 years before the rest of the world. Successful protectors of valuable grain stores against ravaging rats, cats soon became sacred animals and were idolised by the ancient Egyptians.

They appeared extensively in Egyptian paintings, murals, ceramics and sculpture, and it is believed they were so highly revered that Egyptian women tried to emulate the features of the cat with heavily made-up, kohl-lined eyes.

Cats served an important role as bestowers of symbolic blessings at the most important ceremonies, such as weddings, births and deaths. It is this link to the rites and cycles of life that helped to enhance the reputation cats have for being able to escape disaster using their 'sixth sense'. A more scientific explanation attributes this ability to the cat's whiskers, which are highly sensitive to vibration and therefore enable felines to 'predict' events such as earthquakes, tsunamis, and even bad storms.

As the Phoenicians and Greeks opened up trade routes, domestic cats appeared in Europe. These highly prized felines were sold as status symbols, and so loved were cats in Greece that even today a cat lover is known as an ailurophile — from the Greek word for cat, *ailouros*. Later, cats started to appear in India, China and Japan, where their rodent-catching prowess continued to ensure their pride of place in the family.

After enjoying such an elevated position in society, the dark Middle Ages were a turning point for cats and the people's total adoration turned swiftly to fear and hatred. As in Egypt, many ceremonial rituals in Europe included cat worship, but the continued rise to power of the Christian church led to suspicion of such pagan rituals — and cats — quickly turning into widespread rumour and fear. By the fourteenth century, the cat was no longer a god and had sunk lower than a rat in the eyes of the general population. The order went out for all cats to be sacrificed and for all cat lovers in Europe to be burned as witches. Many believed that witches had the power to survive by turning themselves into cats; a magical feat they could apparently perform nine times.

As if invoking the wrath of these former feline gods, the dramatic order to exterminate all cats had powerful consequences for the history of Europe. The sudden and rapid decrease in the number of cats induced a surge in disease-carrying vermin, which allowed the bubonic plague, or Black Death, to sweep through Europe. Almost a quarter of the population was wiped out by this horrific disease. It is thought that one reason this disaster finally came to an end was because people were too busy avoiding the plague to destroy the surviving cats — leaving them to once again flourish and ultimately save humanity from the diseased rats.

By the seventeenth century, cats were again held in high esteem in Europe, lauded in art and literature as fashionable, useful companions — and this state of affairs has continued to the present day. During the two world wars cats were particularly appreciated as they provided companionship to soldiers and kept the mice at bay in the trenches. They were also credited for their uncanny ability to detect the high-frequency sound of planes approaching long before their owners could, giving residents time to rush down into bomb shelters and thus ensure their own survival.

Living Proof … that cats do *have nine lives* is a celebration of this much-loved creature and its amazing ability to survive against all odds. As with many myths, the true origin of the expression 'cats have nine lives' is unknown. One belief is that in ancient times nine was considered a lucky number because it is the Trinity of Trinities. And, as cats have shown throughout history, they do indeed have an uncanny ability to miraculously escape death time and time again, so perhaps this lucky number is particularly well suited to them.

As you will see in the following collection of true stories, many beloved cats have relied on their lucky nine lives to an astonishing degree, whether by defying medical science, surviving a world disaster or taking a marathon hike across the roughest terrain to return to home sweet home. All of these cats were fortunate enough to land on their feet — quite literally in the case of the miracle cat who fell from a great height! — leaving the devoted owners in no doubt that their cat at least must indeed have nine lives.

Acts of Human Kindness

It's hardly surprising that cats are one of the most popular choices for a domestic pet. Ask any cat owner, anywhere in the world, and they will happily regale you with stories of the unique loyalty and personality traits of their cat — just as they would for any other favourite member of the family. Which may explain why some humans will go to extraordinary lengths to help cats and kittens who might otherwise face an uncertain future. It seems that in the case of cats, unconditional love can work both ways.

FROM DUBAI WITH LOVE

Cats are masters (and mistresses!) of the art of seduction. Established cat owners are always keen to acknowledge how much their cats have enriched their lives. Their winning combination of entertaining antics, intuitive affection and unwavering loyalty means that most owners would go to any length to shield their cat from harm. Non-cat owners, they claim, have no idea what they're missing out on. But then, it's never too late to find out …

Lynne and John McDermott had never been cat people. Surrounded by neighbourhood pets in their inner-west suburb in Sydney, Australia, they never really felt the need to have a cat or dog of their own. So when Lynne and John set off on a working contract to join the expatriate community in Dubai, they never dreamt they would return with a new family member.

In 2001, Lynne and John left Australia for the United Arab Emirates, where John had been contracted to work as engineer on the Festival City building project in Dubai. They quickly settled at the Metropolitan Hotel Apartments complex, joining the rest of the overseas community.

Lynne and John were aware that the Metropolitan Hotel was home to an established group of street cats. They were a tough yet scrawny gang, spending their days and nights roaming around the complex. Some of Lynne and John's neighbours were members of a stray cat support group, called Feline Friends, that used to leave out food and water and capture the cats to neuter them, before returning them to the community, to help keep the stray population down.

As Lynne commented, 'Cats are not looked after as they are in Australia. Many of these cats were just abandoned by their expat owners after their contracts finished and they had to leave the UAE. So many of these cats, after having lived most of their lives in pampered luxury and being regularly fed, suddenly found themselves having to fend for themselves, competing for scraps of food against established groups of street cats. You could always tell these loners because they were always the scrawniest and dirtiest. The Feline Friends would capture these and try and find new homes for them.'

One such cat was a small, white, female Domestic British Short-hair kitten, who was to become one of the luckiest ever Middle Eastern street cats.

She was first discovered by the McDermotts' Polish neighbour, Cheisa, who was a member of the Feline Friends. 'Cheisa was a real cat lover who used to allow all the street cats into her apartment to sit on her Persian silk rugs and play in her Venetian glass vases!' laughed Lynne.

Cheisa discovered this pretty kitten on one of her feeding rounds in the complex car park. Only five months old, she had been abandoned and was in a very distressed state — malnourished, dehydrated, black with soot and petrified. She had also recently been through a significant operation as she had fresh stitches on both her sides from a botched neutering job. 'She had been existing on scraps found in the streets and was living under the cars, which must have been terrifying because of the noise and pollution,' said Lynne.

After receiving food from Cheisa, the kitten followed her home and sat outside her back door and meowed all night. 'The next day, 26 January 2002, Cheisa came to the door and asked us whether we could take care of her for three months while the Feline Friends tried to find a new home.

'It was obvious that she could not fend for herself and would not have survived long in the car park,' explained Lynne, so the McDermotts reluctantly agreed. But with strict instructions: 'As long as it's only for three months.'

'We were not really cat people,' laughed Lynne, 'but we offered to feed this little kitten in our front courtyard because we had a lovely, shady tree which she loved to climb into!'

Unused to having a pet around, and determined not to let this new cat rule their lives, Lynne wanted to make sure that she was an outdoor cat. Every night for the next week the McDermotts fed the kitten and put her outside in a makeshift bed before they retired to bed. Little did they know that their other neighbour, Sabine, a German cat lover, would take the kitten inside her apartment and make up a bed for her in her bidet.

The little kitten was on her way to a luxurious life! She was taken along to the Feline Friends and received the necessary health shots to protect against disease. 'We also discovered she had a damaged and infected ear from a previous attack, her teeth were poor through lack of nourishment and her eyes had suffered a fungal infection.' She also had to heal from the recent operation, and the McDermotts quickly realised she would need a lot of loving attention.

By the end of the first week, the little kitten had gained her confidence around the McDermotts and was meowing for their attention, tapping at the villa doors and turning somersaults like a showgirl! 'Of course, by now we were hooked and we couldn't help but fall in love with her,' said Lynne. 'She really enjoyed our attention and was happy to be picked up and cuddled — amazing considering the state in which she was found. And after finding out how quickly she had picked up the luxury lifestyle, choosing a name for her was easy — especially as she had come to us on 26 January, Australia Day. It had to be Priscilla, Queen of the Desert — Priscilla for short — after the famous Australian film!'

After the three months of fostering Priscilla were up, the McDermotts had to make a decision. 'All these offers came in from new owners wanting to take Priscilla, but in just three months she had become part of the family and we had become cat lovers.'

From having had no desire to own a cat, the McDermotts now found that Priscilla had started to rule their lives — and had taken over the neighbourhood. Even though their neighbours had cats of their own, they were no match for Priscilla's charms. 'The other cats got so jealous of the attention that Priscilla got from their owners that she still bears a scar on her nose from when one of the cats took a swipe at her,' commented Lynne.

'She managed to get away with the most amazing antics in their villas. One of her favourite tricks was to climb to the top of Cheisa's shelves and then climb into her expensive Venetian red glass vase. It was a tall thin vase so to get in she had to leap in. John and I would sit there going pale as the vase would teeter and rock back and forth on the edge of the shelf. Then she would pop her head up and meow and Cheisa would laugh and call her down as calm as you like.'

Priscilla continued to thrive in the care of the McDermotts and regained her health, becoming a lovely, friendly and very contented cat. She enjoyed this new life of luxury, in a comfortable villa with her own courtyard, complete with activity tree, and an abundance of gourmet food, including Australian beef fillet! She became a real desert girl and would often wander into the neighbouring property, which happened to be owned by a Sheik and was a part of his extensive horse racing stables. 'There was a sand training track about 100 metres from the back porch and every morning the Sheik's multi-million-dollar thoroughbreds would be training. And there would be Priscilla, sitting in the sand at the side of the track just watching the horses gallop past. We were just hoping that she wouldn't decide to walk into the middle of the track while these expensive animals were thundering past. That could have been a disaster and I'm sure the Sheik would not have been impressed!'

However, as all expatriates experience, the joy of living with a new pet in a new country is also tempered by the realisation that one day, when they return to their home country, they may have to make a difficult choice: to leave their pet behind or take it with them. 'But this wasn't the case with us,' said Lynne. 'We were so overwhelmingly attached to Priscilla that, after six months of having her around the house, we knew we were smitten. We had become devoted cat people and there was no doubt that Priscilla would be returning to Australia with us!'

Lynne and John sought advice from their local vet in Dubai and he confirmed that vaccination, a blood check for rabies and a one-month quarantine period would be the only requirements for Priscilla's migration to Australia. 'Everything is bureaucratic in Dubai,' explained Lynne, 'so we organised Priscilla's trip with an enormous amount of help from Dubai catteries.'

In February 2003, Priscilla landed at Sydney's international airport, complete with her own passport, as a new Australian citizen. After checking through Customs, she was immediately whisked off to Eastern Creek, the quarantine centre. Although jetlagged, Lynne went straight out to see that Priscilla was comfortable. 'The staff there were wonderful but, even though Priscilla was always delighted to see me, I could tell that she was not happy to be locked up in a room.'

Lynne visited Priscilla regularly during the quarantine period, eagerly anticipating the day she would be able to bring her home. Then, in April 2003, Priscilla arrived at the McDermotts house in Balmain to great fanfare and excitement — especially as all the neighbours were keen to meet this new local celebrity!

'Her first tentative step outside the back door was so funny to see, as she just couldn't quite work out what grass was and she certainly hadn't seen trees quite as tall as the giant jacaranda we have in our backyard,' laughed Lynne. 'She hesitantly walked out the back door to the edge of our porch and just stared at the grass for a while. She then put a paw out to touch it; she sniffed it and then tasted it. Once she worked out that the grass wasn't going to bite back she was hooked. She just wanted to keep rolling in it.'

Priscilla was initially in awe of the tall trees and magpies but, after suffering the embarrassment of being rescued from the top of the jacaranda by John and his ladder, she quickly gained confidence in climbing all the neighbourhood trees.

And so Priscilla soon settled into the Australian way of life and, aside from a few scuffles with the local 'designer' Burmese cats, made many friends. 'She loves to sit in the front street tree and demand all passers-by stop and pat her. Many a time we have opened the front door to discover a neighbour sitting in the gutter talking to and patting Priscilla,' commented Lynne.

'We feel very lucky to have Priscilla, not only because she is such an amazing cat, but also because she introduced us to people who have become good friends. Our former neighbour in Dubai still writes to us to find out how Priscilla is getting on!'

From a barely alive street urchin in the Middle East to a pampered princess in a wealthy Sydney suburb, it's true to say that Priscilla, Queen of the Desert has survived and conquered. And fortunately, she is not the only deserving cat to receive such human kindness. Thanks to the Feline Friends, many cats who are adopted by expatriates working on building and factory projects in Dubai and Abu Dhabi, have successfully migrated with their owners to start new lives all over the world! Each year the Feline Friends produces a calendar to tell the stories of these lucky cats and kittens. Copies of the calendar are available from: www.felinefriendsuae.com

RAILWAY KITTENS
In the United States, it is the snowy white cat — like Priscilla, Queen of the Desert in Sydney — that is considered to be a symbol of luck and good fortune. In other parts of the world, if a black cat crosses your path, then you can rest secure in the knowledge that your destiny will be nothing less than perfect.

However, black, white, or neither, it seems that some cats

are simply luckier than others when it comes to finding the perfect human companion. The more superstitious among us may believe in the concept of fate, or other spiritual forces, to explain a fortuitous meeting of souls. For others, it's simply the law of probability that accounts for how a cat can be fortunate enough to be in the right place at the right time.

On a country train line in the northern United Kingdom, a commuter train was completing its regular run one cold winter's day when, suddenly, it was brought to an unexpected halt by a red signal light. The driver had not received a radio message to explain the stop light, and when he radioed to the next station to find out the reason, they were unable to offer an explanation.

After waiting at the light for twenty minutes, the driver got down from his cab to explore. As he walked along the side of the track, he suddenly noticed a medium-sized, brown cardboard box sitting close to the outer rails. Although he knew this couldn't be the cause of the red signal light, he was also concerned that he should remove the box in the interests of safety.

'I walked across to the box and assumed it was just another piece of rubbish that had blown onto the tracks,' said the driver. But as he approached the box, he suddenly noticed that it was moving. 'I couldn't believe what I saw in it when I bent down to pick it up. Nestled together at the bottom of the box, were five tiny kittens — at the most a week old! My first thought was how cold and hungry they must be — they were mewing and huddling together, as if they were missing their mother.'

Luckily for the kittens, the driver was a genuine cat lover, ever since he'd owned his first kitten as a young boy. He carefully picked up the box and carried it back to the warmth of the driver's cab. 'I'd practically forgotten all about the commuters on the train. My main concern now was to get back to the station and to visit the nearest vet!'

The driver radioed to the station to find out the latest news on the red stop light — and also to let the station master know about his find. 'Then the most extraordinary thing happened,' he said. 'As I was calling the station, the red light suddenly turned to green.' While the station personnel were still unable offer an explanation for the red light, they could confirm that the line was all clear and safe for the train to continue, and so the driver continued the journey to the next station, with his new passengers snuggled safe and warm in their box.

As soon as the train pulled into the station, the driver made a call to his local vet and arranged to take the kittens for a check-up that afternoon. 'News had got around the station by this time, and all the train staff came in to the office to have a look at the kittens,' commented the driver proudly. 'We even nicknamed them "the little miracles"!'

The vet confirmed the kittens were under two weeks old and suggested that the vet staff take on the careful nurturing they would need over the next couple of weeks. 'I reluctantly agreed,' said the driver, 'but I went to visit them every other day during my break!'

All five kittens grew strong and healthy and all found new homes within a week of being pronounced fit and ready to join the big wide world. The driver, of course, was one of the first adoptive parents.

Meanwhile, the stationmaster continued the investigation into the red stop light which had mysteriously caused the train to stop midcourse, in the middle of nowhere, for no apparent reason. Curiously, to this day, no amount of equipment or personnel checking has produced an explanation — and it hasn't happened since. 'I'm not usually superstitious,' declared the driver, 'but I think I was meant to find those kittens — and something triggered that red stop light so that I could to be in the right place at the right time.'

FROM RAGS TO RICHES

The relationship between an owner and their cat is always unique. Indeed it is easy to understand why some proud cat owners exclaim that it was their treasured feline friend who actually chose *them* rather than the other way around! As with the train driver and his box of kittens, it's all a matter of being in the right place at the right time.

But once the soul mates have been brought together, the years shared as the new kitten grows into a cat result in a close bonding. Trust and loyalty develop, together with those quirky habits and fun games that contribute so much to the partnership. For owners adopting kittens and cats who might otherwise face an uncertain future, the rewards in developing a relationship that brings such utter enjoyment are almost limitless.

Kathy, a committed cat lover from South Australia, has lost count of the actual number of cats she has looked after, although she can recall that at least 25 of them have been disabled cats with special needs. 'Somebody's trash are my treasures,' she announced, as she described the many cats and kittens she has adopted over the years.

On her way to work one day, always on the lookout and ready to stop and say hello to the neighbourhood cats, Kathy suddenly noticed a pair of shining eyes in the storm drain near her local grocery store. Two days later, when she was shopping at the store, Kathy made some enquiries about the mysterious drain-dweller. The shop owner confirmed it was a cat, although no one had actually seen it in clear daylight. 'The shop owner had also spotted the eyes and had looked into the drain and seen the cat's face, but that's all. And he had started to leave out scraps of bread for the cat to eat and … wait for it … cola to drink!' Kathy exclaimed.

She started leaving small amounts of more nutritious cat food near the drain, in the hope that it might entice the cat to come out. Winter was approaching and Kathy worried that the animal might not survive the cold and rain. However, after a month of gentle coaxing, there was no sign that the cat was prepared to leave the sanctuary of the drain. Clearly, this feline was in a very distressed state. So, armed with many years of dedicated experience in dealing with traumatised cats, Kathy decided more drastic action was required.

Smothering her hand and arm in cat food, Kathy lay down in the street next to the storm drain and waited for the cat to come close. After half an hour, just as Kathy was starting to think that her plan might not be successful, the cat edged closer and started to lick the food from her hand. Gently, but firmly, Kathy closed her arm around the cat and swiftly pulled her out of the drain. Before the cat could realise what was happening, Kathy had placed her in a cosy box and was already striding home!

Back at the house, Kathy opened the box carefully and peeked in at the tiny cat. 'She was nothing but a bundle of bones, covered in thick, caked-on dirt,' described Kathy. 'She couldn't have been more than five months old and certainly looked like she had experienced a tough start to life. And to add to her difficulties, I quickly discovered that she was completely deaf.' Kathy couldn't even imagine the cat's true colour, but after several weeks of gentle washing and cleaning, the cat was revealed as an attractive, blue-eyed, pure white princess. 'Tinkerbelle was the first name I thought of — because she was so delicate and so pretty,' smiled Kathy.

During the following months, Kathy kept Tinkerbelle in isolation from the other cats in the household while she treated her. After a diet of little more than bread and cola, it came as no surprise that Tinkerbelle had badly decayed teeth and was severely malnourished. Her deafness also meant that she was very anxious and wary of anything that moved — except, that is, for Kathy. In this short time, Tinkerbelle had instinctively come to regard Kathy as a trusted and loyal friend and consequently allowed Kathy to handle her without a struggle.

During her time in the storm drain, despite the confined surroundings, Tinkerbelle had also developed a nervous habit of continuously cleaning herself — to the point where she had licked her white fur yellow! Now, under Kathy's care, she enjoyed the regular washing and grooming ritual that was introduced and didn't even mind having a blow-dry with a hairdryer!

Kathy continued to nurse Tinkerbelle to optimum health with a combination of nourishing food and lots of love.

Tinkerbelle was gradually introduced into the household and she began to enjoy the companionship of the other cats, along with Kathy and her husband. 'After a few years, Tinkerbelle transformed dramatically to become a sociable and extremely beautiful cat,' commented Kathy proudly.

So incredible was the transformation that Kathy decided to enter Tinkerbelle in the Cat Council of Australia International Show, which attracts only the very best cats throughout Australasia. 'By this time, Tinkerbelle was proving to love the limelight. She was always the show cat at home and people always commented on her grace and beauty. So we decided to see if the rest of Australia thought she was as amazing as we did.'

Tinkerbelle was preened and pampered until she glowed, and by the time they were lining up for the judges, Kathy was in no doubt that she looked as good as all the other cats at the show, if not better. And, like a traditional rags to riches fairytale, Tinkerbelle stunned her owners by winning not only Best Domestic Cat, but also Supreme Domestic Cat in the show! 'The judge even announced that pedigree owners should take note of Tinkerbelle!' laughed Kathy. 'And the expression on the judge's face was priceless when he asked where I had found this magnificent cat. "She came out of a drain," I replied!'

'Tinkerbelle loved being the star and always took

everything in her stride,' added Kathy. 'I think her deafness probably helped this too.' This incredible cat seemed to thoroughly enjoy her new life and over the next few years she continued to win local show prizes. She always attracted attention and loved being cuddled and cosseted by the many cat lovers who couldn't resist her charms.

But finally, her poor beginnings caught up with her and she passed away at eight years of age, leaving behind many very happy memories for Kathy and her husband. 'I think her start in life had been so severe that she was never destined to live to a ripe old age,' said Kathy fondly, 'but Tinkerbelle will always be a real inspiration to everyone who knew her, because she so brilliantly proved that it doesn't matter what your roots are.'

A CAUTIONARY TALE

While Tinkerbelle slipped into her new, privileged and pampered life in true Cinderella style, for some cats the relaxed way of life is not an option. Always on the lookout for adventure, the ever-curious cat is always ready to explore the tallest tree in the garden or test the boundaries of the neighbourhood. Fully testing their nine lives, there are no limits to the kind of scrapes these cats can get into — leaving owners no choice but to develop nerves of steel, or degenerate into a bundle of neuroses!

Todd Sherman of Florida in the United States is a cat lover who rose to the challenges posed by his adored cat Raisen better than most owners could manage. After years of being confronted with Raisen's heart-stopping, life-threatening antics, he managed to hold it together by treading the fine line between shrugging off imminent danger with cool bravado and collapsing into complete, hysterical decline.

Raisen was no ordinary family cat. She always managed to find herself in *real* danger, side-stepping certain disaster just in the nick of time. This uncanny ability started early in her life, as Todd discovered to his dismay. 'I was first aware of Raisen's die-hard personality the time when there was the juvenile with the pellet gun next door, who very sadly shot her sister, Bran. Raisen managed to bolt in time, and after searching throughout the night, I finally found her, terrified, up at the very top of a 70-foot [21-metre] tall pine tree in the dead, 10-degree cold [−12 degrees Celsius] at 1 a.m. the next morning.' Already distraught by the cruel death of Bran, Todd was determined to save Raisen and patiently waited at the base of the tree with a bowl of cat food, trying to persuade her to come down. 'It didn't immediately work and I deliberately kept leaving the scene hoping she'd get up the nerve [to come down on her own] if I was gone and not giving her all that silly, loud attention,' recalled Todd with a smile.

Raisen recovered from this terrible experience and in a short time became a happy member of the Sherman household. Like any family cat, Raisen was given the run of the house and enjoyed exploring both inside and outside the property. That is, until she became over-curious one day and almost lost her life to her trusting nature. 'She was out on her usual exploration of the garden when suddenly she was struck on the nose by none other than a baby rattlesnake,' grimaced Todd. 'She was always a very friendly cat — particularly with other animals — and, seeing it in the grass, she must have thought it would make a good playmate. Poor Raisen's face immediately puffed up and there was a real danger that her throat would swell and she would stop breathing. I was terrified, but knew I had to keep my head.' Luckily Todd managed to keep Raisen calm and got her to the vet in time. 'I can't describe how lucky I was. The vet said if I'd been even a moment longer, I would have lost her. I'm so relieved that Raisen lived to tell the heroic tale.'

As if these experiences were not dramatic enough for a young cat, Raisen was always getting up to tricks that seemed designed to test Todd's devotion. Like her passion for plastic shopping bags — the kind that are renowned for their potential to suffocate young children and animals. Raisen slept on these bags and played with them; she even climbed into them so that Todd could scoop her up in them and then tip her out.

Of course, Todd was aware that she shouldn't really be encouraged to treat plastic bags as toys and tried to deter her, but Raisen had her own ideas. 'She had got her head caught in the handle of the bag before and it was no problem for her. She knew how to back out of it. They're not exactly "tight" and backing out is easy after all. But then, having worn collars, harnesses, and used to being on leashes, this was probably not something considered "out of the normal" to her. So she never got into a panic,' explained Todd wryly, 'until this particular occasion …'

Raisen was playing in the kitchen when Todd arrived home with some groceries. Somehow, she managed to get the handles of a brand new plastic bag wrapped firmly around her neck. 'I can't explain the ensuing hysteria, from myself, Raisen and the other cats, which definitely resulted in all of us losing a life!' laughed Todd. 'My advice is, if this happens to your cat, don't rush around the house after it yelling or making a big fuss because, without doubt, you will end up making the experience far worse and the cats will forever be paranoid about that object — whatever it is — from then on. In my case, because Raisen was in a panic, the other cats raced to see what was going on. All of them saw me running around the house, chasing Raisen, yelling worried screams. So they assumed there was a dangerous operation going on. Before I knew it, the entire episode had become the household's worst nightmare, requiring lengthy recovery time and resulting in an inconvenient, permanent fear of plastic carrier bags amongst the entire household.'

Raisen's mishaps with neckwear didn't end there. One afternoon, Todd's niece was playing with the cats, when she decided that a thick rubber band would make the perfect accessory around Raisen's neck. 'Sounds pretty unreal? Well believe me, it was pretty terrifying — and my poor niece was so young she didn't realise what she had done,' said Todd. Immediately, Raisen started to cough, and started running frantically around the house, knocking things over in panic. 'You hear the fray going on, you rush to the scene, and immediately begin screaming "OH NO! NOT THAT!" And because I was chasing Raisen and shoving furniture out of the way to get to her, she was in an even greater state of fear. Now it was not just the rubber band scaring her!'

Todd grabbed a pair of scissors and tried to catch her — but she was in such a panicked state that, when he tried to pick her up, Raisen lashed out and clawed a 1-inch-deep [2.5-centimetre] gash in his arm. At the second attempt, Todd managed to cut the band away, and Raisen leapt out of his arms and vanished straight under his bed. 'Without exaggeration, Raisen hid under my bed for a month and she wouldn't allow anyone near her — not even me. I really had to work to earn back her trust.'

Such adventures would curb the curiosity of most cats — but not Raisen. Always interested in what Todd was doing, Raisen was intrigued by the sound of his electric shaver. 'She would come into the bathroom as soon as she heard me switch on the shaver and sit and watch me,' explained Todd, 'until the day it dropped on her when it accidentally slipped out of my wet hands. The impact on her head, I'm sure, was enough to take a life, and the loud buzzing noise it continued to make as it lay next to her on the floor, apparently "moving", only served to make her believe it was quite probably alive and about to attack.'

Once again, Raisen sought shelter under Todd's bed and it took a week for her to return to a calm and collected state. 'Amazingly her bravado returned, but turn on that electric razor … ' laughed Todd.

In spite of her lust for adventure, Raisen probably still had a few lives left after all her death-defying experiences but, sadly for Todd, Raisen was unable to conquer the illness that finally claimed her. 'Raisen had a bout with Hypertrophic Cardiomyopathy which she couldn't beat. But she lives on and remains continually loved in my memory, and I'll never forget her,' said Todd fondly. 'She was the most intelligent and "with it" cat I'd ever known in my lifetime. Raisen was "there". She knew what was going on around her. That put her far above the rest. I would have gone to any lengths for her.'

KISS OF LIFE

As illustrated by Todd and his beloved Raisen, an extreme circumstance will often generate an extreme reaction, particularly in times of apparent disaster. The adrenaline rush is instantaneous and reactions are on the spur of the moment, overcoming any obstacle in an attempt to protect loved ones from harm. Ziggy, one very lucky tortoiseshell cat in Melbourne, Australia, was on the receiving end of a true act of impulsive bravery during a crisis which would otherwise have proved fatal — and all from a complete, though animal-loving, stranger!

The story of Ziggy starts on a hot summer's day in his owner's apartment in central Melbourne. It was just a normal weekday in the heart of the city. Ziggy followed his usual habit of crawling under the half-open kitchen window to visit his neighbourhood friends, while his owner was making a hurried breakfast of toast and coffee.

After climbing through the empty cardboard boxes outside the shop below the apartment, and rolling around the grassy backyard with the neighbour's ginger cat, Ziggy hopped back onto the fence and made the leap onto the ledge to crawl back through the kitchen window. His owner had already finished breakfast and was preparing to leave for the office. As usual, he closed the kitchen window and checked that Ziggy had plenty of water before giving him a quick goodbye cuddle.

But as soon as his owner had left the apartment, Ziggy must have been aware that something was not quite right. His owner had been rather flustered and in more of a hurry than usual. He had left both the bedroom door and the bathroom door wide open — and he usually made a point of ensuring they were closed before leaving. He also hadn't bothered to put away the milk or the bread after preparing his breakfast. Ziggy probably would have liked this, particularly as the milk had also been left open!

But what would have been very disturbing for Ziggy was the still-smoking toaster. In his haste, the owner had left the toaster switched on — and even worse, it still had a slice of bread toasting inside it. The smoke from the burning toast would have been distressing enough, but poor Ziggy was about to endure a far more harrowing experience.

The toaster quickly caught alight and, within a matter of minutes, the fire started to spread through the kitchen. From the kitchen it moved swiftly across the hallway and into the living room, bedroom and bathroom. As it crept through the apartment, destroying everything in its path, the thick, black, choking smoke was joined by a lethal cocktail of poisonous gases emanating from furniture, carpets and plastics. Ziggy would have been terrified. Without a refuge from the flames, smoke and gases, he was facing certain death.

As the fire spread to the front of the apartment, facing the street, a passer-by suddenly noticed smoke and flames billowing out of a window. It was estimated by onlookers that the local firefighters arrived around ten minutes later. They asked if anyone knew the owner and if it was likely that anyone might be in the flat. A neighbour confirmed that no one was likely to be home — except for a tortoiseshell cat. As soon as they were safely able to enter the building, two firefighters climbed into the flat. They walked from room to room calling out, but heard nothing. Then, just as they were about to descend to the street, one of the team stopped by the bedroom — and saw a very sooty cat lying beside the bed. He gently touched Ziggy then gathered him up in his arms.

Although he hadn't been burned by the flames, Ziggy had been overcome by the fumes and smoke and was unconscious. The rest of the firefighting team had assumed he was dead; however, this firefighter was a real cat lover and, although he couldn't feel a heartbeat, he knew he couldn't just leave Ziggy. He had to try to revive him.

As soon as he was back on the street, the firefighter surprised the bystanders by laying Ziggy on a rug in the street. Instead of covering him up, ready to be identified by the owner, he started to administer mouth-to-mouth resuscitation and heart massage!

After what seemed like minutes, a miracle occurred. Ziggy suddenly twitched his leg and regained consciousness. The feline kiss of life from a firefighter with a big, cat-loving heart had saved his life.

Ziggy's devastated owner returned to his flat just moments later and was both astonished — and delighted — to hear of lucky Ziggy's survival. Even though he had lost practically everything, he was lucky enough to still have his faithful companion, thanks to a complete stranger who had put his own life at risk to bring Ziggy out of the fire to safety.

After several visits to the local vet, Ziggy's health was restored and he soon re-established his daily habits in the new apartment. Meanwhile, his owner made sure he developed some habits of his own, like checking the toaster before leaving for work.

MY CUBAN CAT

Cat lovers always seem to attract cats — and vice versa — wherever they are in the world. It's almost as if cats recognise the mutual appreciation. Just like Ziggy and the firefighter, for some cats these chance meetings can be literally lifesaving.

Cleo may be lucky enough to have a quiet, comfortable existence in Chelsea, London, but she began life as a humble, hungry stray in Havana, Cuba. Fortunately for Cleo, she was unofficially adopted by Flavia Campilli, a woman renowned in Havana for her extraordinary benevolence to the local neighbourhood cats.

It all started in London, where Flavia have been living since leaving Italy in 1971. She had decided to take early retirement from a hectic financial job, but just as she was starting to enjoy her new life, her happiness was cut short. Soon after leaving the city her best friend and loyal companion Elsa, a beautiful, miniature West Highland White Terrier, left her for a better world. Feeling lonely and missing Elsa, Flavia decided to accept an offer to work overseas in Cuba. And here began Flavia's love affair with Cuba's cats!

Flavia moved into a hotel close to her offices in Havana but, knowing no one, she used to spend her evenings sitting next to the swimming pool. One night a beautiful cat appeared and strolled by her chair. She was long-haired and her colour was a mixture of light silver-grey and white. They looked at each other and, immediately, Flavia was smitten. 'I was touched by the warmth in her expression — she had marvellous light-blue eyes. I tried to stroke her but she ran and hid behind a palm. Cats in Cuba are not used to such attention from humans. From that night onwards, every night that I sat by the swimming pool, I expected her visit and she never failed,' explained Flavia.

The following day, Flavia visited the local supermarket and bought some minced meat. She also bought some canned cat food from the only existing pet shop, which mainly catered to the foreigners — the only ones who actually bought pet food, when available, for their animals.

And so she and the cat became close friends. Flavia called her Lady, because she really was so elegant — except when she was eating. 'Like all animals in Cuba, she was always hungry and it was then that her savage instincts blossomed in full. She would drink the water from the swimming pool and I used to treat her to my ham and cheese sandwich, which she would quickly devour.

'Every morning when I opened the doors that led to the swimming pool, Lady would appear and I would set down a plate of minced meat or dry food — both real luxuries for Cuban cats. In the evenings, we just kept each other company like two old friends who often do not need to talk because they have already said it all,' recounted Flavia.

One day Lady appeared with a friend — a big male cat covered in scratches. Flavia liked his orange coat and yellow eyes and offered him a dish of minced meat. Now she had two friends visiting her in the mornings and often in the evenings too.

Flavia arranged for the local vet, Mario, to visit her hotel bungalow to carry out health checks on both cats and was prepared to foot the bill to neuter the cats to maintain their health. By now the staff working in the hotel were used to Flavia's philanthropic gestures. 'They thought I was a bit crazy to care for the cats or at least an eccentric,' laughed Flavia. However, some of her kindness must have touched them, as they soon developed a fondness for the cats they used to chase away, and were happy to take care of Lady and Orange when Flavia had to take short trips back to England.

And so it happened that one day after returning from England Flavia noticed a tiny, dark brown, little kitten who greeted her from the bushes on her arrival back at the hotel. 'I later learned that one of the bodyguards had found her in one of the streets outside the hotel, close to the busy main road and picked her up saying, "Do not worry, there is a crazy — *loca* — client in our hotel who will probably take care of you!" ' exclaimed Flavia. And so it was that Cleo — an abandoned, tiny kitten, who had diced with danger on the main road — came into Flavia's life. She would become a dear and precious friend.

Cleo had never really had any close contact with humans — or at least had not experienced help from humans. She watched Lady closely and realised that Flavia was generous and kind. 'After a time, my bedroom became Cleo's favourite place and she would always come there at night or when she was anxious. The hotel staff could not see why I loved Cleo so much as she was very tiny, rather scrawny with patchy hair and not at all attractive. They thought she looked a bit like a rat! Of course, I never saw her like that and later, as she started growing older, with all the good dry food that she was eating, her hair became a beautiful dark-brown colour with orange highlights and the colour of her eyes flashed green and yellow.

'Cleo's trusting nature won me over and she soon became very special to me,' continued Flavia, 'so you can imagine how I felt when, one day rushing out for work from my bungalow, I was opening the door to go out and Cleo, who was still a small kitten, caught her paw under the door. Still today I feel the pain when I talk about it. She screamed in pain and terror and I realised there was nothing I could do.' As she was an undersized cat, the bone in Cleo's leg was completely crushed. Mario the vet explained that surgery was not possible, but Cleo was strong and resilient and proved not to be affected by one front leg being slightly shorter than the other.

So Flavia felt even more protective of Cleo. She loved to go out in the hotel gardens in the evenings but Flavia could not rest until she knew she was back in the bedroom. 'I used to call her, going around the gardens in my pyjamas, hoping no one else would see me — a crazy woman — calling out "Cleo!" and banging a spoon against the food dish until she would appear from under a tree or bush and follow me to the bungalow,' laughed Flavia.

Finally Flavia's work contract ended and she had to return to London for good. 'It was a horrible decision, nights of tears and fears, but I could only take one cat back with me — and without question, it was Cleo. Lady was never completely happy indoors; she preferred the outdoors, roaming way of life. Orange, forget it. He used to disappear sometimes for days. Both were too independent and I, as I live in a small house in the heart of Chelsea, I could really only manage one ... my baby Cleo.'

A few weeks prior to her departure, Flavia had started encouraging the cats to move away from the hotel by feeding them far away from her bungalow. 'There was no one to place them with and in any case no one had the means to take care of them,' explained Flavia. 'I left enough dry food for about six months, and the staff promised to take care of them. What else could I do but promise to keep in touch?'

On her return to London, Flavia visited Cleo in quarantine three times a week, but she was not pleased at being left and would often hide in her sleeping area. Finally, the quarantine ended and Flavia drove home with Cleo. From the backstreets of Cuba, an abandoned, barely alive kitten, Cleo had been whisked to a new life of unrivalled privilege in Knightsbridge, London!

The moment Cleo arrived at her new home, she behaved as if she already knew the place. She went straight upstairs to Flavia's bedroom and jumped on her bed. But this drastic change in her fortune almost cost her life. 'I left to go to the bathroom, but when I returned, I couldn't see Cleo anywhere. I looked under the bed and called out her name — but nothing,' described Flavia. 'Then, I noticed the curtain flapping at the window and as I reached out to move it aside, there was a loud screech and then a stomach-churning thump. My poor Cleo had been hiding behind the curtain and had panicked when I moved it — falling straight out of the window with nothing to break her fall!' On instinct, Flavia rushed outside in her pyjamas. She was prepared for the worst and Cleo's life flashed though her mind: she had survived poverty and illness on the streets of Cuba and was now supposed to start a new, luxurious life in England. Flavia couldn't bear to think that she might now not have this chance. Miraculously, as she searched around her neighbours' gardens, she suddenly heard a faint meow. There, lying in some low bushes, was Cleo. She was terrified and it took Flavia a while to coax her gently into allowing herself to be picked up. Her heart was beating frantically — as was Flavia's — but luckily Cleo was fine and had not sustained any injury.

Cleo enjoyed her new regal life over the next few months without incident, until one day the local black-and-white bully tomcat, Pickles, decided that he would like to meet the new, beautiful, exotic Cuban cat. Renowned in the neighbourhood for getting his own way, even the toughest tomcats had been known to give in to Pickles. On this night, he waited until nightfall and then tried his luck through the cat flap. Flavia's friend and cat-sitter, Mary Ann, was woken by an ear-splitting commotion: SHRIEK, MEOW, GRRRF! She quickly ran down to see Cleo in the conservatory in an incredible gladiator-style fight with Pickles. Cleo may have been pampered but she certainly gave Pickles the message that her fighting skills were in a different class. After being chased all around the kitchen, he finally shot off out of the cat flap and scuttled back over the neighbours' gardens.

Cleo was shaken but stood proud, as if she had protected the whole house from this brute.

Cleo is now nine years old and still doted on by Flavia. 'She still has her good looks and she is very happy. I love to tell her stories about Orange and Lady — she jumps up onto my lap and purrs contentedly when I remind her of the old life in Cuba. I feel so lucky that I had the opportunity to meet these wonderful cats.'

Survival of the Fittest

Admired for their uncanny intuition and aristocratic grace, cats have an incredible ability to bounce back from the brink of adversity. Whether it's a considered leap from rooftop to rooftop, or an unfortunate, mistimed tumble that always, miraculously, results in kitty landing squarely on all fours in the style of a dismounting gymnast, the evidence points to the fact that, when it comes to survival of the fittest, cats have more than their fair share of luck.

THE (VERY) EXTREME ESCAPADES OF TOMMY THE TOMCAT

Some cats give up the thrill of high jinks and double-dare as they reach cat-dotage, preferring instead the easy-going life of prepared, regular gourmet meals, and a reliable, cosy lap to snuggle into. Others, it seems, are honour bound to test their nine lives to the absolute edge of the outer limits.

A very well-loved pet of children Nora, Johnny and Jimmy Lowton in early-1940s northern England, Tommy was possibly the biggest tabby tomcat ever to survive in the post-war period. Each experience he encountered, and survived, seemed to drive him further in the quest to exceed his capabilities — like extreme sports for cats!

The harried life during World War II, with air-raid warnings and food rationing, took its toll on animals of lesser courage. But Tommy always managed to heed the deafening sirens to find his way to the air-raid shelter, and Nora, Johnny and Jimmy made sure that Tommy didn't go hungry.

In the years following the war, Tommy was popular among the local farmers because he helped to control the mice and rats in the grain and hay stores. After breakfast every morning, Tommy would wait until the children had left for school before dashing out the back gate to cross the fields to the nearby farms.

'He was known as King Mouser amongst the local farming families because he would spend a large part of the day in the barns — and would then leave a display of his catches outside the door, like trophies,' explained Nora. 'And it's not surprising that he was the biggest tom around, because he used to eat up everything he caught, leaving only their tails.'

Tommy loved this idyllic life — hunter by day, pampered pet by night — but he never underestimated the importance of keeping his guard up. He may have been rather round and heavy, but he was still stealthy and quick on his feet. 'I've actually witnessed times in the barns when Tommy only narrowly escaped being crushed by a couple of falling bales. But we used to worry about him more during late summer with the local harvests,' said Nora. 'The farms used huge tractors with threshers during harvest and Tommy still insisted on running across the fields, darting in between this machinery as if it was a friendly version of Russian roulette! And because he was a tabby, he blended into the landscape too well. The farmers asked us to keep him inside, but that was virtually impossible. It was like he had a hungry instinct for danger.' As one farmer said to Nora, 'That crackpot cat of yers is gunna lose his nine lives, the ways he's carryin' on!'

Luckily Tommy survived the harvest every year, and continued to be a welcome sight on the farms, earning himself a regular saucer of fresh milk.

But tomcats will be tomcats and one of Tommy's characteristics was not quite so popular amongst the neighbours. Well-fed and with high self-esteem, Tommy rather fancied himself as the local Lothario and Nora's neighbours soon found themselves overflowing with pregnant cats and the subsequent kittens that resulted from his late-night antics. Thorough soakings with bucketfuls of water hardly deterred him, less so the heavy thwack of dustbin lids and even a sharp-edged coal shovel on one occasion. 'Most of the time, fortunately, they missed, but once Tommy arrived home with a very deep gash in the side of his head. It was bleeding quite a lot, but we managed to stop the flow and cleaned him up. Tommy was very unsteady on his feet and we were worried about him, but as it was post-war, we couldn't afford vet bills, so our mum patched it up with our own first aid rations! He wasn't quite himself for a few days afterwards, but within the week, he was back up to his old tricks.'

One such trick was to loiter around the pigeon loft of older brother Jimmy. 'Jimmy would get really annoyed with me if Tommy was in the back garden at "homing" time,' laughed Nora. 'As if he didn't get enough food, Tommy would sense the time of day and look out of the window with eyes gleaming, licking his lips. Somehow, he often managed to squeeze into the back garden just at the very second that Jimmy was successfully calling in the last of the pigeons. Naturally, one look at Tommy sent them scattering back up into the sky! Jimmy even chased me down the street one day, because he thought I'd let Tommy out on purpose!'

One day, however, Tommy was a bit too quick to pounce. As Jimmy watched the last pigeon fly into the loft, Tommy swiftly nipped around the side and slipped in through the door. Jimmy could hardly believe his eyes and ears as a thick cloud of feathers scattered and the air was filled with terrified squawking. Jimmy pulled open the door and quickly slammed it shut, hoping to minimise the escape of the pigeons. Unfortunately, Tommy's leg was caught in the door and he was making matters worse by struggling. 'Jimmy was so angry about his precious pigeons that I had to beg him to let Tommy go,' remembered Nora, 'although really, Jimmy is such a softie with animals, like everyone in our family!' Jimmy did let Tommy go and he quickly scuttled into the house — bedraggled with peck marks on his back and a very noticeable limp.

Tommy never recovered from this limp and it certainly hampered some of his more acrobatic exploits. When Nora came home from school one day, it was fortunate for this hyperactive cat that she went straight into the back garden. Although he was now wary of the pigeon loft, Tommy had climbed on top of it — most probably to tease the pigeons — but had slipped off the roof and landed in a quarter-full rainwater barrel. When Nora found him, he was literally treading water. 'It must have only happened seconds before I arrived, because even though the water wasn't very deep, Tommy would have had no chance at all of climbing out of that barrel alive. Like all cats, he hated water and he was in the most frightened state I had ever seen him. He wouldn't jump off my lap all evening.'

It was Tommy's natural curiosity that led to his lifetime of near-fatal escapades — and possibly his family's devotion that made possible his continued survival. In the early 1950s, Nora's family decided it was time to have their wooden floor in the sitting room replaced. The carpenter arrived with the wooden planks and the necessary tools. 'Tommy was very interested in the carpenter — he always hung around visitors hoping to charm them into giving him food, but he seemed to really like the wooden planks and tools. Maybe it was the scent of the wood.' Tommy lay on top of the wood and watched as the carpenter prepared the area for work. But as soon as the hammering of nails started, Tommy scarpered. He hated the noise and wanted to seek refuge. The family left the carpenter to get on with the job and came back at the end of the day to find it finished, all neat and cleaned up as good as new. But Tommy couldn't be found anywhere.

Uncharacteristically, Tommy didn't return for days, and the family went out into the garden and the street to look for him, but to no avail. 'We thought he must have been really scared off by the carpenter, but after a week we started to get very worried. He usually never failed to come home for dinner, even though afterwards he would disappear out into the night,' said Nora. Then, miraculously, on the quiet Sunday morning, they heard a muffled meowing that sounded like Tommy — but he couldn't be seen anywhere. They checked the garden and the rainwater barrel and all the kitchen cupboards and the sideboard in the sitting room. Suddenly they realised where he was. 'Johnny, my younger brother, knelt down and put his ear to the floorboards and then laughed. "He's under here, the beggar!" Tommy must have been exploring underneath the floorboards when the carpenter had stopped hammering, and had been trapped under there when the new floorboards were nailed down! We had to call the carpenter back in to loosen one of the new floorboards and I remember it cost a fortune,' smiled Nora, 'but we couldn't have left him there. Tommy was part of our family. Luckily he was so big, he had survived without food for all this time — although he was very thirsty when we pulled him out.'

This must have been Tommy's final challenge because, according to Nora, he lived a very quiet life after this. Preferring to hang around the house and garden, enjoying the benefits of his revered position in the family, Tommy survived to a very ripe old age. 'And,' added Norah wistfully, 'we will never forget him. He will always be remembered in the family and the stories of his escapades are like treasured heirlooms that we have passed down the family.'

A NIGHT WITH THE CROCODILES!
A local hero because of his larrikin behaviour, Tommy Tomcat earned his reputation by always preferring to go a few steps

beyond a comfortable existence. But some cats have no choice and are literally thrown into an extreme circumstance. It is the courage they display in response that earns them their resulting heroic celebrity status.

The Northern Territory in Australia is a beautiful place, renowned for its vast areas of unspoiled and picturesque wilderness. But for a cat it can be a tricky place to survive with long, very dry and very hot summers, and an indigenous wildlife population that includes venomous snakes, poisonous spiders and crocodiles.

Kathy Roberts, working for Australia's Cat Adoption Centre Program, was a regular traveller around the Northern Territory, bringing help to homeless cats and kittens. She would fly the three-and-a-half-hour journey to visit the local animal shelters, taking along extra supplies and also helping to re-home some of the cats by bringing them back to a Cat Adoption Centre in Adelaide, South Australia.

'I am such a cat lover that it was always hard to part with any of the cats I brought back with me,' explained Kathy, 'but it was always made slightly easier because the Program ensures that all the cats and kittens are adopted into good homes.' However, on one particular trip to Alice Springs in the Northern Territory, she visited the local RSPCA and found the staff were still buzzing with excitement and amazement at the latest feline friend to join them.

Big Boy, as he came to be known, was a magnificent, three-year-old, black, long-haired cat. Well-nourished and hefty in stature, it seemed strange that he was in the shelter at all. 'He was such a good-looking cat and didn't appear to have been living a hard life on the streets,' said Kathy. But poor Big Boy had experienced something far more precarious than street life.

Only a couple of days earlier, some very distressed Rangers had brought Big Boy to the RSPCA straight from a nearby tourist wildlife park. 'Apparently they were just as much in a state of shock as Big Boy,' exclaimed Kathy. 'The story is one of amazing cruelty but also of incredible survival instinct.'

The Rangers had been patrolling the wildlife park, carrying out the usual morning checks. They reached the crocodile park and, at first startled, then horrified, realised that an animal had somehow found itself in the middle of the enclosure — in full view of the fearsome crocodiles.

The Rangers worked quickly to distract the crocodiles — some of them huge and almost full-grown, but all of them potentially lethal — while they prepared to rescue the animal. 'He was curled up into a tiny, tight ball and even when the Rangers reached down and picked him up, he refused to relax, so they weren't even sure if he was alive,' Kathy explained. Once on safe ground and with some gentle stroking and coaxing, slowly the animal started to move and uncurl. 'They were amazed to discover that the animal was a healthy, black cat — possibly even someone's pet.'

The Rangers then carried the über-fortunate cat — affectionately referred to as Big Boy — to the park vet where, after a thorough feline medical, it was established that he had survived this unbelievable incident with no physical injuries at all, although he was in a state of severe shock. The vet and the Rangers concluded that, although he must have been terrified beyond belief, mercifully Big Boy had had the instinctive intelligence to lie perfectly still, in one spot, for the duration of the night and early morning. Consequently, even though they had been prowling around him, forever on the alert for their next meal, the crocodiles had left Big Boy alone.

'I could hardly believe this story,' said Kathy. 'Even the Rangers were describing it as a miracle. If you have ever seen how crocodiles leap into the air or move with the speed of light, snapping their jaws, just for a morsel of meat, it seems incredible that Big Boy survived. It's amazing that he saved his own life by not moving an inch.'

How he came to be in the crocodile park is something that the Rangers can only guess at. The park itself is located near a highway and away from residential areas, which rules out any assumption that Big Boy may have fallen into the enclosure by accident. 'As a main road runs alongside the edge of the crocodile park, the Rangers felt that Big Boy must have been thrown over the wall deliberately, which makes it all the more distressing. It's terrible to think that someone may have been so cruel. Big Boy must have been in shock, wondering what was happening to him — and then to be faced with such a near-death experience.'

Of course, Kathy had no option but to bring Big Boy back to Adelaide, to help him get over the shock and nurse him back to his former health. And he enjoyed living in Kathy's animal-filled household, slowly regaining his confidence.

A couple of months later, Kathy attended the Royal Show in Adelaide to take part in the cat competitions with her own cats. As a regular at the show, Kathy had become good friends with one of the stewards at the pavilion and enjoyed recounting Big Boy's incredible story to her with great pride.

Fate stepped in once again for Big Boy. The steward was so impressed by the story that she asked Kathy if she could adopt him. 'Big Boy is such a huge cat and had developed such a strong personality that I knew he would do well with my friend — especially as she has three big, strapping, teenage sons to keep him in line!'

So Big Boy went off to his new home and another new life. His ordeal with the crocodiles had obviously left him with a finely honed awareness of hierarchy, because he rushed straight into the house and into the arms of the eldest son, wrapped his front legs around the boy's neck and head-butted him! Having established his status in the household, Big Boy resumed his soft and cuddly nature and would happily leap up to anyone who would, or could, hold him!

Kathy is lucky enough to hear the latest news about Big Boy every year when she attends the Royal Show. 'Apparently the teenagers really cherish Big Boy — he even takes a shower with them in the mornings! They give him all the hugs and kisses he needs and he really does live a life of luxury. Their mother thinks he has had a taming effect on the boys, but I prefer to think that Big Boy has learnt something from his death-defying experience and, as a survivor, he is giving something back.'

HITCH AND HIKER

Without a doubt, good fortune played an important hand for Big Boy, making his a heart-warming, albeit incredible, story of the instinctive will to survive combined with the ultimate luck of being in the right place at the right time for his loving, adoptive family. For Big Boy, it was definitely a winning result. Such an outcome wouldn't be out of place in Las Vegas, the city of luck and opportunity, where the many hopeful who visit have a chance of leaving with a treasure trove. For Clint and Kathy Frederick, however, it wasn't until they left their Las Vegas hometown to go on a road trip that

Lady Luck shone down on them and they hit the jackpot big time — with their own very special feline treasures.

Clint and Kathy were getting ready one Friday afternoon to head off to a weekend getaway at Laughlin, about 160 kilometres from Las Vegas. They loaded up their truck, including Boozer the dog, and Hooter the squawking cockatiel.

By 6.30 p.m. they had arrived and were settled in at the Riverside RV Park. Later that evening they ventured out to find dinner and a couple of lucky slot machines. Inevitably, they stayed out late.

'Saturday we were slow getting around,' explained Clint and Kathy. 'Around noon we had finished our second pot of coffee as we sat under the shade of our awning … just a lazy day, roughing it. All around us was quiet and peaceful. In the distance we heard the powerboats cruising the Colorado River, but we also heard the faint cry of what sounded like a bird. Maybe Hooter had picked up a new noise. We sat quietly, waiting to hear the noise again.'

Suddenly a 'fuzzy black blob' appeared under the rear of their motorhome. 'We lost no time coming out of our chairs. We had lived in Arizona and learned if it crawls around on the ground you jump first, ask questions later.' A second glance revealed that what had appeared to be a black ball of fur was in fact a tiny kitten!

'It barely had its eyes open and crawled along on its belly — too young and too weak to walk, all black with diesel soot. Its eyes and nose were clogged with residue from the exhaust. We realised the kitten had ridden on the engine all the way from Las Vegas! The "bird" sounds we heard earlier were from this half-dead orphaned kitten. What a miracle it survived the trip!' One hundred and sixty kilometres is a fair distance to drive as a passenger in the warm cabin of a motorhome, but as a kitten, clinging on to the underbelly of the vehicle as it races along the highway, it defies belief!

Both Clint and Kathy were aware that the kitten needed to eat immediately. The other main concern was that dehydration might have set in since the daytime temperature in the desert was over 40 degrees Celsius. Using a medicine dropper, they slowly fed the kitten with tiny drops of milk, taking great care not to overfeed it. Already they had decided they would keep this lucky little survivor; it would be easy to introduce a kitten to Boozer and Hooter.

Knowing that the garage in Las Vegas where they stored their motorhome was home to some feral cats, Clint and Kathy also searched underneath and inside their vehicle for the possibility of more kittens or even a mother cat. However, they found no more stowaways.

By Saturday night the kitten appeared to have stablilised so, after checking it was comfortable, Clint and Kathy went out to dinner and continued in their pursuit of Lady Luck. At midnight, while searching for the motorhome doorkeys they heard the same tiny meows as they had heard twelve hours before. At first, Clint thought it was the kitten, which they had left safely in a cosy shoebox in the shower recess. But it was too loud to be coming from inside. 'We opened the door, grabbed a flashlight and proceeded to the rear of the "rig". The cries stopped and we couldn't see anything in the engine, just filters, fans and belts. What would the neighbours think? Our search and rescue effort had to look real strange to anyone still awake. Here we were, middle of the night, under the coach with flashlight in hand, making mother cat noises! We expected security to arrive any minute!'

Finally, after much searching and human-meowing, Clint and Kathy switched off their torch and were about to climb in for the night when a second kitten dropped out of the motorhome and onto the ground! It had been completely still and silent while Clint and Kathy has searched with the torch — most probably out of fear — but once this little bundle landed on the grass it soon found its voice and meowed plaintively for its brother or sister, who had already been discovered twelve hours before. And this second, very brave and very strong, miracle kitten was just as dirty and covered in diesel soot as the first!

'Of course, we were totally prepared to feed and care for

this one too, and we just knew the kittens would thrive because they had each other.' After all, if the kittens had managed to hang on for dear life during their unbelievable journey, they were hardly likely to give up now.

Clint and Kathy are understandably proud of their feline heroes and love to tell the story, particularly when people ask the history of their names. 'Naturally, it didn't take long to name them Hitch and Hiker because of their incredible journey, and their will to survive!'

LEAP OF FAITH

Cats may have nine lives to play with, but it seems that in near-fatal circumstances, as in the cases of Hitch and Hiker, a physical effort of almost super-feline proportions is an absolute requirement. And sometimes fate steps in with a little helping hand too.

Vicky Byard, of the Academy of Veterinary Dental Technicians in Pennsylvania, United States, is used to dealing with all manner of animal emergencies. But one case in particular will stand out forever in her memory as the most amazing study of cat survival.

It was late afternoon on 26 March 2004 and the veterinary team at Rau Animal Hospital in Glenside, Pennsylvania, were preparing to close for the day. The weather was surprisingly warm for this time of the year and, naturally, they were looking forward to enjoying the rest of the afternoon. However, just as they were about to leave, the loud speaker announced that an emergency case was already on its way to the hospital.

The hospital receptionists passed on the details to the team as advised by the owners. The case of Cleo, a beloved family cat, was indeed an emergency.

'Having been a technician for over 24 years, my experience is that owners are typically under great stress and frightened during emergency situations and therefore most exaggerate the condition and situation,' explained Vicky. 'However, I couldn't have been more wrong. In these many years, I have witnessed many emergencies — but this was one of the rare times my stomach actually turned when I saw Cleo enter the practice.' As soon as Vicky saw Cleo, her first thought was that this situation had to be photographed for other professionals to appreciate. Cleo had sustained a most horrific accident and it was beyond belief that she was actually still alive.

Responding to the warm spring breeze, the family had left a first-floor window open while they were out. Cleo had decided to make the most of this opportunity by squeezing through the window and onto the roof. Clearly, her innate feline skills were not as finely honed or trustworthy as they should be — but then she was a pampered, 4.5-kilogram, almost eight-year-old, silver tabby Maine Coon cat. Cleo must have spotted a favourite nearby tree branch and taken a flying leap in that direction. However, she had seriously miscalculated and had fallen straight onto the 5-centimetre-diameter fence spikes rearing up from below.

It was the mother and daughter who were unlucky enough to find their family pet impaled on the fence, but they acted with extreme speed and bravery. 'Although in shock, the fifteen-year-old daughter and the very concerned mother maintained their calm and had the amazing foresight to bind Cleo to the fence with wide brown packing tape. The police were called to the emergency but unfortunately they did not have the tools needed to remove the portion of the fence that held the tightly bound cat. So, the fire department was called to the site. The family kept Cleo calm by speaking to her as the firefighters cut through metal and removed the cat and fence as one. I first saw Cleo as the mother and daughter carefully carried her and the fence portion to the treatment room,' recounted Vicky.

Vicky was not alone in her amazement at Cleo's response to her ordeal. The attending veterinarian leading the emergency team made an initial evaluation which included the comment that, in spite of her incredibly traumatic experience, Cleo was remarkably calm with normal respiration!

'It was impossible to assess the extent of the damage because the lifesaving packing tape covered much of the cat,' explained Vicky, 'but it was determined that the primary concern for this cat was for oxygen supplementation, access to a vein and pain control.'

The family remained with Cleo, talking softly to help reassure her and keep her calm. Even with the veterinary team working around her Cleo kept her cool and moved only slightly when the attempt was made to find a vein to administer pain control. 'The family was shown to the waiting room now that their critical role in keeping Cleo calm was over, to spare them the grim reality of treatment. The next task was to remove the tape securing Cleo to the fence. What we found was that Cleo had actually been impaled by only one of the fence posts. By a stroke of amazing luck after such a fall, the post had entered through her axillary [armpit] region and exited through her back by her scapula [shoulder blade].'

After study of the radiograph and much discussion amongst the team, the leading veterinarian made the decision to remove what was effectively the skewer. As Vicky explained, 'Finally, half of the team supported the cat and half of the team grasped the fence. A good tug pulled the fence through the cat, finally freeing her. The staff was amazed to find that there was very little bleeding, and there appeared to be no sucking of air at either site. All of Cleo's vital signs remained amazingly good throughout the procedure.'

After cleaning and suturing, the injury was radiographed once again. Miraculously, even though the fence spike had passed completely through Cleo's body, the internal injuries amounted to bruising around the lung area and a fracture of the left shoulder blade. Cleo was made comfortable with a sling and then moved to a cage for recovery. After only twenty minutes, she was reunited with her family and actually responded to their voices!

As the Rau Animal Hospital does not operate on a 24-hour basis, Cleo was transferred to the Veterinary Specialty and Emergency Center in Langhorne, Pennsylvania. There, she was kept under observation for the next couple of days where they reported that Cleo appeared comfortable and was enjoying eating small amounts of food. She still required careful monitoring and veterinary care, but by 29 March — only three days after the accident — it was agreed that Cleo could go home as long as her owners took care to maintain her medication.

After spending four days at home, the owners noted that Cleo was lethargic, her temperature was 39 degrees Celsius, there was excess saliva on her lips and her hair was matted on her chest. The veterinarian instructed the owners to stop Cleo's medication for 24 hours to rule out any adverse reaction. Sure enough, the owners reported that Cleo was faring far better without her medicine.

Five days later, on 9 April, the family returned to the Center for suture removal and Cleo was found to be healing quickly and doing well. As Vicky commented, 'For a cat that had sustained extensive injury after such a dramatic fall, combined with a feverish reaction to her medication, Cleo had made a miraculously swift recovery.

'I am delighted to say that we have had the pleasure of seeing Cleo a few times since the accident, for wellness visits and typical feline issues. I am certain that the level-headedness of the mother and fifteen-year-old daughter and their ability to keep the cat calm was one of the most critical contributions made towards Cleo's positive outcome.

'But most illuminating to me was how this cat showed no obvious signs of pain. Her heart rate remained normal, her respiration was not affected, her pupils remained normal throughout. The miracle of nine lives or not, our practice's standard of care is that if the situation would be painful to the staff, it is considered painful for our animal friends. So we administered pain relief and we believe it was as a result of this that Cleo was possibly able to bounce back from her horrific experience more quickly than expected.'

Beyond Courage

The mysterious traits of felines have been celebrated throughout history, and even the most sceptical among us have to admire how some cats and kittens survive against all odds. Whether you are a believer in the concept of lucky nine lives or not, these animals' courage and ability to endure extremes of emotional and physical hardship is almost inexplicable.

JOSH THE THREE-LEGGED CAT

Any cat with an exceptionally courageous personality will inevitably put the nine lives theory to the test. Some people may call them foolhardy but these determined cats have no issue with going the whole nine yards to extract as much from their lives as possible. In fact, larger-than-life characters like Josh, in this heart-warming story, seem to positively enjoy it!

'Josh. He's a cat you can't help but like — even my friends who don't like cats really adore him!' exclaimed Marjory Parish. But there's more to Josh than a cute face …

Marjory and Doug Parish of Devon, England, are understandably proud of Josh. Together with his sister, Missie, he came to stay with Marjory and Doug in May 1994 after their owner, a very close family friend, died of breast cancer. Both cats were then four years old although Majory had known them since kittenhood. Settling in was less traumatic than they had anticipated and soon Josh and Missie were very much at home with their adoptive owners.

For four years, Josh and Missie enjoyed a comfortable and relatively fuss-free existence. However, this charmed world was turned upside down when Josh turned eight. Marjory was out in the garden with friends when she noticed Josh limping towards them. His behaviour was quieter than usual and he wasn't at all interested in attention from the group in the garden. 'I took him to the vet when I discovered a large swelling on his joint,' explained Marjory. 'I thought that he had been in a local fight and that he would need a shot of antibiotics.' The vet gave Josh a thorough examination and agreed that the leg was swollen and prescribed antibiotics. But he was also suspicious of the swelling and suggested that Marjory and Doug bring him back in a week's time.

'Josh was still limping and wasn't comfortable at all, all week, and when we took him back to the vet, the swelling was larger. We tried not to think the worst, but the vet said he thought it was cancerous. But he also did not think there was time to check, as his instinct and experience told him it was nasty.' Marjory and Doug were in shock — they had known this vet for quite a number of years and completely trusted his judgement.

Josh stayed at the vet clinic and, without delay, his leg was amputated. The vet sent the leg off for analysis and his instincts were confirmed. Apparently it was a particularly unpleasant kind of fast-growing bone tumour. 'Our concern now was whether the amputation had happened in time,' said Marjory. 'We certainly didn't need to worry about Josh adapting to his new status, as he took it totally in his three-legged stride! He wasn't having any of that nonsense about staying in and using a litter tray while he looked like an oven-ready turkey; he insisted on going outside as usual!'

Marjory and Doug had a worrying few months while they waited to see if the amputation had caught the tumour in time or whether the cancer had spread. But Josh didn't seem to worry about anything. As if the entire incident had been just a regular check-up at the vet, he carried on with all his old pursuits — although he found his tree-climbing ability was no longer what it had been!

Then, just after his fur had grown back and Josh was back to his former humorous self, dashing around with his funny, three-legged gait, he fell prey to another accident that juggled with his second life.

'It could have been fatal but luckily timing was on his side — again,' smiled Marjory fondly. 'We're not sure why it happened but all we know is that somehow a heavy plant pot fell off the garden wall and straight onto Josh. Fortunately it missed his head and body but landed on his tail, cutting it to the bone.' Poor Josh was rushed off to the vet again — this time coming home with fifteen stitches to pull his tail back together, although the vet was concerned that there was too much damage and he might actually lose the tail. The vet made Josh wear a plastic ruff which made him look quite intimidating to Marjory's two female cats, while the other male cat walked backwards into a corner with his eyes fixed on Josh in astonishment. Rather than risk the nerves of the family pets, Marjory removed the ruff, confident that after his experience with his leg, he would not gnaw at his stitches. This judgement proved to be right and, as luck would have it, Josh's tail healed well.

Josh recovered from these indignities and carried on being 'Jack the Lad' in the local area. 'When we moved house in 2001,' laughed Majory, 'Josh instantly set about whizzing up and down the road making sure everyone, including all the local children, knew he was there and he was "the boss". For some reason, he took against a harmless cat over the road and even now will go and sit in front of his cat flap to prevent him from coming out! Josh is now almost fifteen years old but still thinks he's a youngster, and doesn't pay any attention to the fact that (to quote the legendary Peter Cook of that great British institution, *The Goons*) he is "deficient in the leg department".'

Marjory is fortunately spared the weight of Josh on her lap, as he is a big-boned rangy cat, but he always lies beside her — although she suspects this is more to prevent Missie or either of the other two cats from snuggling in than anything else. 'Without doubt, Josh is a big rascal but he has survived the trauma of losing his first owner plus some very narrow escapes without a fuss. We are proud of him; he is a very special, heroic cat and, of course, we love him dearly.'

A GOOD CHRISTMAS FOR RUDOLF

The 'miracle' has often been adopted by authors and filmmakers as a good fictional device. In this true story, however, a small kitten named Rudolf actually brings the idea of the miracle to life. His story is made even more special because it all began on Christmas Day.

Christmas Day is a special shift day at the Animal Welfare shelter in Adelaide, Australia. Volunteers are rostered to carry out the cleaning, feeding and exercising duties, although there is no vet present to carry out medical duties. On Christmas Day in 1995 one of the volunteers arrived at the shelter to find a ragged cardboard box at the front gate. She picked it up gently and carried it into the office to open it up. Inside she saw a tiny little kitten looking up at her. Hardly ten weeks old and barely breathing, he was quietly mewing. The volunteer picked up the kitten and quickly realised that his mewing was more like a cry for help — the central area of his face, particularly his nose, was covered in cigarette burns, leaving terrible, painful facial injuries. On closer study, the kitten also exhibited other signs of neglect, including malnourishment, ear mites, fleas and gingivitis. He was in such poor condition that it was surprising he was alive at all.

Usually in such cases, when kittens are so young, neglected and suffering such terrible injuries, the shelter vet would administer pain relief but would not hold out much hope of survival. Unfortunately animal welfare shelters the world over are under-resourced and cannot offer a high level of intensive care. However, as this was Christmas Day, the volunteer knew she couldn't leave the kitten and decided to take him home with her where she could give him her undivided attention. On the way home, she christened him Rudolf — a sad reminder of his facial injuries but appropriate to the festive occasion!

The volunteer gently bathed Rudolf's wounds and he gradually started to accept a little food. Despite everyone's assertion that it was unlikely he would survive, time passed and courageous Rudolf grew stronger as his injuries started to heal. His coat started to grow back until he transformed into a very healthy, white, semi-long-haired domestic with the most captivating gold eyes. But the volunteer discovered Rudolf had a more permanent disability: he was deaf.

As if for security, Rudolf followed the volunteer everywhere and at every opportunity would curl up in her arms. He used to suckle with one paw and knead with the other, and was most content when he was wrapped up in his blanket. He was clearly appreciative of the kindness that had saved him on Christmas Day.

But Rudolf still had many fears to overcome. It was obvious he had been severely abused, and even after living in an atmosphere of comfort and kindness with the volunteer and her husband, he was terrified of men. Rudolf insisted on living behind the fridge for nearly two years and would only come out when the volunteer was around.

Because Rudolf was deaf, he spent a lot of time simply watching the other cats as they leapt up to sit on the husband's knee, enjoying the pampering and fuss. Gradually, Rudolf started to become more trusting. After months of gentle stroking and petting, finally Rudolf leapt up onto the husband's knee. A major triumph!

With his growing confidence and marked handsomeness, the volunteer decided that it might be interesting to enter him into a local cat show. More and more people had commented on Rudolf's beauty with his angora-like coat and glinting gold eyes, and it would be wonderful to show him off.

Amazingly, Rudolf loved the spotlight and impressed the female judges and stewards so much that he won Domestic Show Cat of the Year for two years running in South Australia! Like the story of Tinkerbelle earlier in this book, perhaps his deafness helped him to ignore distractions and stand aloof and proud! He even warmed to the male judges and became a favourite amongst the stewards at the show.

Now, twelve years later, Rudolf is still going strong. 'I think of Rudolf as my miracle and he is my inspiration for helping animals,' smiled the volunteer. Thanks to that lucky Christmas Day in 1995 and a positive strength of character, Rudolf managed to overcome the pain and neglect of his early life to rise again as prince of the show. A Christmas fable come to life!

A MOTHER'S INSTINCT

Until discovered by the volunteer, it was Rudolf's own instinctive determination that helped him survive his battle for life. This same overwhelming instinct to preserve life at all costs is even more exaggerated in the case of a mother cat. No matter how extreme or horrific the situation may be, a mother will summon every atom of courage and energy to ensure that her young survive.

Cleo, a 'teenager' of around ten months of age, was a regular tortoiseshell cat who, since she was well-nourished and healthy, seemed to have been living in an apparently normal household. So it must have come as a terrible shock to her when, one day, Cleo's life was threatened by the humans she most trusted.

'Cleo's case was one of the most sad, but also one of the most rewarding, we have tended to in our clinic,' commented Sally, a veterinary nurse in New York. 'She seemed to be such a trusting cat and that made it seem even more heartless that she suffered such ill-treatment.'

It appeared Cleo had been taken out for a drive in the family car. While the car was still moving, she had been thrown out of the open window onto the roadside — and the car had continued to drive on, leaving Cleo to her fate.

Luckily for Cleo, a kind-hearted passer-by witnessed this unbelievably callous and inhumane act and rushed to help her. At first glance, Cleo appeared to have no serious visible injuries, so the passer-by very gently picked her up and carried her home. On the advice of the local vet, Cleo was immediately taken to the clinic. 'When she arrived, Cleo was in a state of shock but she did not struggle when we started to help her,' said Sally. 'She seemed to respond to softly spoken words of encouragement.'

The passer-by recounted what had happened and this only

added to the mystery. 'Cleo had obviously been looked after as a pet. Why would anyone want to do anything so cruel?' wondered Sally.

A thorough examination from the vet offered a possible, although disturbing, explanation. Miraculously, although the car had been moving when she was thrown out, Cleo had only sustained superficial wounds. However, the vet very quickly discovered that she was also pregnant — heavily pregnant, in fact. 'Cleo had obviously surprised her owners with her pregnancy. But I can't understand why on earth they would react to their pet in this way,' said Sally.

Sally and the vet were concerned that the combination of shock from the accident, together with the impact of the fall may have caused serious damage to the unborn kittens. 'At this stage it was a matter of "wait and see". It was amazing in itself that Cleo had managed to survive the fall.'

Cleo was watched around the clock to make sure she was comfortable until, only ten days later, to the delight and excitement of the veterinary team at the clinic, Cleo successfully gave birth to four healthy, playful kittens. As Sally remembered, 'It was just fantastic to see Cleo with her kittens. We all felt it was a great demonstration of her sheer determination and will to live.'

And the happy ending continues ... several months later, as soon as the kittens were weaned, Cleo and her offspring were all re-homed and are now living happily with their own pet-loving families.

PEG-LEG TWINKLE

The work of Animal Welfare organisations can expose some horrific and emotionally disturbing circumstances — as with the case of Cleo and her unborn kittens. But for the many volunteers and the paid members of staff, the chance to help these animals and witness the near-miraculous acts of courage and survival is all the reward they need. Peg-Leg Twinkle is possibly one of the most courageous cats that animal welfare worker Sarah Hartwell in the United Kingdom has ever had the good fortune to meet.

'Nobody held out much hope for the pretty Calico cat that one of our Humane Society officers had just taken to the vet's clinic one day in 1995. The cat had been found dragging a leg-hold trap, which are sometimes set to trap foxes, despite the fact that these barbaric devices are completely illegal in Britain,' recounted Sarah.

The cat had horrific injuries: the trapped paw was almost severed just below the dewclaw and one of the cat's hind legs had almost been stripped to the bone. As Sarah explained, 'At first we thought she had dragged herself out of one trap and then stumbled into another one. We'd heard of animals gnawing legs off to escape from traps; this looked as if she'd gnawed all the flesh off her back leg, or as if it had been pulled off by the jaws of the trap, like rolling back a shirt sleeve.'

Sarah and her colleagues decided to call the cat Twinkle, in reference to the lucky stars they were all hoping would shine on this brave cat. Leg-hold traps inflict such terrible injuries that usually amputation is a necessity, but in Twinkle's case it seemed impossible to amputate both the damaged forepaw and hind leg.

Although it seemed as if Twinkle had got to the end of her nine lives, Sarah also acknowledged that she looked far too healthy to be euthanased. She was friendly and in relatively good condition, which meant that she might have been someone's missing pet. 'Twinkle was fit and even a little plump and the only blood was from her lacerated forepaw and from her mouth where she had bitten at the trap.'

While performing the surgeries, the vet realised that the hind leg was actually an old injury that had left Twinkle with a pirate-style 'peg-leg' which allowed her to walk, run and jump, but not climb. 'The vet was surprised that Twinkle had not died of blood poisoning when the leg became mummified. The bone felt light and seemed fragile, but it was evidently strong enough for Twinkle to use,' said Sarah. 'Twinkle recovered well from surgery, but still nobody had reported losing a pretty Calico with a peg-leg, so she was released to a local animal shelter. If she was still unclaimed after two weeks she would be made available for adoption, though few people would be attracted to such a disfigured cat when there were plenty of perfectly formed kittens needing homes.'

One of the shelter helpers took on the role of looking after Twinkle during this period, but by the time the two weeks had elapsed, no fewer than ten people had already fallen in love with the 'personality cat with the peg-leg'. However, as the real owner had not come forward to claim Twinkle, the shelter helper decided to take her home.

A couple of weeks after being taken home, Twinkle surprised the vets and the animal shelter staff with the news that she was pregnant! Discounting the fact that her hind-leg injury may have been hereditary, the vet agreed that it was safe for Twinkle to go ahead with the pregnancy.

'Twinkle produced five darling kittens, three ginger and two black and white — and all normal. Despite the problems of only having three-and-three-quarter legs, she was a perfect mother. In fact Twinkle loved all kittens. After her own kittens were weaned and went to new homes, her owner took in some motherless kittens and Twinkle washed and cared for them as though they were her own,' smiled Sarah.

But the demands of pregnancy and birth took their toll on Twinkle and the vet noticed signs of infection in her peg-leg, which had suffered additional strain. 'There were signs of infection which ordinary antibiotics could not solve and there was a real danger of blood poisoning or gangrene if it was not treated.' Rather than risk Twinkle's life, the vet decided to amputate the leg, leaving Twinkle with only two-and-three-quarter legs.

'Without her "peg-leg" for support, it is a little harder for Twinkle to get around and cavort as other cats do. She moves with a lopsided gait as one fore leg is shorter than the other. But, despite her physical problems, Twinkle is still an active, happy cat who loves people and washes any kittens she can find,' commented Sarah.

Clearly Twinkle has extraordinary courage and the spirit to keep fighting. As Sarah so perfectly summed up, 'She has survived an illegal trap, the amputation of a front paw, a pregnancy when the odds were against her, a life-threatening infection and the amputation of a hind leg. She had also survived whatever illness or injury damaged her hind leg. You might expect this Calico survivor to be grouchy or bitter, but she has come through it all with a purr and a head-butt. Everyone who has met her says she is a true survivor!'

Home Sweet Home

Like humans, many animals are adept at finding their way home if they follow a regular route — homing pigeons even make a career out of it! Rest the reins on the homeward stretch of a pony-trek or let go of the dog's leash on the walk home and they will switch to autopilot as they find their way back to their warm and comfortable place of rest, food and love.

Cats, however, seem to take this natural homing instinct a giant leap further. In fact, some cats will literally go to extraordinary lengths to find their way to the safety and comfort of their favourite lap.

THE ULTIMATE FAITHFUL FRIEND

While cats are renowned for their 'pickiness' in trying out all members of the family and friends before choosing their favourite human to dote on, when the feeling is reciprocated the loyalty of a cat has no boundaries. Your feline friend will remain faithful and true, no matter what trials they may face. The story of Cosmic is an incredible tale of one cat's undying loyalty to his owner and his struggle to be reunited with the object of his affection — and it's got an ending worthy of a Hollywood screenplay.

Cosmic was the beloved childhood pet of Carolyn from Kiama in New South Wales, Australia. Inseparable friends and totally devoted companions from childhood through to the high school years, Cosmic used to travel on Carolyn's shoulder as she rode her bicycle to visit her school friends. 'People used to say he looked like a fur scarf,' laughed Carolyn. 'He literally used to spend every second with me — except during school time. He would curl up to sleep at the end of my bed and then hop on my shoulder in the morning to go downstairs to breakfast!'

Cosmic was always treated as 'one of the gang', and when Carolyn and her friends experimented with a new look, Cosmic enjoyed his own makeover swapping his usual white-and-ginger coat for a pet-friendly pink or purple hair rinse! Not surprisingly, Cosmic was well known in Kiama as a bit of a local character — adored not only by Carolyn and her friends but also by all the locals. The local butcher would save tasty morsels for the 'crazy cat', and during his rounds the postman would always linger to have a cuddle with Cosmic. 'I think everyone loved Cosmic because he was so entertaining. He would do really cute things on cue — like close his eyes in anticipation of a tickle! He was quite the local showman.'

After completing school, Carolyn realised that her future career plans would mean moving to the city of Sydney. Knowing how much Cosmic loved his favourite haunts in Kiama — and how much he had become part of the local landscape — Carolyn made the tough decision not to take Cosmic with her. 'It was heart-wrenching, the thought of not having my closest buddy with me. But I knew that Cosmic would not fit into my new city regime. It would have been cruel to take him with me, away from the open fields and his neighbourhood friends.' So, in 1990, Carolyn left Kiama for Sydney, and this marks the exact time when Cosmic mysteriously disappeared.

The family looked everywhere locally and asked everyone in the town if they had seen Cosmic. 'When I was living at home and still at school, Cosmic had been a real roamer during the day, so we all thought he had gone off on one of his expeditions,' explained Carolyn. 'When he didn't come home that night, we put up posters around Kiama, and everyone promised to let us know if they heard anything.'

But as the days turned into weeks, Carolyn and her family had no choice but to fear the worst. Cosmic would never stay away for more than a night, even when Carolyn had gone away on a holiday with her friends. 'We were all devastated at the thought that Cosmic may have had an accident and was lying somewhere, alone. I was so upset and blamed myself for moving to Sydney,' recalled Carolyn. The locals, including the vet, continued to look out for the white-and-ginger feline friend — but no sightings were reported.

Time passed and the weeks turned to months, and then it was already a year since Cosmic had disappeared. 'My family decided against getting another cat,' said Carolyn. 'We were so shaken and heartbroken at losing Cosmic that we couldn't even imagine getting to know another cat.'

Carolyn continued to live her busy life in Sydney and looked forward to hearing the family's news by phone in between her trips back to Kiama. So when her mother called her one summer's day in 1999, Carolyn had no idea that she was about to hear the most incredible news.

Out of the blue, on this sunny afternoon, Carolyn's mother had been busy with housework and had heard a persistent, loud 'Meow!' at the front door. Curious, she opened the door and looked down to see if she recognised a neighbour's cat. Right there, to her astonishment, stood the old family friend! After an unbelievable lapse of nine years Cosmic had come home!

Carolyn's mother hardly dared to believe her eyes! 'Mum thought he was a stray at first because he was a lot worse for wear, as you can imagine,' smiled Carolyn. 'But remember, Cosmic was more than a cat in our family, he really was another sibling — and my best friend. Mum looked at him closely and called "Cosmic" and he ran straight up to her and purred with his eyes closed.'

After receiving this startling news, Carolyn had no choice but to drive straight back to Kiama the next day to be reunited with her beloved Cosmic. 'It was a very teary reunion, as you can imagine, and I was concerned that he might be suffering from ill health. There were so many questions that would never be answered. Where had Cosmic been all these nine years? What had he been doing? He looked so unkempt that he couldn't possibly have lived with another family.'

The family and many locals believed that when Carolyn had left Kiama nine years ago, Cosmic had been heartbroken and had tried to follow her all the way to Sydney — a distance of 120 kilometres. But somehow he had lost the trail and failed to find his way, becoming completely lost. The vet confirmed that he had developed skin cancer, which accounted for his dishevelled appearance. This, coupled with his advanced age, meant that Cosmic didn't have that many more years left. 'It was almost like he'd survived just so that he could come back home to say his final farewell,' commented Carolyn.

His place in the family reinstated, Cosmic was treated like a king from that day onwards. 'Mum made sure he had the best quality morsels to eat, and I came home regularly. It was really amazing to have him back, almost surreal really, considering the amount of time he had been missing. I always felt that Cosmic was a particularly special cat, but to think of what he must have been through — and to come back home to be with us — it makes him into a true hero.'

Despite his ill health, Cosmic lived a life of cat-splendour for quite a few more years in the care of Carolyn's family — and brought more than a little heroic colour back into the local life of Kiama.

SCOTT THE INSCRUTABLE

When cats are loved and nurtured from kittenhood in a comfortable family environment, like Cosmic was, their determination to do whatever it takes, whatever the distance, to re-unite with their loved ones is incredible. Yet some cats, like Scott from Balmain, New South Wales, Australia, in this next story, only discover a unique sense of loyalty and belonging at a later stage in their life.

Scott was a real bruiser. He looked like a bouncer and behaved like a gangster. In fact, he was so tough that even his new family eventually re-christened him Begbie — in honour of the meanest character in the film version of Irvine Welsh's book *Trainspotting*. But above all, he was a lovable rogue who displayed the true fighting spirit of a born survivor.

A huge tabby, Scott was of indeterminate heritage. His corpulent body and relatively short legs, topped by a slightly misshapen head with a permanently bemused expression, gave him a decidedly quirky air. So his arrival at the home of the Thomas family came as more of a shock than a surprise!

Rosie Helena Thomas was only four years old when she arrived back from the park one Saturday, with her brother Jake and her mum and dad, to find an enormous and strange-looking cat sitting at the front gate of the family home. The family had to squeeze past him to walk through the garden into the house, and he had no qualms about following them inside. Rosie noticed that he was limping, so he immediately won the sympathy vote and was awarded a saucer of milk to help him on his way.

The family ushered him out of the house and through the front gate and encouraged him to go home. But he didn't move — and was still there the next morning. So Rosie's mum decided they should take him to the vet to see if he was microchipped.

'The cat was so big that I thought he was a bit scary a first,' remembered Rosie, 'so Mum carried him into the car to go to the vet. Although we already had a cat, Minxie, a cute little tortoiseshell, I was very excited about having a new cat.'

The vet told Rosie and her mum that the cat must have been living rough for a couple of months because, in spite of his size, he was in a poor state of health and was probably lacking in love and attention. The vet went on to tell them that the cat was certainly in a great amount of pain because he had a badly damaged mouth — it actually looked as though it had been burned and there were some teeth missing. 'The vet thought maybe he had bitten into an aerosol can or something, when he was out looking for food. So it was pretty amazing that he had managed to survive, because eating and drinking must have been very painful for him,' explained Rosie.

After the medical examination, the vet checked the cat for a microchip but found none, which meant that it would be virtually impossible to locate his owner. So there was nothing for it but to take him home.

Both Rosie and Jake were very excited about the new family cat and decided to call him Scott. 'I was really happy and spent all day with him, giving him little bits of food. The vet had told us he was about two years old, but he was still a huge cat for his age. Scott just wanted to stay out in the front garden — he wasn't really bothered about coming inside. But he started to spray everywhere to mark his territory, which Minxie wasn't very happy about. He also tried to scratch and bite if we tried to pick him up. Mum explained that it was probably because he had been treated very badly and was now not very trusting of humans. I thought he looked like a

Fishing Cat — a small tiger — like one I had seen at Taronga Zoo in Sydney.'

Scott immediately settled into his adoptive family's life — after all, he had researched and handpicked his new home. 'It felt like he had chosen us to be his new family,' smiled Rosie, 'and after a while, Scott didn't mind if Jake and I patted him, and he even started to let Mum pick him up. Dad was still a bit afraid of him and would have to throw a towel over Scott to pick him up! Scott used to hide behind doors and then jump out on Dad or swipe him with his claws — Mum thought it was like Kato leaping at Inspector Clouseau in the *Pink Panther* films.'

Although the family had never noticed Scott in the neighbourhood, he seemed to know where he was going when he went off exploring during the day, always making sure he returned for supper when all the family were home. 'He was pretty independent, even though he loved being around us,' said Rosie. 'One day he made the mistake of jumping off the fence into the next-door garden — and into the territory of our neighbour's cat-detesting dog! We heard a lot of barking and loud meowing and then it all went quiet. Mum rushed around and saw the funniest thing: Scott had the dog backed into a corner and was snarling at him, swiping out with his claws! Mum finally managed to pick Scott up and carried him home. He acted as if the whole thing didn't bother him, and then he sprayed my shoes, so he got put outside again.'

Family life was never quite the same in the Thomas household after the arrival of Scott. Rosie's mum explained that it just like having a stroppy teenager in the house to complete the family! For Rosie and Jake, Scott was the source of many hilarious stories that kept both themselves and their friends entertained. 'One day, Scott was chasing a bird up a tree in our garden, which was hanging over the swimming pool. He climbed higher and higher and then the bird flew away. Mum could hear the leaves rustling and she said Scott looked so funny up there because he was so enormous. The branch wasn't very big and it started to bend right across the pool. It got lower and lower, and then Scott slipped and fell with a huge splash into the shallow end. Mum rushed outside and ran down the steps of the pool, still wearing her trousers, to scoop Scott out! She got soaking wet and Scott was a bit quieter that night — but he did sit on Mum's knee all night to thank her.'

After Scott had been living with the Thomases for a year or so, the family decided that the time was right to introduce a new puppy to the family — Betty, a Staffordshire Bull Terrier. After making sure that Scott was safely locked outside in the back garden, the Thomases went after school to collect Betty. But when they returned home, somehow Scott had found his way back into the house and was sitting on top of the kitchen bench, like a judge waiting for the trial. What ensued was the kind of physical 'relationship test' that is thankfully unique to cats and dogs. 'Betty saw him and immediately jumped after him,' explained Rosie. 'Scott slipped off the bench and landed on his back, but got up really quickly and started to have a fight with Betty. I remember being scared, and so was Jake. We were shouting at Mum and Dad to get them to stop the fight. Betty seemed to have jumped on top of Scott but he was going mad. Mum finally pulled Betty off and Scott tried to jump up to attack her, but Dad threw a towel over Scott and put him outside. The next day, we were nervous about leaving them while we went out, but after about a week they were the best of friends and Scott and Betty even used to sleep in the same basket!'

Scott seemed to single out Betty as his favourite member of the family — possibly because they were both newcomers and they shared a passion for food. Rosie remembered, 'They used to wait in the kitchen when Mum was cooking but poor Scott always used to get the blame if any food went missing. And once, when he was hovering around Mum, she tripped over him and accidentally dropped a hot baking tray on his head. He dashed out of the kitchen and didn't come back for ages, even though Betty was getting all the scraps.'

Rosie and Jake were rightly proud of Scott for his unflinching involvement in family life! A lesser-spirited cat may have deserted them at the first sign of trouble. Both Jake and Rosie felt privileged that he had chosen their household to be his home. 'Scott was such a cool cat to have as a pet and we were all really, really sad when he finally died,' recalled Rosie fondly. 'He must have been about eight or nine years old when he died, which isn't very old for cat years. But he had had so many adventures that I think he must have finally worn himself out. We still miss him — and so do our friends. They loved our stories about him and they all thought he made a great guard dog because of the way he used to jump on anyone coming into the home!'

STOWAWAY!

Home is where the heart is — and all cat owners know this is just as true for cats as it is for humans, no matter where 'home' may be. In the case of Scott, his true home was discovered with the love and affection of the Thomas family. For Colin's, a friendly tortoiseshell cat, home is somewhere a little less conventional, but no less loving.

With her own website, www.westgate.co.nz, and a stack of regular international fan mail, Colin's, the unintentionally well-travelled cat, has achieved world celebrity status!

As a permanent resident at Port Taranaki's tanker terminal in New Zealand, Colin's is considered to be just as important as any other employee. She has her own Staff Identification

Card — in charge of Fridge Security — and the office is littered with photographs of Colin's 'doing' the paperwork and other office jobs! In fact, it seems like she runs the office with all eight, strong, tanker terminal men responding to her every request.

The tanker terminal has been her home away from home ever since 1992, when she was discovered there as an abandoned kitten by the then manager, Colin Butler. Colin decided to adopt the cat as the terminal mascot, and from that moment she was known around Port Taranaki as 'Colin's'. Adored by all, Colin's soon forged a bond with the terminal team and discovered that, by being vocal, she could ensure a steady supply of food and treats! However, it was this newfound skill combined with her insatiable appetite that explains how, nine years later, she suddenly ended up taking an unforgettable journey.

It was on Monday, 19 November 2001, that Colin's was first discovered to be missing. The Tanker Terminal Manager was naturally worried and sent an internal email to all staff to keep a look out for the much-loved feline.

From: Newton King Tanker Terminal Manager
Sent: Monday, 19 November 2001 11:14
To: Everyone List Member
Subject: [Everyone] NKTT cat {01}

Colin's (the Cat) has gone AWOL since Thursday 16/11/01. If anyone has seen her since, please advise the terminal or the watchhouse. Colin's is a nine-year-old tortoiseshell cat. We are waiting for her safe return. Finder gets a chocolate fish award and a special mention in a newsletter.

Thanks

Arun Chaudhari, NKTT Manager.

As a precaution, a message was also sent out to all ships that had departed from the port, since Colin's had the habit of hanging around the tankers in the hope of coaxing food from the kitchens.

Shipping agent Mr Larry Stewart soon received an email from the Master of a Korean vessel, MT *Tomiwaka* — and the missing cat mystery was solved. The email read:

Good morning! Mr Larry. Currently our 2nd engineer has managed the cat. He said that the cat was following him but crying and supposed the reason of crying may be hungry. Therefore, he brought the cat on board to give some food and intended to land ashore again prior to sailing. But he forgot it due to sleeping. Therefore, please advise what kind of measure I can take if necessary. I will do all necessary steps to follow your requirements, if any.

Colin's was now an official stowaway heading for South Korea!

The Korean crew members were as smitten with Colin's as the Port Taranaki team and, anxious to let everyone know that she was well, they emailed photographs of her to a local New Zealand newspaper, *The Daily News*, to show that she was happy and, of course, well-fed.

On hearing that she was safe and well, the Port Taranaki team was keen to find a way to bring Colin's home safely. The potential problem was that if she were taken ashore in Korea to await a returning tanker, she would have to face quarantine for several months before being allowed back into New Zealand. The only way around this was to organise a ship-to-ship transfer rescue mission … mid-ocean!

By this time, Colin's had already been aboard the MT *Tomiwaka* for two weeks and was somewhere north of Papua New Guinea. Although she was a tanker terminal cat, she had never developed her sea-legs and reports from the ship confirmed that she had suffered sea-sickness for a couple of days into the journey. This, however, didn't last long and soon she was happily tucking into salmon and beef followed by a rest on her bed — the sofa in the second engineer's cabin. For Colin's it was just a holiday; she had no idea of the international dealings that were now underway to bring her home!

The Port Taranaki team worked hard to try to arrange a mid-sea ship-to-ship cat transfer but, after much negotiation, the idea was abandoned as being too risky. The MT *Tomiwaka* was a methanol tanker and any possible collision could cause an explosion. It seemed that the only option was for Colin's to arrive in South Korea and then wait for another New Zealand-bound tanker for the return journey. But how could they arrange for someone to look after Colin's and where would she stay?

Just when it all seemed impossible, the perfect solution turned up. During her escapade, the adventurous cat's story had been followed closely by the world press and, as a result of the widespread media coverage of her plight, a donation was made that would cover the costs to fly the Port Duty Superintendent and cat lover Gordon MacPherson out to South Korea and return with Colin's. 'From the beginning I've said I would go and bring her back. I suppose I'm the number one provider. When Colin [the original owner] left, he was concerned because he couldn't take the cat with him, so I took over,' Gordon told local newspaper *The Daily News*.

After eighteen days at sea and some 9600 kilometres later, the incredible adventure ended at the South Korean port of Yeosu. Reunited with Colin's, Gordon didn't hesitate to scoop her up for a hug which was recorded for posterity by the local and international TV crews that had turned up to record the event.

From there, Colin's and Gordon travelled to Seoul to ensure that the correct quarantine procedures were carried out ready for the trip home. Already, Terminal Manager Mr Chaudhari had talked to the Ministry of Agriculture and Forestry officials and shipping agents and had got clearance from local quarantine officers, since Colin's would be travelling in a sealed cage from the tanker *Tomiwaka* to Seoul airport and would therefore not need to spend time in quarantine in either Korea or on her return to New Zealand.

On 5 December 2001, Colin's arrived back in New Plymouth, New Zealand, to a hero's welcome. More than 50 workers, New Plymouth Mayor Peter Tennent and Taranaki Cat Club representatives cheered her arrival along with international television camera crews. A white limousine took her on her final journey home — as befitting her newfound celebrity status.

New Plymouth Mayor Mr Tennent publicly thanked Colin's for bringing publicity to New Plymouth and awarded her an honorary ambassadorship of the city in recognition of her involvement in the enhancement of international relations. Colin's was also made an honorary member of the Cat Club.

Today, Colin's takes her fame in her stride and relies on her own website to do the talking for her. 'Colin's doesn't stray far from her home these days. She occasionally wanders down the wharf with me, though she doesn't go onboard vessels any more,' said Terminal Superintendent and rescuer, Gordon MacPherson. 'She's never been as adventurous since her epic voyage; she's now an older and wiser cat. She still hunts, stalks seagulls occasionally, though the last time she caught anything was about a year ago when she got a bird. So she's not really earning her keep, which I guess is understandable since she must be about twelve years old by now. She's still cunning, timing it well with getting fed before people go off duty and then approaching the next person for another feed after they start their shift.'

A true adventurer, Colin's overcome what many cats will never endure — sea-sickness and jetlag — to make it back home to the unconditional love of her extended family at the tanker terminal.

FEELS LIKE HOME

Popeye, the cherished white cat in the Dives family, was rather less excited about his adventure than was Colin's. Not only was he a poor traveller, he was also adamant that he would not be moved from his beloved home.

Imagine the scene: 25 years ago Popeye was happily living in Newcastle, New South Wales, Australia, alongside the family Labrador, Cleo; a red canary; Natalie Dives, aged eight; brother Brad, aged five; and little sister Angela, one.

Comfortable in his territory, with a good relationship with his cat neighbours, Popeye had an enviable existence. Then, one day, Mum, Trish Dives, announced that the family was moving 275 kilometres away to Tamworth, where her husband Jimmy Dives had been relocated for his work as an ethical drugs representative prescribing to GPs.

Somehow everyone — humans and animals — would all have to fit into the family's Ford Cortina for the trip to Tamworth. Cleo would share the passenger seat in the front, while Natalie, Brad and Angela would squeeze in the back with the red canary, complete with cage, resting on their knees. But Popeye posed more of a problem. As he was renowned for his reluctance to sit still for even the shortest amount of time, Trish was not prepared to risk sanity and safety by putting him in the back with the children and the canary for the four-hour journey.

Jimmy had a great idea. He would consult with one of his doctors, who was also a huge cat fan, to work out the best way to transport Popeye. After much deliberation, Jimmy returned home with a tiny pillbox containing the perfect solution: Valium. The doctor had suggested that, as a reliable relaxant, Valium might be the best solution to get Popeye through the journey with the least amount of trouble. Although unsure of the amount to prescribe, the family tried two tablets, crushed into Popeye's food in the morning.

Within a short period of time, Popeye fell into a peaceful sleep and Trish popped him into his comfy catbox stowed in the boot, ready for the journey. The plan was to check on Popeye at each car stop.

Trish was the nominated driver and at hourly intervals she stopped the car to let the children and Cleo stretch their legs. She checked on Popeye at every interval but each time Popeye was in silent slumber, oblivious to the journey.

Finally, after the four-hour trek, the Dives arrived in Tamworth, where they were greeted by torrential rain — the worst rainfall experienced in the region for many years — which succeeded in cutting off one end of Tamworth from the other. As if this wasn't bad enough, when they pulled up outside the house they were intending to rent for the first year, it was still occupied by the previous tenants — two adults with teenagers and their Labrador! There was no alternative but for both families, plus animals, to stay in the house.

In the pouring rain, Trish unloaded the children, Cleo, canary and Popeye and took them into the house to make them comfortable. All had survived the trip admirably and Popeye was still cosily asleep in his catbox. Realising that he might be completely disorientated when he awoke, Trish decided the best place for him was in the outdoor toilet — a dry place that was well away from the Labradors and close enough to maintain regular checks.

Twenty hours later, Popeye finally woke up in Tamworth, in the outdoor toilet, to find a small bowl of food and water awaiting him. But instead of enjoying his new surroundings, Popeye noticed that the door was slightly open and took off. When Trish went to check on him, she found him gone.

At first the Dives thought Popeye was just checking out his new neighbourhood and would be back by the end of the day. He didn't have the character of a runaway cat and was certainly more accustomed to a comfortable life as part of the family. But he didn't come back that day or the next. Trish tried to keep up the family's spirits by suggesting that everyone call out his name in the garden, while searching under the bushes — but to no avail. Naturally the children were devastated. Days turned into weeks. The Dives were finally left with the house to themselves and so set about making it into their family home — which only made Popeye's disappearance even more evident. Every day the children would take it in turns to go out into the garden to bang the spoon against the can of cat food, in the desperate hope that Popeye would leap across the garden.

After six long weeks, Trish and the rest of the family finally resigned themselves to the thought that Popeye might have met with an unhappy fate. There had been no sign of him since he'd disappeared and none of their new friends and neighbours had spotted him.

Then, one evening, Trish and Jimmy said goodnight to the children and the babysitter, went into the garage and climbed into their new family car, ready to go out. Jimmy turned on the headlights, preparing to drive out the garage, when Trish yelled out, 'It's Popeye!' As if by magic, there on the driveway stood Popeye, looking emaciated and very dishevelled with scabby ears. Trish could hardly believe it. Poor Popeye looked desperate, as thought he hadn't eaten for weeks and had been in a hefty battle for his new territory. But, above all, he looked very relieved to be home. Trish picked him up and he nestled into her as she carried him inside the house. He demolished a small bowl of food and water in seconds and then spent all evening sitting on Trish's knee. When the children woke up next morning they could hardly believe it: Popeye was back with the family.

It took less than a week for Popeye to fit back into the swing of Dives family life — and the children were delighted to discover that he enjoyed cuddles more than ever. A trip to the vet revealed that Popeye was not suffering from anything more serious than lack of good-quality food and some love and attention. However, the mystery of his disappearance still puzzled the family. Some of the neighbours thought he may have been living in the timber yard at the end of the road all this time and had returned because he had heard the children in the garden. Trish wondered if he had perhaps just tried to find his way back to Newcastle.

The mystery was never solved, but it seemed like history was repeating itself when, a couple of months later, Popeye disappeared once again. Just like the first time, he simply took off into the bushes and then failed to return. It seemed like, even though he loved being in the company of everyone in the family, he just couldn't find a place to settle in the house. Of course, Trish and the children were beside themselves with worry again and, together with friends and neighbours, organised a search of the surrounding area, including the timber yard. Popeye was nowhere to be found. Then after a couple of weeks, just like before, Popeye suddenly reappeared, starving and very grubby. Popeye was lovingly welcomed back into the family and was even granted permission to sleep on the children's beds in an attempt to make him feel at home.

By now the Dives had been living in Tamworth for almost a year, and the house they had been building across town was finally ready. As Trish was planning the much-awaited family move, she was also on her guard at the thought of uprooting poor Popeye yet again. But then she remembered an old wives' tale that someone had told her after Popeye's first disappearing act: if you put butter on a cat's paws when you move house, it will never stray. The cat will be so busy cleaning its paws in the new surroundings, that it will have no time to think about running away!

On arrival at the new family home, Trish unloaded the children, Cleo the Labrador and the canary and then carried Popeye straight into the kitchen. There, she dabbed butter onto each of Popeye's paws before allowing him to jump down. Popeye took off, but this time ran from room to room leaving greasy pawprints throughout the house! Finally he settled in the new sitting room and started the long and thorough ritual of paw cleaning.

Whether it was the settling effect of the butter or the comforting aura of the new home, Trish couldn't say, but Popeye established himself in the house from the first day they arrived. He quickly found his favourite spots for eating, sleeping and sunning himself and became friends with the neighbours' animals. 'It was like he had found his true home,' said Trish, 'and thankfully for the family, he never tried to run away again.'

KIT-KAT AKA JAMES BOND

Cats are highly praised for their amazing agility and balance — and both can be essential requirements when they have to switch on their homing radar. Ben Davies, the owner of Kit-Kat, believes his cat was, without doubt, inspired by James Bond when faced with astonishing challenges on her journey home — but though her determination was shaken, it was definitely not stirred.

Ben Davies, his sister and mother lived on the outskirts of the northern coastal town of Forster in New South Wales, Australia. Life in such a rural setting was perfect for the Davies family and their much-treasured family cat, Kit-Kat, a beautiful eight-year-old, black Persian. The Davies had raised Kit-Kat from a kitten so she was as much a part of the family as the children. Thoroughly cosseted with plenty of cuddles and only the very best gourmet cat food, Kit-Kat was also very much in touch with her instinctual feline side. She liked to think of herself as adventurous and loved the countryside, climbing trees and spending hours exploring in the garden and beyond during the daytime, while she waited for Ben and his younger sister Kylie to return home from school. Then she would wait at the front door, ready to leap on them with a furry welcome!

'Kit-Kat had been around for as long as I could remember,' said Ben. 'She was a truly adored cat even though she had a bad habit of coming inside from the rain, soaking wet, and pushing her way down to your feet under the blankets when she thought you were asleep! Not to mention leaving the insides of rodents on the kitchen table in the morning as a present from her … yuck!'

But on one particular evening in spring, Kit-Kat's daredevil determination was put well and truly to the test.

Ben's mother was in a hurry. She was already running late

for the fifteen-minute journey into town and she couldn't be late for the school's annual music concert. An accomplished recorder player, Ben was to be the star performer with the school orchestra. So, without a second thought, Ben's mother grabbed her bag and car keys, dashed to the family car — a reliable Audi, resplendent with roof racks — jumped in and drove off into the night.

As she drove along the quiet, lonely, winding roads at around 60 kilometres per hour, she realised that the driver of the car behind her was flashing his lights and beeping his horn. Since it was an isolated area she didn't really feel safe pulling over, especially for a stranger, so she kept driving. The driver behind her kept beeping his horn and made a few attempts to overtake her, despite it being unsafe to do so on the winding road. By now Ben's mum was increasingly concerned that this person might be dangerous and trying to scare her. She decided to accelerate until she could at least reach somewhere safer and more public, like the caravan park up ahead.

Then suddenly she heard a strange thumping noise on her car. In a state of panic, thinking that she had either hit something or that something may have been thrown at the car, she decided to pull off to the side of the road and hopefully allow this intimidating driver to pass. Once she had stopped, the driver — a man — pulled up alongside and shouted, 'Couldn't you see me trying to get your attention? I've been beeping my horn and flashing my lights. You had a cat on your roof racks for the last ten minutes and it's just fallen off back down the road.'

Ben's mum was devastated. She knew instantly what had happened. Kit-Kat, the much-loved family cat, had always loved to lie on the car roof! But with Ben's mother running late, she'd been in such a hurry she hadn't even thought to check whether she was there. Poor Kit-Kat must have been terrified hanging onto the roof rack at 60 kilometres per hour for all that time!

Ben's mum leapt out of the car and thanked the driver, and then ran back to look for Kit-Kat. She looked all around the area where she could remember hearing the bump, and further down the hill too, in case Kit-Kat had rolled to safety. Of course, the search was hampered by the fact that it was, by now, pitch black. The area was also known to be inhabited by dingoes, snakes and other potentially deadly bush creatures. So, very reluctantly and in a state of shock, Ben's mother gave up the search, assuming that poor Kit-Kat could not possibly have survived her ordeal.

Of course, when Ben's mum finally turned up in town at the school concert to tell the family what had happened, everyone was distraught. Kylie had always treated Kit-Kat as her own cat and had loved to feed and groom her. For Ben and Kylie it was like losing a sibling — their wonderful black Persian cat had literally grown up with them. Over the next few months, Ben's mum gradually recovered from the combined shock and guilt of the accident and the rest of the family slowly accepted the loss.

Then, out of the blue, six months later on a rainy Saturday afternoon, Ben's mum opened the front door to go out to the car. There, on the doorstep, dripping with rain, and a little angry, stood a very bedraggled version of their own precious Kit-Kat! A closer look confirmed it was indeed her — although in a heart-breakingly terrible state — so Ben's mum gently lifted Kit-Kat and carried her into the house to dry her and give her a much-deserved cuddle and a dish of food.

The family was delighted, relieved and incredulous. Kit-Kat was a truly miraculous survivor! She had endured the breakneck car ride astride the roof racks — possibly hanging on by her claws — had managed to land in one piece after falling from the moving car, had survived a six-month trek through bushland inhabited by deadly snakes, spiders and dingoes, and had managed to find her way back home. She must have been the luckiest cat alive!

A thorough check-up at the vet revealed that, amazingly, Kit-Kat was suffering nothing more than treatable malnutrition and lack of care. The Davies family gratefully nurtured Kit-Kat back to health and gradually managed to calm her understandably over-anxious behaviour. 'She must have been through so much and so many lives,' said Ben, 'but so had we, because we had missed her so much as part of the family. It was so great to have her home.'

Cat Heroes

Unconditional love is one of the greatest rewards showered upon all cat owners. As a valued member of the family, a cat's loyalty and empathy can know no bounds, drawing on their uncanny sixth sense to protect or fuss over owners during the most vulnerable and needy times. Yet while some owners joke that their cat would do anything for them, some very brave felines have literally risked life and limb to protect their loved ones in the face of adversity.

TO CATCH A THIEF

There are many fictional accounts of how the most unlikely candidates rise above themselves to become heroic figures; like Superman or even Forrest Gump, it's the stuff that the most popular Hollywood films are made of. Agatha, a gentle family cat, could easily be a contender for such international celebrity on account of her incredible intuition and determination to safeguard her owners.

Lynn Seely of Mechanicsburg, Pennsylvania, in the United States, was the proud owner of a blind and amazing Calico cat called Agatha. In spite of her disability, Agatha was never short of an adventure — and she always seemed to come out of her scrapes with flying colours! On one cold winter's night, Agatha surpassed even her own high standards when her quick and heroic actions won her the admiration of not just the Mechanicsburg police force but the entire town!

Lynn and her husband lived with Agatha in a comfortable two-storey home in a quiet neighbourhood. On this particular night, a thick blanket of snow covered the streets, so Lynn was happy to turn in early for the night, ensuring that all windows and doors were tightly shut against the cold winter air. However, at about 3 a.m., while Lynn and her husband were sleeping, an unexpected event occurred in the alley that ran between their home and the house next door.

A man — definitely not a local, but someone who had clearly familiarised himself with the neighbourhood — slipped into the alley and located the small side window of the house. From there, he was completely concealed from the street, making it easy to remain undetected. He carefully removed the screen, then pushed up the window slowly, shining his torch into the room to check that nothing was blocking his path. He must have noticed the large, 2-metre-tall cat tree that was positioned partially in front of the window, but it didn't deter him; he still had plenty of room to climb in without making any noise.

However, he failed to notice the large Calico cat who had been carefully listening to the sounds of the screen being removed and the window being opened. Agatha was crouched inside a tunnel in the cat tree and was already poised for action. She knew her owners were tucked up in bed, so who was this stranger who had opened the window to the cold night air?

For Agatha, war had been declared. Her house was being invaded and the household's safety was at stake. Her fur was on end and her ears were pitched forward, attentive to the slightest sound. It was up to her and she was ready!

The burglar slowly eased one leg through the window, then stuck his face through as he gripped the sides of the window and prepared to jump into the room. In that split second, as his face was coming through the window, Agatha acted. She leapt up, fully wired for the attack. Jumping straight at his face, her enormous claws scratched and tore while she sank her teeth into his cheek for good measure. The burglar was completely caught off guard and, in a mixture of surprise and terror, yelled out and fell backwards out of the window. In a state of pure panic, with blood pouring down his face, his foot caught on the way out and his shoe was left dangling as clear evidence on the window latch. The fall was soft, but freezing, and the maimed burglar was up in an instant and running for his life, leaving extraordinary patterns of shoe and sock prints in the snow.

Lynn and her husband were awakened by a blood-curdling scream that sounded too close to be from outside. They both got up and quietly went down the stairs.

'As we crept down the stairs and into the dining room we could see that the window was open! We turned on the light and there in the open window was a shoe. My heart was pounding as my husband dialled the police,' explained Lynn. 'Then I noticed Aggie. She was fluffed up larger than I believed was possible. She was turned towards me and her tail was swishing back and forth like it did when she was really happy about something. How odd! Why would she be happy? As I came over to where she was, she chortled at me in her sweetest voice. She was really proud of herself for some reason.'

Lynn noticed that Agatha had something on her white paws and was shocked to see that it was blood. Her first thought was that Agatha had hurt herself — particularly as there was also blood on the cat tree. 'But then it became clear to me that Aggie had attacked the robber as he tried to enter the window!' Lynne said, 'What a cat!'

The police arrived shortly after the call and checked out the alley. The first thing they noticed were the odd footprints left by the burglar. 'The policeman just stood there shaking his head as a big grin spread across his face,' recalled Lynn proudly. 'He agreed that it did appear as if our cat had stopped the robber from entering the house. There had been a few crimes in the area recently and the policeman suggested that he probably preferred two-storey homes because that meant he could plunder the lower level without being detected. That was where the TV, VCR and other valuables usually were. He also would go up to the bedrooms and check for cash and jewellery as well as credit cards — but so far, no one had woken up to catch him.'

While the evidence was being gathered and documented, Agatha strutted around the room, enjoying the attention and adoration from Lynn, her husband and the police team. 'The policeman said that this robber had been particularly thorough in his research and would not go to a home that had a dog,' continued Lynn, 'but he added that he'd probably think twice about one with cats now, too! We all laughed, but later I must admit that it was frightening that a robber had almost gotten into our home except for the very brave actions of Aggie!'

Approximately one month later, a man was arrested in the area for selling stolen property — and he was particularly noticeable for the terrible scratches on his face. Although Lynn and her husband were unable to identify him as their burglar, it was a rather incredible coincidence. 'The policeman contacted us to advise us of the arrest, and he told us how the burglar had been asked if a "lion" had attacked him,' Lynn chuckled. 'He was also told that a "poor little blind kitty" had attacked a robber in Mechanicsburg … did he happen to know who that robber was?'

The house-burglar never admitted responsibility for this crime, but justice prevailed and he was given a prison sentence for other burglaries. However, Lynn discovered that he wasn't going to get off lightly for the crime against their household. Word had quickly spread and the police as well as his fellow criminals in prison teased the burglar mercilessly with the nickname 'Attack Cat Jack'.

Agatha basked in the attention from the community for some time after this memorable evening. After all, she had single-handedly put an end to the spree of neighbourhood burglaries.

Sadly, after a gradual decline in health, Lynn's beloved hero-cat Aggie passed away in January 2005 and is greatly missed by her many friends and admirers.

PUSSKIN THE HERO

As Agatha's story clearly shows, loyalty and bravery come in all guises. Although blind, Agatha put her size and strength to good use! This is a remarkable tale about a very small but also very brave cat: Pusskin. Pusskin's owner, Elsie, regarded her cats as working animals rather than pampered pets, but she would find herself greatly indebted to Pusskin for her extreme loyalty. Like many treasured pets. Pusskin was prepared to go to any lengths — even to risk her own life — to protect her owner.

Pusskin was a tiny black cat who weighed no more than 2 kilograms even though she was a fully-grown adult. Usually, a cat of this size would serve little useful purpose on a busy but remote cattle station located in rural Australia. She had been the runt of a litter of four kittens and, rather uncharacteristically, Elsie had taken pity on Pusskin and decided to help her to survive by feeding her by hand. Pusskin repaid the favour by following Elsie absolutely everywhere.

Elsie tried to encourage Pusskin to follow the example of the other cats on the cattle station — all independent felines working hard, day and night, catching rats and mice. There was no room for the luxury of a pet kitty. Life on the cattle station was tough for cats, with the risk of dingoes and other wild animals combined with the danger of potential injury from cattle and machinery. It was important that Pusskin learned to work for her living and look after herself. But this tiny black cat continued to follow Elsie around and, instead of adopting the working habits of the other cats, she became Elsie's unofficial assistant.

One day, as Elsie was walking toward a sheep pen, her mind on the rest of the station chores that needed to be completed before dark, she was suddenly distracted by Pusskin. The little cat had raced ahead and was now hissing and jumping around a patch of grass. Elsie moved forward cautiously until she was almost on top of Pusskin. Incredibly, her little cat was leaping around the biggest and deadliest Red-Bellied Black Snake Elsie had ever seen. Pusskin kept teasing the snake as it raised its head and tried to strike at the little black bundle of fur.

Heart thumping, Elsie realised she only had two choices: she could try to rescue Pusskin from the snake and risk getting bitten by the venomous and potentially dangerous creature; or she could leave the cat and snake to their deadly fight and save herself whilst the snake was distracted. Elsie knew of bush stories that recounted how people had actually been chased by Red-Bellied Black Snakes.

Knowing that she probably would have stepped right onto the snake if Pusskin hadn't alerted her to it, Elsie had to make the heart-wrenching decision to back away and save her own life, while inwardly thanking the brave little cat for sacrificing its life for hers. Elsie went back to the station homestead with a sad heart. In spite of herself she had grown attached to Pusskin and the extent of her loyalty had deeply touched Elsie.

Three days later, while Elsie was busy with her station work, she was amazed to see a very sick and dishevelled Pusskin staggering into her homestead. In a state of disbelief, Elsie gently picked her up to assess her injuries — it was incredible that the cat had survived, and even more so that she had managed to make her way home.

Pusskin in arms, Elsie drove the station truck out to the sheep pen where the savage fight had taken place. There lay the biggest Red-Bellied Black Snake that Elsie had ever seen — dead. Somehow, in the style of an age-old fable, the smallest cat had killed the biggest snake.

For the rest of her time on the cattle station, in gratitude and admiration for her heroism, Pusskin was relieved of her duties and lived the life of a pampered pet as Elsie's constant companion. Later, when Elsie retired and moved to the city, Pusskin and her reputation went with her. Elsie was proud of her tiny cat and loved to tell her miraculous story. Indeed, Pusskin was considered by all who knew her to be a mighty hero, and when Elsie wanted to rent an apartment even the real estate agent agreed to waive the 'no pets' rule when he heard how Pusskin had saved Elsie's life. Who said black cats are unlucky?

ONE GOOD TURN DESERVES ANOTHER
Gratitude can take many guises. For Pusskin, Elsie's kindness

towards her meant that she was prepared to make the ultimate sacrifice when it came to safeguarding Elsie's safety. Other cats are no less dedicated to their families and will also do everything they can to save the lives of their loved ones.

The story of Brother, a cute five-year-old cat, begins before he was born. His mother, a stray cat, had found her way into the Reiman family's backyard shed in Utah, in the United States, where, shortly afterwards, she gave birth to her litter on a mattress wedged in the rafters.

The Reimans were oblivious to their new tenants, even though the kittens and their mother lived in the rafters for a few weeks. Then, on Mother's Day morning, the mattress slipped, probably because of the wriggling little kittens, and they all tumbled down into a gap behind the wall. The plaintive meows of the kittens were clearly audible to Jon and Kimberly Reiman, who were relaxing in their yard. Satisfied that the cries were not from their own two cats, Jon followed the direction of the meows and determined that the sounds were coming from behind the wall in the shed.

Jon quickly removed a section of the wall and there, snuggled together, he discovered the litter of young kittens. The family was delighted that the recovery had been successful, but the mother cat's reaction was not so positive. She wouldn't take the kittens back. Without hesitation, Kimberly and her daughters took over the role and shared the bottle-feeding shifts until the kittens were old enough to be adopted.

The kittens were adorable and the Reimans had no difficulty in finding good, responsible adoptive homes. But they decided to keep one of their little charges — and they called him Brother. Five years later, after Jon and his family had saved his life, it was Brother's time to return the favour.

Brother was devoted to his adoptive family right from the start, following them around the house and checking where they were just like a guard dog! And it was this unrelenting attentiveness that would help to save the lives of the entire family. On 5 April 1999, Kimberly followed her usual evening ritual, which included turning on the dishwasher before preparing for bed. Pacing around the kitchen, the ever-loyal Brother kept meowing and meowing at Kimberly. Her first thought was that he wanted extra food, but she found his bowl full. So she opened the front door to see if he wanted to go out. He didn't. But he continued to pace around the kitchen looking distressed. 'I thought he was just being silly,' recalled Kimberly. So she continued upstairs to her bedroom and closed the door.

But Brother did not give up. Instead, he went downstairs to the bedroom where the Reiman daughters were also settling down for the night. He pushed open the door, leapt on daughter Chelsea's bed and started to nudge and press her arm. 'Go away, Brother,' mumbled Chelsea, slightly irritated, as she continued to read her book. But the persistent cat would not give up. He meowed again and clawed her leg as if to say, 'Listen! This is REALLY urgent!' Assuming he just wanted to go out, Chelsea finally gave in and got out of bed to walk to the front door. It was as she was walking through the house, that she suddenly smelled smoke. Looking into the kitchen, Chelsea was confronted with a frightening vision: the dishwasher was engulfed in flames and already the fire was spreading! Ironically the smoke alarms had been temporarily disconnected that night, ready for the latest upgraded models to be installed. With no smoke alarm, and everyone in the family turned in for the night, the outcome could have been fatal. 'Without Brother, it could have been really tragic,' noted Kimberly. 'We could easily have died from smoke inhalation.'

Fortunately Chelsea managed to rouse the rest of the family and they successfully evacuated the house in time. Meanwhile, thanks to the swift action of the fire service, the fire was safely contained in the kitchen area, minimising the damage to the rest of the family home.

It may have taken Brother five years, but he more than repaid the Reimans for rescuing him from the storage shed. His persistence in ensuring that his family was safe in the smoke-filled heat of the fire was a true act of bravery.

In honour and recognition of the love and determination

he displayed in saving his family, Brother was presented with the Lewyt Award for Heroic & Compassionate Animals by the North Shore Animal League in America.

MINOU

Brother's single act of bravery was enough to earn him the badge of hero amongst his family and community. For Doug Smith, a cat called Minou was his greatest childhood hero because of the many adventures they shared — and survived — during his boyhood in the United Kingdom. Minou was Doug's friend and ally during the most mischievous years of his life. The influence a cat can exert on children and grown-ups, and the mutual feelings of loyalty that can result, should never be underestimated.

In memory of his much-loved Minou, Doug wrote this wonderful eulogy that marvelled at her amazing ability to make use of every one of her nine lives.

'Minou was my first cat. My father introduced her to the house the same day my mother and I came home from the hospital. The theory was that my two-year-old older sister wouldn't be quite so jealous of the new baby (me) if she had a new pet to play with. I'm not ashamed to admit that I stole her.

'Minou was a small, long-haired black cat, named Minou because my mother thought she fussed around like a little French maid.

'I always remember Minou as being rather aloof — she always used to sit slightly away, watching me carefully. No doubt, I must have gone through the "annoying small child" phase, and she never quite recovered from it.

'The thing I remember most about her was that whenever I held her, cradling her on her back, she'd reach one claw-filled paw up and rest it on my nose. I like to think she was intrigued by the funny thing sticking out of my face; however, it was probably more intended as a gentle reminder that she wasn't quite defenceless.

'She seemed to appreciate us. The first time we went on holiday as a family, she was left home with the neighbours dropping in to feed her. We were away for one week, and when we got back, there were seven small voles lined up on the doorstep. She would never bring them inside — that was not allowed.

'She took full advantage of all of her nine lives. She was shot by some people hunting pheasant in the woods behind the house; she fell in the septic tank when it was being drained; she had a fight with one of the local dogs which left her missing a piece of her ear; my mother ran her over in a car (well, Fiat 500!); and, worst of all, the boy who lived across the street tied a piece of string round her neck with a brick on the end of it. She ended up hanging between the house next door and its garage for two days before we found her. If you ever meet an Andrew Pratt, ask if he ever lived at 19 Torksey Avenue.

'She survived all these trials, and started to get more mellow. More and more often you would see her chasing things in her sleep, and if you could persuade her to fall asleep while you were stroking her she would sleep so soundly that you could lift her head up and drop it an inch or two without her waking.

'Her glossy coat faded from a rich shiny black to a dull, reddish colour and we had to groom her to prevent it getting matted. Her hunting forays turned into a doze under the rose bush — she still caught the occasional bird that would settle in the bush above her, but only very rarely. She would sometimes lie in the sun so long without moving that her long hair would singe.

'When I was sixteen, my parents divorced, and my father and I moved to a small town called Gainsborough, 12 miles [19 kilometres] away. We took Minou with us, but the area around the house already had an established cat population. She wasn't really capable of creating her own domain, and ended up sulking in the house most of the time.

'Eventually, she was claimed by the busy road outside the house. Her difficulties establishing her own run forced her to cross the road; she never used a litter tray, and would only "go" outside.

'She was run over by a Ford Granada two days before I left home to go to university. I was out the night it happened, so mercifully I didn't see her in that condition. I miss her, I still carry her little pet ID tag on my key ring. Somehow losing Minou marked the transition from childhood to adulthood; part of my life was gone and it was time to move on.'

Catastrophic Circumstance

While some cats count off their nine lives by narrowly escaping random, but regular, domestic incidents, others have the misfortune of risking their full quota with one, world-headline-making disaster.

MIRACLES AT GROUND ZERO

September 11, 2001 is a date in our recent history that has become irrevocably associated with terror and tragedy in the Western world. Sheer disbelief and utter helplessness were just some of the feelings that were experienced as media images showing the devastation of the World Trade Center in New York on that fateful Tuesday loomed on television screens across the world. As people watched the Twin Towers slowly crumble to acres and acres of rubble, it wasn't difficult to imagine the panic of the unwitting victims and the ensuing horror at the loss of innocent lives.

Nancy, a veterinary nurse in New York, was among those watching the 24-hour TV coverage. Astounded by the real-time, real-life footage, and fired by compassion, Nancy's instant reaction was concern for the animals. Without a second thought, she rushed out of the door and made her way to the scene to find a way to help the 'forgotten' victims of the immediate and surrounding areas — the pets.

Organisation of a pet rescue operation was already being discussed and planned at a nearby empty municipal pier, but on arrival all Nancy found was chaos. 'I was ill-prepared for the total chaotic crowd that I found. Hundreds of distraught pet owners, all waiting for permission to go into Ground Zero, all becoming more and more desperate as time ticked by and their animals had gone another hour without food, water or company.'

Nancy used her knowledge of veterinary medicine to try to help answer questions such as: how long will my cat survive without water? Can my pet manage without its medication? A raised toilet seat and the availability of food containers that could possibly be ripped open reassured some owners that their pets could at least drink and eat. However, as Nancy was well aware, shock, smoke inhalation and asbestos dust were factors that caused mounting concern as the days ticked by. 'I didn't let them know how hopeless I felt when I met pet owners who had kept their animals in locked rooms or had not left food out for them on that day.'

Finally, two-and-a-half days later, on 13 September at 8 p.m., Nancy was allowed to enter Ground Zero with a Park Ranger. 'The strange thing is that New York looked as alive as ever, except the only people who were around were in uniform — policemen, firefighters and armed soldiers. The air was thick with smoke and the acrid smell of burning rubber — which I later found out was caused by office furniture. We had to walk the last six blocks on foot, slogging through 4 inches [10 centimetres] of grey, sludgy mud, concrete dust, papers and shattered glass.'

Nancy had volunteered, along with a resident, to go into one residential apartment block to search and hopefully rescue a number of pets. With no electricity, and therefore no elevator, they had just 30 minutes to search the pitch-black apartments.

Fueled by anxiety and a surge of adrenaline, the resident climbed all the way to the 28th floor to his own apartment, and there he heard a tiny meow followed by some scratching. Following the sounds, in complete darkness and eerie silence, he finally discovered his three beloved, but very bedraggled, dusty cats, tucked behind the sofa. Incredibly, all were alive, although in a state of shock, and were visibly relieved to see their owner. 'It was a moment of real joy after two days of utter sadness,' said Nancy. 'The cats were dehydrated and in urgent need of medical attention because of the smoke and dust they had inhaled, combined with the immense shock of the last few days. But you could see they were overjoyed at being reunited with their owner. He of course, was in tears of relief and joy at the miracle of finding them alive.'

Nancy also managed to locate six more cats from the same apartment building — all of them were suffering from dehydration, malnutrition and suspected respiratory conditions, but nevertheless they were the survivors of a very tragic event. 'Back at the pet rescue centre, we were met with applause — the same tireless applause that greeted all 400-plus rescued animals that arrived over the next three days. It was very moving to say the least.'

A nine-month-old Bengal cat was among the last of the pets to be rescued, because his owner, a photographer, lived only a block away from Ground Zero. When the photographer had heard the first aeroplane attack on the World Trade Center, he had dashed outside with his camera. He had no idea that he would be in danger until the Twin Towers began to fall and he had to literally run for his life. Four days later, neither the pet rescue operation nor the photographer had been given permission by the authorities to go back to the apartment. Filled with concern for his loyal companion, he anxiously confirmed that at the time his cat had water in his dish, but no food. The pet rescue team offered him little hope since the proximity to Ground Zero meant that the water was probably unfit for consumption anyway. 'The photographer was feeling very distraught and even guilty at abandoning his cat just so he could get his photograph. Although we tried to offer comfort, we were also feeling helpless,' said Nancy.

On 16 September, the photographer and the rescue operation were finally allowed to go back into the apartment. 'The apartment was unrecognisable,' said the photographer. 'Even though it was very dark, it was clear that everything was completely covered in thick black soot and grey dust — even the cat's water. He must have been so scared.' The cat was indeed terrified and suffering extreme dehydration and malnutrition — but amazingly he was alive!

'You can't begin to imagine how delighted we were. None of us could believe it. It was a real miracle!' smiled Nancy. 'The volunteer vets on the team examined and treated this amazing cat who really had defied death. And thanks to all the donations of the necessary supplies, we were able to make him comfortable and ready for complete recovery.'

He was, indeed, one of the lucky pets to survive this horrific catastrophe. Many cats and other animals were left unclaimed, making their situation even more desperate. Publicity about their plight gave some people a much-needed sense of purpose and the response from the American public was inspiring. Over 300 people visited the pet rescue operation and registered to foster the unclaimed animals for an unlimited period of time.

'I was honoured to be a part of such a truly amazing effort in such an unbearable situation,' concluded Nancy. 'I was moved beyond words by the strength of humanity, but moreover I was stunned by the resilience of these amazing animals. For cats to survive in such conditions is nothing short of miraculous.'

TSUNAMI SURVIVORS

The reality that cats and other animals could actually survive a catastrophe of such epic proportions as Ground Zero offered both a distraction and a sense of hope to people in a time of great tragedy and sorrow. Only a few years later, in 2004, inspiring stories of feline survival were to emerge again following the disastrous effects of the Asian tsunami.

Australian Lynda O'Grady could not have imagined she would find herself in the middle of one of the world's biggest humanitarian disasters when she packed her luggage for an eagerly anticipated holiday in India. In November 2004, Lynda set off on her trip, looking forward to revisiting the sights, sounds — and animals — of this vibrant country. As former manager of the Cat Protection Society of New South Wales, Lynda naturally couldn't help but seek out the local animals. Indeed, on past trips to India she had often stepped in to help with injuries or offer a supply of cat food.

During this particular trip, Lynda was enjoying travelling around India, and by December 2004 she had reached Pondicherry in the south of the country. A picturesque, French-influenced place, with an abundance of local dogs and cats, Lynda was thoroughly entranced. From here, she could easily travel to other southern Indian towns and cities. But all plans came to a standstill on 26 December when, deep in the middle of the Indian Ocean, a tsunami developed with such incredible strength and power that it devastated the entire region.

On the day the tsunami hit, Lynda had woken up early to catch the bus into the town of Chennai. On arrival in Chennai the place was like a ghost town. Shops were closed up and the streets were unusually quiet, with no sign of people or animals. After walking around, Lynda caught sight of another tourist. The tourist was in a state of shock and explained that a wave had hit the coast, causing untold damage and the loss of many lives.

In Chennai the local church soon became the place where families gathered for shelter, food and support as the gravity of the disaster became apparent. Aid agencies were quick to move in and the food drops were vital. 'There was such a strange feeling in the air, I can't quite explain it. This once bustling idyllic beachside town, littered with cats and kittens, had been changed forever,' said Lynda.

During her discussions with locals and tourists, Lynda discovered that just before the wave had struck the coastline — without any warning — the town's cats had disappeared completely. Habitually hanging around the tourists for food, their sudden departure had been noticeable in the town, although the locals had attributed it to an impending storm. 'A cat's intuition is fairly reliable. Their whiskers are highly sensitive to vibration so it's not unusual that they would run to a safe place if a storm was brewing,' explained Lynda. But on this occasion, instead of running into houses or shops and hiding under chairs, they ran up into the high ground as far away from the coastline as they could. How different things may have been if the town's population had taken advantage of this 'sixth sense' premonition.

Feeling a little helpless and not wishing to hamper relief efforts, Lynda decided to go to Mahaballipurum, a coastal town which supposedly had not been devastated. Before the tsunami, most of the town's cats had survived by scavenging scraps from local families, restaurants and tourists. Now, even though the tsunami had not badly affected it, the tourists had abandoned the town, meaning the food supply had suddenly dried up. 'Seeing these starving cats and pitifully thin, mange-ridden dogs was just too much. I decided to spend each day until my departure to Australia feeding what animals I could.'

Lynda walked through the town scouring the shops to find nutritious cat food. However, as the cats were strays, they were not accustomed to canned pet food and were reluctant to eat it. 'These cats had been through so much. The fear and terror they must have experienced — it was truly miraculous that they had survived at all. The saddest thing is that there were so few kittens … and I can't bear to think what may have happened to them.' Those kittens that Lynda did find were given milk.

Every day, more cats reappeared and, in an effort to support local food vendors, Lynda decided to buy their cooked dishes to offer to the cats and kittens on the streets and the beachfront.

The animals soon came to trust Lynda and would come up to her for their daily nourishment. The locals and especially the many beggars could not believe that Lynda would spend her time and money on food for the stray cats. Often she had to buy the locals food or provide the children with sweets before they would allow her to continue her work. She was like a modern-day Pied Piper, as children gathered around to see what this strange cat woman was up to. As Lynda commented, 'It was very difficult contemplating that I should possibly be helping the people. Many of these animals, particularly the cats, are used to struggling on a daily basis to get by. Was I just interfering? It was an extremely confronting situation.'

Lynda was finally able to catch a flight out of India to return home to Australia — but the wrench was hard. She had to leave behind all the animals she had helped nurse back to strength, hoping somehow they would make it. 'I can't describe how emotional I felt in leaving those cats behind — I had come to know them and I could only hope that I had inspired the locals to continue to look after them as they rebuilt their own lives after the tsunami. In the back of my mind I know there is so much animal welfare work required in countries such as India, even more so since the tsunami, that I may have to return.'

AFTER HURRICANE KATRINA

For Lynda, it was amazing to witness at first hand the uncanny phenomenon of feline sixth sense. Without it, the many cats and kittens of southern India that ran for the hills at the very first tremor of the tsunami would almost certainly have perished. This amazing ability to sense danger and hold onto life was also apparent in the aftermath of the devastating Hurricane Katrina, which ravaged the southern United States in August 2005.

Betty and Gregory Speyrer of East New Orleans were the proud owners of six pampered cats: Rainbow, Tiger, Charlie, Giuseppe, Michael and Campanita — plus the old family dog, Kelly. When Hurricane Katrina struck their region, the

Speyrers and their cats were amazingly lucky and all of them managed to survive the floodwaters and destruction that devastated the area. However, like most of the buildings, their home did not escape the impact and the resulting damage was so extensive that it was rendered uninhabitable for both humans and cats.

Homeless and in shock, Betty and Gregory were temporarily relocated to Baton Rouge, where they set about making arrangements to get a government-donated trailer to set up on their property. The idea was that they could live there with their family and their cats while the house was being renovated. The Speyrers, just like so many other New Orleans residents, believed they'd be home in a couple of days, so they accepted that it was best to leave their beloved cats behind — with feeding instructions — in familiar territory.

But they hadn't anticipated what turned out to be the next stage of the Hurricane Katrina catastrophe. The force of the initial impact had wreaked havoc on the environment, putting incredible strain on the city's defences — so much so that, a few days later, the levees finally broke, resulting in a disaster area that was now completely underwater. On top of this, in mid-September, Hurricane Rita hit the area to devastate anything that might have remained.

Days turned into weeks and the Speyrers were unable to return to their flooded hometown. Naturally their distress as they thought of the possible fate of their beloved cats was almost unbearable. But the story of four of the cats — Rainbow, Tiger, Charlie and Giuseppe — is a compelling example of the strong connection between animal and man.

Cathy Scott was a journalist covering the rescue events in New Orleans. In mid-January 2006, a caregiver rushed over to Cathy to tell her that a cat was being reunited with his owner. 'We had not had many cat reunions in recent months,' explained Cathy, 'so I grabbed a pen and notebook from the table I was working at and hurried over to the cat area of the building. Rescued Katrina cats were being kept in kennels in a fenced-off area inside Celebration Station — a former arcade — in Metairie, Louisiana, a suburb of New Orleans. Best Friends Animal Society, based in Kanab, Utah, had set up a temporary triage centre at Celebration Station in December for one last effort to pull the remaining homeless Katrina pets from the streets of New Orleans. I stayed at Celebration Station for three-and-a-half weeks to write about the rescue effort.'

Cathy introduced herself to Betty Speyrer just after she walked into the centre looking for Tiger, one of her cats. She had received a phone call first thing that morning, advising that her cat had been found at her house in East New Orleans near City Park. 'Betty told me that when she and her husband returned in late September to their home for the first time, their six cats were nowhere to be found. For the next several months, Betty sent photos and notices to more than 100 shelters and rescue groups across the United States, to no avail. "I contacted them all," she had said. "No one had them. I'd given up." '

So when six months after the hurricane Betty answered her phone, she couldn't believe what she was hearing. A rescue worker told her that they'd received the notice about her cats and that Tiger, the tortoiseshell, had actually been found near their house! He had been taken straightaway to the temporary triage centre for assessment.

Betty had hung up the phone, grabbed a cat carrier, and run out of the apartment to make the 120-kilometre drive to their storm-damaged home. 'Her first thought,' smiled Cathy, 'was that, if rescuers had managed to find Tiger, their other cats could still be there too — they always stuck together.' At the house, Betty had leapt out of the car and started to call out, using their family generic call-cry 'Kitty, Kitty'. After several attempts, seemingly out of nowhere, appeared Rainbow, their fifteen-year-old cat — as if all he'd been waiting for was someone to call him! Betty picked him up, held him for a moment like a long-lost friend, and then placed him in the carrier in her car. She then drove to the Best Friends' triage centre to be reunited with her other boy, Tiger.

'I was standing there with her when she walked to a kennel where Tiger was staying,' recalled Cathy. 'She bent down and looked inside. "Yes, it's him," she said. "It's Tiger." Betty picked him up and held him against her. It was an emotional moment. She pressed his face against her cheek and they both closed their eyes. It was difficult to tell who was happiest, Tiger or Betty! I remember Betty saying that the reality of getting Tiger and Rainbow back on the same day was nothing short of incredible.'

Despite weathering both hurricanes Katrina and Rita and then surviving outside, Tiger was in fairly good shape. 'A little skinny, but still healthy. Betty gave a thumbs-up for the cats as she headed out the door with Tiger in tow, then added, "Two down, four to go!" '

This was almost a premonition, because about a week later Betty received another phone call from a rescuer telling her that yet another cat fitting one of the descriptions on the Speyrers' notice had been found near their home. This time it was Charlie, and he too had been taken to the centre for assessment. Then another week went by and Giuseppe was found! By this time, Betty had become a regular, and very happy, visitor to the temporary centre as, one by one, four of the Speyrers' six cats were rescued. And, miraculously, they all were in good shape.

The ability of these cats to survive two hurricanes and

then to fend for themselves in such devastated circumstances for six months is astounding. 'I kept in touch with Betty,' said Cathy, 'and she reported that it took no time at all for the cats to settle back into the same daily routines they had before Katrina. And as if in celebration of the regeneration efforts in the area, including the replanted and newly grassed garden at the Speyrers' house, the cats like to go out in the garden at dawn and stretch and play around in total enjoyment.'

The remaining two cats — Michael and Campenita — have been spotted in the Speyrers' neighbourhood but have been too skittish to be caught. Betty and Gregory, now back on the property and living in their temporary trailer, continue to leave food and water outside their home, hoping they will finally return. Because Campenita, who is shy, was always so attached to Michael, Betty believes that's why Michael has not returned yet. 'Betty explained to me that they played a lot and cuddled up all the time,' commented Cathy. 'Everywhere Michael went, Campenita followed, so Betty is sure that Michael is staying out there with her.'

Sadly, the Speyrers' fourteen-year-old dog Kelly did not manage to survive the hurricane. The Speyrers found her in one of the upstairs bedrooms of their home, where she used to sleep. 'Betty told me that Charlie now sometimes goes into the house and sleeps under the bed, where Kelly was found,' said Cathy. 'Apparently she was like a mother to the cats —

she groomed them and took care of them, and when they were kittens, she would pick them up by the scruffs of their necks and put them in their basket. So it's not surprising that they are really missing her.'

For Betty — and obviously for the cats too — the family is not complete without a dog. So when the repairs to their house are finished, the Speyrers plan to adopt a puppy for their cats. 'Then the puppy can grow up with the cats,' laughed Cathy, 'like the way the kittens grew up with Kelly.'

'Our cats are the continuation of the life we had before Katrina,' Betty told Cathy. 'With our animals here, even though we have to rebuild our home and it's a lot of work, everything is okay. It's a rebirth. The cats are the thread — our connection — to our previous lives.'

Working as a journalist on the Best Friends Animal Society magazine, Cathy stayed in New Orleans for over three months to capture the amazing pet reunion stories following Hurricane Katrina. In total, Best Friends ended up rescuing 4500 dogs, cats and other pets. Between 15 and 20 per cent were returned to their original — and overjoyed — families.

Feline Facts and Frivolities

BUILT TO SURVIVE

So why do cats have this amazing ability to survive against all odds? While myths and legends abound, the apparent superpowers of the cat can possibly be explained in more scientific terms by way of the cat's physiology.

Finding their way home

'PSI trailings' is one suggested explanation of a cat's ability to travel vast distances to find its way home. PSI is a parapsychological term and is defined on Wikipedia as 'the active agent by which mind influences matter and is able to receive extra-sensory perception impressions'. The theory is that cats use the earth's gravity to determine their place, or home, in the world and have developed the ability to return to this place by 'trailing' or using the magnetic field on earth, the sun and their own biological clocks. However, the 'active agent' which allows them to do this remains unexplained and no specific physical or biological feline mechanism related to this ability has been identified.

Falling from great heights
If a cat begins to fall, the inner-ear canal, which controls balance, will help the cat right itself and therefore it will, in most cases, land on its feet. Severe injury is often avoided because a falling cat will always right itself in a specific order. First its head will rotate, then its spine will twist, rear legs will align themselves, and finally the cat will arch its back, thus lessening the impact of the landing.

The mysterious 'sixth sense'
The whiskers of a cat are extremely sensitive and can detect even the slightest changes in air pressure. This may explain why cats can apparently predict the onset of storms and even earthquakes. The whiskers also act as an alternative sensing device to enable cats to 'see' well in the dark. (Interestingly, if a cat is overweight and his sides stick out further than his whiskers, he will lose his sense of perception and stability.)

The 'sixth sense' ability of cats is further assisted by the fact that cats have incredible hearing. Cats are able to hear sounds that move faster than 45,000 hertz — which means they are capable of hearing the sound of a bat!

Detecting in the dark

In addition to superpower ears and personal-radar whiskers, cats have a greatly enhanced visual capacity. Cats need only one-sixth the amount of light that humans require to see. Consequently, their night vision is incredibly finely tuned and their peripheral vision extends to about 285 degrees. Perfect for finding mice — or unwanted intruders!

Having said this, you won't find your cat doing any close-up work. Like long-sighted humans, they cannot see detail very well and, while they are not colour blind, they can only see red, blue and green.

CATS AND LUCK

Of course, all cat owners believe their pets are lucky, but across all cultures and throughout history the cat has been associated with the concepts of omens and luck. Here are some of the most common.

- In Britain and Australia black cats are considered lucky.
- White cats are a symbol of good luck in America, while black cats are a sign of bad luck.
- Blue cats are the bringers of luck in Russia.
- In Japan, a model of a waving cat in the doorway of a shop will bring good fortune to the shopkeeper, while in China it is said to beckon customers inside.

- In Britain and most parts of Europe, to see a black cat is usually fortunate, especially if it crosses one's path. In some places, the luck only occurs if the cat is politely greeted, or stroked three times. Sometimes it is considered unlucky if the cat runs away from the person, or turns back on its own tracks.
- If a black cat comes into a house it is considered a very lucky sign. The cat should never be chased away or you risk it taking the luck of the house with it.
- Sailors avoid the word 'cat' while at sea, but to have a cat on board is lucky, especially if it is a completely black cat. If the cat is thrown overboard, a violent storm will ensue.
- In Yorkshire, England, it was believed that if a sailor's wife kept a black cat, her husband would always return safely from the sea. This sometimes led to black cats being stolen.
- A white cat sitting on your doorstep just before your wedding is a sign of lasting happiness. If the household cat sneezes near a bride on her wedding day, she will have a happy married life.

CATS AND CULTURE

Cats have even been celebrated in literature for their amazing powers and superior wisdom, as the following selection of quotes reveals.

'I believe cats to be spirits come to earth. A cat, I am sure, could walk on a cloud without coming through.' — *Jules Verne*

'I love cats because I enjoy my home; and little by little, they become its visible soul.' — *Jean Cocteau*

'A cat has absolute emotional honesty: human beings, for one reason or another, may hide their feelings but a cat does not.' — *Ernest Hemingway*

'If animals could speak the dog would be a blundering outspoken fellow, but the cat would have the rare grace of never saying a word too much.' — *Mark Twain*

'The smallest feline is a masterpiece.' — *Leonardo da Vinci*

'There are no ordinary cats.' — *Colette*

'The cat is domestic only as far as suits its own ends …' — *Saki (H.H. Munro)*

'Cats are a mysterious kind of folk. There is more passing in their minds than we are aware of.' — *Sir Walter Scott*

'One of the most striking differences between a cat and a lie is that a cat only has nine lives.' — *Mark Twain*

Sources

I am indebted to the following people, articles and websites for supplying me with the relevant material for the stories contained in this book.

From Dubai with Love — Lynne and John McDermott
Railway Kittens — Danielle Parkinson
From Rags to Riches — Kathy Roberts
A Cautionary Tale — Todd Sherman, Gainesville, Florida, United States; www.blakjak.com
Kiss of Life — Danielle Parkinson
My Cuban Cat — Flavia Campilli
The (Very) Extreme Escapades of Tommy the Tomcat — Nora Hayward
A Night with the Crocodiles! — Kathy Roberts
Hitch and Hiker — Clint & Kathy Frederick, Las Vegas, Nevada, United States; www.blakjak.com

Acknowledgements

Love and thanks to my mum and dad, Keith and Kelli, Jackie and Ian, Cath and Russell, Catherine O'Keefe, Andy and Denise, Susie and Sam, Lawrence and Nesrin, for all their fantastic support while this was in progress.

Thanks also to Dr Barbara Fougere, Dr Katrina Warren and Danielle Parkinson for introducing me to the inspiration for this book: the Cat Adoption Centre Program.

And finally, not forgetting the unfailing support of Benny, Gareth and Anouska — thank you for making this happen.

Also by Exisle Publishing …

For the Love of a Cat
A Publisher's Story

Few people can appreciate the joy that being owned by a cat brings better than David St John Thomas — the latest in a long line of publishers and authors to pay homage to the very special cats who have entered their busy lives. This is a book for everyone who really cares about cats. Vividly written, sometimes serious, sometimes light-hearted, it is bound to uplift anyone who has fallen for a cat, however much against their better judgement. While cat people are nice (Hitler couldn't stand them!), the real heroes in this book are naturally the cats themselves. A rich portfolio of feline characters — inclu_____ ____ _uthor's own cats — step off the page, or perhaps lie ___ ___ _____ _uctive curves on it, so vividly that you can feel ____ ____ ___ hear their purr! Rich in entertaining anecdotes ___ ___, *For the Love of a Cat* will enhance every cat ov____ ___ _nderstanding of their feline friend and remind the___ ___ _nd again just how lucky they are to share their lives with this most fascinating of creatures.

ISBN 978 1 921497 36 0